Helping
BOYS
Succeed
in School

Helping

BOYS

Succeed
in School

A
PRACTICAL
GUIDE
FOR PARENTS
AND TEACHERS

TERRY W. NEU, PH.D., & RICH WEINFELD

PRUFROCK PRESS INC.
WACO, TX

Library of Congress Cataloging-in-Publication Data

Neu, Terry W., 1959–
  Helping boys succeed in school : a practical guide for parents and teachers / Terry W. Neu & Rich Weinfeld.
      p. cm.
  Includes bibliographical references.
  ISBN-13: 978-1-59363-198-7 (pbk.)
  ISBN-10: 1-59363-198-7 (pbk.)
  1. Boys—Education. 2. Sex differences in education. 3. Academic achievement. I. Weinfeld, Rich, 1953- II. Title.
  LC1390.N48 2007
  371.823—dc22
                          2006020734

ISBN-13: 978-1-59363-198-7
ISBN-10: 1-59363-198-7

The "Da Vinci's Car" activity in Chapter 10 was compiled and developed by Bill Brown, Director, Eli Whitney Museum and Workshop, in conjunction with Terry W. Neu, Ph.D., Project Coordinator, Project HIGH HOPES, for Javits Act Program #R206R00001. The activity is adapted here with permission from its authors.

The activity, "What's the Difference? An Experiment in Herpetology," in Chapter 10 was compiled and developed by Terry W. Neu, Ph. D., Project Coordinator, Project HIGH HOPES, for Javits Act Program #R206R00001. The activity is adapted here with permission from its author.

Prufrock Press Inc.
P.O. Box 8813
Waco, TX 76714-8813
Phone: (800) 998-2208
Fax: (800) 240-0333
http://www.prufrock.com

To our sons, Jake, Nic, and Jake, as well as the many other boys in whom we have personally seen the potential to do great things.

Contents

Acknowledgements

We would like to thank Kenneth Caputo for his contributions to the bullying information in Chapter 7. More about Ken can be found in the About the Contributor section of this book.

Introduction

Over the past 6 years, we have been combining our skills to bring information and stories about the boys we've worked with to audiences at conferences and workshops across the United States. We are dedicated to helping boys succeed in school and life. As educators who have worked extensively with the gifts and the special needs of boys, and, often, the combination of both within the same boy, we have years of experience to share. As the fathers of boys, we have the understanding of the hopes and fears that parents have concerning their sons' success.

You may notice that this book encompasses several voices: Terry's, Rich's, and those of the boys we've worked with over the years. Our partnership as coauthors reflects our personalities: Rich is the "facts guy," and Terry is the storyteller. In parts of this book you may hear more of Rich's voice, as you hear about the statistics, describing the problems and providing the data that support our solutions. In other parts of this book, you will hear more of Terry's voice as he tells the tales of the boys we have worked with. In some parts, you may hear the boys themselves, as we put the stories they've shared with us to paper. Although these stories may be composites of several boys, they are based on actual boys we have worked with over the years. We hope that from all these voices, you will gain an understanding of both the facts and the emotions that are involved in ensuring boys' success. Most importantly, we believe you will be given practical tools that you, as parents and educators, can immediately use to help your boys. We hope that our words, and those of the boys we've worked with, can help make a difference in the lives of other boys, both those who struggle, and those who need a simple nudge toward the path of success.

chapter 1

What's Going on With the Boys?

t was standing room only for the presentation on boys' issues in education at a national conference on education. We were there as concerned educators who had noticed the overrepresentation of boys in the special education programs that we had worked in and administered over the years. We were also there as the fathers of boys who were already expressing a dislike for the reading and writing that they were required to do in school. Along with the rest of the crowd, we nodded our agreement as the presenter talked about the problems facing boys in our schools. We waited in anticipation for the speaker to offer solutions to these problems. Our enthusiasm soon turned to disappointment, for nearly all of the solutions offered by the speaker had one common theme: Our boys would be OK if we could just teach them to be more like girls—more sensitive, more cooperative, and more able to understand and verbalize their emotions and those of others.

While this theme seemed to find approval with many in the audience, we left the presentation feeling that a major point had been missed. We saw the truth in the value of helping boys become more sensitive and in touch with their emotions so that they could be more cooperative members of their class and better able to relate to the emotions presented in their reading and writing assignments. On the other hand, we left feeling that the presentation missed the important issue of how, rather than changing the boys to fit our schools, schools might change to capitalize and expand on the strengths of boys.

> **Rather than changing the boys to fit our schools, schools might change to capitalize and expand on the strengths of boys.**

We had seen firsthand the ways boys were suffering and failing in our schools. We had also seen how these same boys could thrive when provided with alternative ways to learn. We left the session determined to do our part to find and share solutions that would capitalize on the strengths, talents, and interests that we had seen over the years in the boys with whom we had worked.

The first step toward making changes in how we educate boys is to have a common understanding of the problems that boys currently face and an understanding of the possible causes of those problems. By now, most of us have heard that boys are not doing as well as girls inside or outside of our schools. First Lady Laura Bush has chosen to make this issue one of her priorities for her second term in the White House. Mrs. Bush and others are voicing concern about some startling and troubling statistics.

HOW ARE BOYS PERFORMING IN SCHOOL?

Nationally, boys are scoring lower in reading and in writing than girls, and their lead over girls in areas like science and math has now virtually disappeared. Results from the 2002 National Assessment of Educational Progress (NAEP) show that in the area of writing boys are 17 percentage points behind girls in the 4th grade, 21 percentage points behind in 8th grade, and a whopping 25 percentage points behind in 12th grade (U.S. Department of Education, 2003). This gap between the genders in writing has increased over the years. The 2002 NAEP reading results also showed a gap between boys and girls at the two tested levels, fourth and eighth grade. In reading, girls outperformed boys by 7 percentage points in fourth grade and 9 percentage points in eighth grade. While in school, boys are less likely to earn good grades, take challenging courses, and be active in school. Besides trailing in academic performance, boys are more likely to drop out of high school than girls and less likely than their female counterparts to graduate high school, to attend college, and to go on for graduate degrees (Mortenson, 2005) The college admission trend is likely to be exacerbated by the new SAT test, which is predicted to favor girls over boys (Cloud, 2003). As Lesley Stahl (2003) reported, somewhat tongue-in-cheek, on a *60 Minutes* segment, if statistical trends were to continue at their current rate, the final male college graduate will receive his bachelor's degree in the year 2068.

Reviewing a variety of statistics from virtually any state, any school district, and nearly every individual school will give evidence of the problems boys are experiencing in our schools. A look at any grade level, any socioeconomic group, and any race will also show that boys are not performing as well as girls. And, statistics from other countries also yield the same types of results. In only 2 out of 32 countries examined were males as likely as females to graduate from high school, and in only one country (Peru) were males more likely to graduate (Organisation for Economic Co-operation and Development, n.d.).

> **Besides trailing in academic performance, boys are more likely to drop out of high school than girls and less likely than their female counterparts to graduate high school, to attend college, and to go on for graduate degrees (Mortenson, 2005).**

Other evidence can be gathered by looking at boys' participation in honors and Advanced Placement classes. A smaller percentage of boys than girls are participating in these advanced courses, providing additional evidence that boys are not doing well in our schools today (Stahl, 2003). Although boys historically have performed better than their female peers, the past 30 years have seen the reversal of that trend (Mortenson, 2005). In 1974, the percentage of male freshmen enrolled in college dipped below 50% for the first time (other than the years during World War II) and that percentage has never again climbed back to the 50% mark. In 2003, the percentage stood at 46.7%. Beginning in the 1980s, the percentage of men obtaining bachelor's degrees had dipped below 50% and this number has continued to decline to the level of 42.6%, as last measured in 2000 (Mortenson).

In 2001, 180,000 more women than men were awarded bachelor's degrees (Mortenson, 2005). This statistic is significant for the individual men who will each earn more than a million dollars less in their lifetime than their male counterparts who have earned their degrees (Mortenson). It is also significant for our society as a whole. As Tom Mortenson, who has done extensive research in this area, points out, " . . . because males make up roughly half the nation's population, unfulfilled male educational potential diminishes national economic, social, political, mental and spiritual health" (p. 1).

SPECIAL EDUCATION ISSUES
AND ATTITUDES

Aside from not achieving or graduating from school at the rate of girls, boys are much more likely than girls to be labeled as having a variety of school problems. Boys constitute a majority of both the students identified as having learning disabilities and those identified with emotional disturbance. Special education programs and classes are vastly overrepresented with boys. At the secondary level, boys comprise 73% of students with learning disabilities and 76% of students who are labeled emotionally disturbed (Mortenson, 2005). In addition, boys are three times more likely than girls to be diagnosed with Attention Deficit/Hyperactivity Disorder (ADHD; Centers for Disease Control, n.d.). Boys also are much more likely than girls to be held back or to repeat a grade. In 2000, 34.3% of boys, compared to 25.8% of girls, were enrolled below their modal grade level for their age (Mortenson).

On the other end of the spectrum, gifted boys are experiencing problems, as well. Gifted boys can be quite misunderstood and are often labeled as troublemakers when they express their creativity in the classroom. In some cases, their gifts and talents are overlooked due to the behaviors they may be demonstrating in the classroom environment (Gentry & Neu, 1998).

After looking at all of these issues, it will come as no surprise that boys' attitudes toward school are more negative than their female counterparts. An editorial in *USA Today* (*USA Today* staff, 2003) referred to a recent survey that showed the disparity between boys' and girls' beliefs and feelings about school. While 67% of girls agreed with the statement, "I often try to do my best in school," only 41% of boys agreed. Similarly, 70% of girls said it was important to do well in school, compared to only 57% of boys. These attitudes may help explain why girls are more likely to be involved in their schools, often serving as student government leaders, as well as leaders of other school organizations. There is also evidence that boys are seeing school as more of a "girlish" activity and are therefore opting out of certain classes and programs (Kerr & Cohn, 2001).

The problem goes beyond academics. As we have seen by the shocking school shootings, including those in Littleton, CO, and West Paducah, KY, in the late 1990s, the school shooters have nearly all been boys. Government authorities and school officials have struggled to understand the reason for the profile of the shooter that has appeared. One consultant to the Secret Service, Dr. William Pollack, believes "they're all boys because the way we bring up boys in America predisposes them to a sense of loneliness and disconnection and sadness" (Dedman, 2000, ¶ 39). Boys are much more likely to be the victim of violent crimes at the hands of others, as well. Not only are the majority of the school shooters boys, 78% of the victims of school shootings between the years of 1992 and 2004 also were boys (National School Safety Center, 2006). In a seemingly related statistic, boys are more likely to bully and be the victim of bullying (more on this in Chapter. 7). Suicides are another indication of the current plight of boys. Although girls make more suicide gestures than boys, boys are 5 times more likely to actually commit suicide among youth ages 15–19 (National Center for Health Statistics, n.d.).

Boys From Minority Groups

Educational institutions have begun placing much of their focus on gathering data in order to analyze students' performances. The No Child Left Behind Act (2001) requires states to gather and report data on a variety of groups. Test results are broken out for most minority groups, as well as over socioeconomic categories and for students who receive special education services. Unfortunately, states are not required to report data on a group comprising 50% of the population that as a whole is being left further and further behind: boys. Furthermore, if we look at the boys through the dual lens of their gender, as well as their minority group or socioeconomic status, we will see even more disturbing statistics. For example, in 1977, 55% of Hispanics who were awarded bachelor's degrees were men, while in 2002 that number had dropped to under 40%. Similarly, in 1977, 43% of Blacks who were awarded bachelor's degrees were men, compared to 33% in 2002 (Mortenson, 2005). Although we will not focus on solutions that are specific to individual minority groups or socioeconomic status in this book, we believe that the suggestions that we offer will cut across and have value for all of these groups.

It's Not Boys vs. Girls

It's important to state at the outset that although we are illustrating the current plight of boys as compared to their female counterparts, this book is not about boys versus girls. The problems that girls face in our schools have only been given attention over the past few decades, and we still have a long way to go to deal with all of those issues. One female participant sarcastically summed things up at a recent Harvard University conference on boys' issues, saying, "Oh, I get it, we paid attention to only men for thousands of years, then we paid attention to women for 20 or 30 years, and now it's time to forget about the women again!" The academic and emotional issues that girls face in our schools continue to demand attention. We do not believe it's a matter of choosing whether to pay attention to the girls or the boys. We believe that as we continue to pay attention to our daughters, we can, at the same time, increase the attention we pay to our sons. Not only boys, but many girls, as well, will benefit when boy-friendly strategies are introduced into our classrooms. The ideal classrooms will incorporate a range of strategies that will help all our children succeed.

It is also important to state at the outset that the nature of looking at the current plight of boys means that we will be talking in generalities throughout this book. There are obviously many differences between and among boys. The problems that we report and the solutions that we offer are what we have found to be true for most boys, but none of these problems or solutions will be true for all boys. It is our hope that parents and educators will look at boys individually to see what is currently true for them and which of the solutions that we offer may be a good fit for the boy or boys in their life.

BIOLOGY OR THE ENVIRONMENT?

Like almost everything, the underlying causes of the problems faced by boys can not be attributed solely to their heredity or solely to their environment. It is clear that the current status of boys in education is due to a combination of both the characteristics that boys are born with and the way that a variety of societal factors shape them.

Biological Factors

As we learn more and more about the biology of humans, we see more differences between men and women. *The Washington Post* recently reported on a study conducted by Massachusetts Institute of Technology (MIT) biologists that found men and women differ genetically by 1–2%, the same amount of genetic difference that separates humans from chimpanzees (Jenkins, 2005). Scientists have discovered hundreds of differences between the brains of men and women. These differences do give us information that offers explanations regarding some of the differences in the performance of boys and girls in school.

There are many differences in the way the brains of girls deal with language as compared to their male peers. More areas in girls' brains are involved with language than in the brains of their male counterparts. Women seem to have more connections between the part of the brain that handles emotion (the amygdala) and the regions of the brain that handle language. While men on the average have bigger brains, brain research is showing more complex connections between the parts of the brain in women. Research shows that the corpus callosum, a large tract of neural fibers that connects both brain hemispheres, is larger in women than in men (Bishop & Wahlsten, 1997). Dr. Bennett A. Shaywitz (Shaywitz et al., 1995), a professor of pediatrics at the Yale University School of Medicine, discovered that the brains of women process verbal language simultaneously in the two hemispheres of the frontal brain, while men tend to process it in the left side only. In fact, these connections, as well as their greater use of both hemispheres of the brain, may explain why women lose less language capabilities than men after suffering a left hemisphere stroke (Kimura, 2002). This could have some bearing on why so many more boys suffer from dyslexia. Perhaps having more areas of their brain involved in language allows girls to compensate for weaknesses in their brains more readily than boys, if one area is not working in an optimal way.

Researchers are suggesting that these structural differences may be related to a greater tendency among females to sense emotional states and use language to describe those states. In addition, the brains of girls generally mature earlier than those of boys. From as early as the age of 6 months, girls show more electrical activity in the left hemisphere than the right. (The left hemisphere is dominant for language in most people.) In contrast, levels of testosterone have been shown to be related to increased development of the right hemisphere, which tends to be dominant for spatial skills in most people. Girls' development is also faster in the prefrontal cortex, which is specialized for affect regulation and executive decision making. This may explain girls' superior abilities to control impulsive behavior and to respond empathetically. Research has also shown major differences between the genders in the typical sequence of brain development, with brain development shifting from primarily the left to the right hemisphere later in childhood for girls, while the reverse happens with boys (Hanlon, Thatcher, & Cline, 1999). Brain-imaging studies have also have shown that when faced with emotional issues boys process these issues in the brain stem, resulting in a "fight or flight" response. Girls' brains tend to move emotional information into the cortex, making them more likely to process emotions and to get help from others, a process referred to as "tending and befriending" (Taylor et al., 2000). As Simon Baron-Cohen (2003) discusses in his book, *The Essential Difference*, the brains of women are set up for empathizing while the brains of men are set up for systemizing.

Baron-Cohen (2003) presents extensive evidence about this "essential difference" between men and women. He discusses the ways in which the female brain is "hard-wired for empathy," defining empathy as the drive to identify another person's emotions and thoughts and to respond to them with an appropriate emotion. He goes on to say that the purpose of this empathy is to "understand another person, to predict their behavior, and to connect or resonate with them emotionally" (p. 2). On the other hand, according to Baron-Cohen, the male brain is primarily hard-wired for understanding and building systems. The "systemizer intuitively figures out how things work, or extracts the underlying rules that govern the behavior of a system" (p. 3). The purpose of this systemizing, according to Baron-Cohen is "to understand and predict the system, or to invent a new one" (p. 3).

Many of the discoveries regarding the differences between the brains of boys and girls support the ideas that are advanced by Baron-Cohen (2003), and these differences clearly are having an impact on school performance. Girls begin speaking earlier than boys, and by first grade are approximately one year ahead of boys in language development. Studies show girls' speech is more coop-erative, reciprocal, and collaborative, and that they verbalize their feelings more readily (Baron-Cohen). In fact, girls perform better in a wide variety of tested language skills such as:

- speech discrimination,
- word reading and spelling,
- reading comprehension skills (especially for fiction),
- verbal memory,
- accurate speech, and
- fluent speech.

Girls have less than half the risk of having language disor-ders than boys do. Even in looking at quantity of language, girls have larger expressive vocabularies and simply put, produce more words in a given period. Rob Becker describes this phenomena in his brilliant one man comedy show, "Defending the Caveman," say-ing that by the time everyone returns home after a long day at work and school, women still have plenty of words left, while the men and boys have used up their allotment for the day. This explains the one-word answers and grunts that a woman may receive as responses from her husband and sons as she tries to talk about the day's events.

Baron-Cohen (2003) also reports on the effects of testosterone on the development of typical male or female attributes. Lower lev-els of fetal testosterone, which is seen more commonly in females, leads to better levels of language, communication skills, eye con-tact, and social skills. Higher testosterone levels are associated with faster and more accurate maze learning and spatial activities.

Also supporting Baron-Cohen's theory are studies that show that boys are better in many aspects of spatial learning. Studies have shown that males are superior at navigation. They excel in geography and building activities. While girls tend to have stron-ger computational skills, boys excel at high-level abstract logic and math reasoning (Baron-Cohen, 2003). Also supporting this theory are studies that show that the right hemisphere skills develop ear-lier in boys, while it is the left hemisphere skills that tend to develop earlier in girls (Hanlon et al., 1999). Boys also tend to have better ability in movement activities, such as aiming, throwing, and catching objects. New studies find evidence that while the female eye has better perception of color and texture, boys' eyes have better perception of movement (Sax, 2005).

There are other observable differences between the behavior of boys and girls that may be related to their biological differences, but are certainly influenced by the environment, as well. Boys need more movement, more variety, and more stimulation. The movement not only helps boys to manage boredom and impulsivity, it actually stimulates their brains, allowing for better learning. Boys also tend to test the rules and tend to be more motivated by competition.

Brain research and a variety of studies are providing us with more and more information about basic differences between boys and girls. In later chapters we will examine what is happening in our schools that may not be taking these differences into account and what we can do to change this situation.

Environmental Factors

Although it is now clear that socialization doesn't explain all of the differences between boys and girls, it is also clear that our environment plays a huge role in shaping who we each become. Expectations do matter. Many of these expectations are communicated in subtle ways not only by family, but by the media and other institutions, including school.

From the beginning, we treat boys and girls differently. Parents respond differently to their babies, even before they are born. Studies have shown that prospective parents respond to the same behaviors in the womb (e.g., a baby kicking) differently if they know they are having a son than if they know they are having a daughter.

American society has made great strides in the past few decades at attempting to raise our children "equally," providing the basis for equal opportunities for both genders. However, what Dr. William Pollack (Pollack & Cushman, 2001) refers to as the "boy code" begins to be taught to most of our sons at the ages of 2–3. It is not always consciously taught, but it is taught nonetheless. As a whole, our society teaches boys to suppress their feelings. As a result, boys don't have experience with and often don't feel comfortable exploring their own emotions or the emotions of characters they meet during language arts activities in their schools. Perhaps, as a result of the boy code, boys also do not see reading and writing as masculine activities. The boy code and its effects on education will be explored in more detail later on in this book.

We believe that boys continue to receive a strong message about what is masculine and what is feminine, or something considered even worse in the minds of many older boys, what is associated with being gay. While the women's movement has helped girls to be open to a variety of possibilities that were not considered feminine a few decades ago, there has been little real movement in helping boys explore and accept nontraditional activities that have not historically been related to the male role. While the notions are slowly changing, parents still tend to impart masculine and feminine characteristics on young boys and girls, dressing boys in blue and girls in pink, giving boys trucks to play with and girls dolls to play with, or allowing boys to get dirty while asking their daughters to stay clean. Some parents subtly relate messages about their fear of homosexuality to boys through their own unacceptance of and uncertainty toward this population, and some boys may even be affected by the way the media or their own peer culture regards gay men. What results is a strong motivation on the part of many boys to avoid anything that would label them as unmasculine, and boys increasingly may be viewing certain school activities as such.

Another related factor is the lack of male role models for literacy. Fewer than 20% of all teachers are men and few male role models for literacy exist outside of school. Furthermore, with a majority of the males who are in education working at the secondary level, the elementary school years are particularly female-dominated. As one 6-year-old boy described, "School is where you sit at a desk all day and listen to women talk." The instructional materials and activities that are chosen by the women in charge generally are more likely to appeal to girls.

Boys are generally more shame aversive than their female peers (Pollack & Cushman, 2001). Once they have experienced being shamed by a teacher, they will tend to react negatively to that teacher. That negative reaction may range from their withdrawal, to their taking on the role of the class clown as a way to protect themselves. The degree of shame that is felt will vary from boy to boy, but it is often the result of the public criticism that is common in our classrooms. Pollack also observes that boys need time to process an event before they are ready to talk about it and are more likely to open up and talk about their feelings when involved in an activity. Opportunities to wait until they're ready to talk about a behavioral incident are not typically available in schools, causing some boys to seem behaviorally more difficult than they might be if they were given the support they needed.

What results is an environment that does not often allow boys to learn in the ways that may be more natural to them. Their need for movement, hands-on projects, and experiential activities has found a smaller place in our schools in recent years. Perhaps even worse, the current school environment tends to punish boys for their natural tendencies to be active and competitive. The punishment that they experience is often felt as shame and leaves boys alienated from the school environment.

The dichotomy between the school environment and the environment that boys experience outside of school has become dramatically different for this generation of boys. While outside of school, students are multitasking and interacting with a variety of technology; inside of school they are expected to maintain focus for long periods of time on information that is primarily presented in the same low-tech way that it has been for years— listening to a teacher talk or reading a book. *TIME* Magazine (Wallis, 2006) reports that this generation of students "tends to be extraordinarily good at finding and manipulating information . . . and

> While outside of school, students are multitasking and interacting with a variety of technology; inside of school they are expected to maintain focus for long periods of time on information that is primarily presented in the same low-tech way that it has been for years—listening to a teacher talk or reading a book.

[students] are especially skilled at analyzing visual data and images" (p. 54). Although the article reports that a growing number of college professors are capitalizing on their students' strengths by utilizing "film, audio clips and PowerPoint presentations" (Wallis, p. 54), our experience suggests that the same teaching trend is not taking place in many of our elementary and secondary school programs.

Although boys may thrive with greater access to technology, it is clear that they continue to need human interaction and contact, as well. Boys and girls thrive when they feel connected to the school environment. In his 1999 book, *Connect*, Ed Hallowell talks about the power of the "feeling of being a part of something larger than yourself" (p. 4). In a study published in the *Journal of the American Medical Association* (Resnick et al., 1997), the students who did the best in school were the ones who felt connected. For a variety of reasons that have been mentioned here and will be explored in greater depth in this book, our boys are feeling less and less connected to their school experiences.

CONCLUSION

There are, however, some reasons to be hopeful. The following snapshot is from a program that is being piloted in Frederick County Public Schools in Maryland.

We had read about the program at Twin Ridge Elementary School in *The Washington Post* and were anxious to see it for ourselves. What we saw exceeded our expectations. Our hearts were warmed to see so many boys actively engaged in their education. As we entered the fifth-grade classroom, teams of boys were engaged in a friendly contest of "Civil War Jeopardy." On each team table was a live lizard that the boys were caring for. From time to time a boy or two would get up from his seat and move around and this was expected and OK, because they were still paying attention. In fact, there were no behaviors that seemed off the task of the lesson or problematic for the teacher.

On the back of each chair hung the boy's current reading material that he had picked based on his own interests or from a recommendation given by another boy. As we talked to them, it was clear that they were all interested in and excited about what they were reading. We interviewed several of the boys, and they told us how great it was to be in this class. They described the "brain breaks" that they took from time to time during the day so that they could move and refresh their brains for more learning. They told us it was OK to be "gross" in their writing and to include action in their writing; as a result, they now liked to write more than ever before. We left, believing even more strongly that the solutions to boys' educational issues that we believed in (and that will be discussed throughout this book) could be implemented and would make a difference.

There is a crisis that is now facing boys in our schools. It is the result of the interaction between who our boys are and the environment in which they find themselves. This book will present an exploration of these issues and will focus on solutions that can make a difference in the success of our boys in school.

Each chapter will end with tools that parents, teachers, and the boys themselves can use to look at their current situation, as well as plan for what could be done in the future. We encourage you to reproduce these, to modify them as needed, and to use them as you try to make a difference for the boys in your life.

CHAPTER 1 TOOLS

Gathering Data:
Information for Parents and Teachers

In order to see how boys in your state, school district, and school are performing, you can collect data on the performance of the boys in your area. Sources for collecting this information might include your state's department of education Web site, your school district's Web site, your school's Parent-Teacher Association (PTA), and your school's administrators.

1.   What standardized tests and assessment results are available regarding my school, my school district, and my state?

2.   How are boys performing on these assessments?

(Tip: Look at your state department of education Web site. Go to http://nces.ed.gov/nationsreportcard and look at the results by gender for your state. Look at your school district's Web site. If assessments results aren't already being reported by gender for your school and school district ask for results to be broken out for boys and girls.)

3.   Chart the results:

Statewide assessment	
Name of assessment:	
Subject area assessed:	
Grade level assessed:	
Boys' score (state):	
Boys' score (district):	
Boys' score (school):	
Girls' score (state):	
Girls' score (district):	
Girls' score (school):	

School district assessment	
Name of assessment:	
Subject area assessed:	
Grade level assessed:	
Boys' score for my district:	
Boys' score for my school:	
Girls' score for my district:	
Girls' score for my school:	

4. Find out what special programs and classes are offered in your school and school district. These may be programs for students with a variety of gifts, talents, and/or interests. Find out what percentage of students who are participating in specific classes and/or programs are boys. Find out how the boys are performing in these classes and programs. Fill out the chart below:

Special Classes (Advanced Placement, honors, GT, advanced)	
Type/name of class:	
Percentage of boys in class:	
Performance of boys in class (average GPA; pass/fail percentage):	
Type/name of class:	
Percentage of boys in class:	
Performance of boys in class (average GPA; pass/fail percentage):	
Type/name of class:	
Percentage of boys in class:	
Performance of boys in class (average GPA; pass/fail percentage):	

Special Programs (magnets, signature programs, talent development programs)	
Type/name of program:	
Percentage of boys in program:	
Performance of boys in program (average GPA; pass/fail percentage):	
Type/name of program:	
Percentage of boys in program:	
Performance of boys in program (average GPA; pass/fail percentage):	
Type/Name of program:	
Percentage of boys in program:	
Performance of boys in program (average GPA; pass/fail percentage):	

Intervention Plan

Parents and teachers who begin to be concerned about a boy's academic performance and overall well-being may want to create an intervention plan to help pinpoint where a boy's problems are occurring and to locate solutions to these problems.

Parents, complete as much of Part A of this intervention plan as you can. Ask for a meeting between you and your child's school to be convened to complete this plan together.

Intervention Plan
Name:
Date:
School:

A. Evidence of Gifts:
Test scores:
Performance in school: (When does the student show interest, perseverance, self-regulation, and outstanding achievement?)
Performance in the community:
Evidence of Learning Difficulties: (reading, writing, organization, memory, specific learning disabilities, ADHD)
Test scores:
Performance in school:
Behavioral/Attentional Problems:
Performance in school:
Performance at home:

Helping Boys Succeed In School, Copyright © Prufrock Press Inc. This page may be photocopied or reproduced with permission for individual use.

B. Current Program:
Gifted instruction:
Adaptations:
Accommodations:
Special instruction:
Behavior/attention management: (Plans, medication)
Counseling: (In-school, therapy)
Case management: (Home to school communication; communication among staff)

C. Recommendations
Gifted instruction:
Adaptations:
Accommodations:
Special instruction:
Behavior/attention management:
Case management:

D. Next Steps:

Note. From *Smart Kids With Learning Difficulties: Overcoming Obstacles and Realizing Potential* (pp. 167–170), by R. Weinfeld, L. Barnes-Robinson, S. Jeweler, and B. Roffman Shevitz, 2006, Waco, TX: Prufrock Press. Copyright ©2006 by Prufrock Press. Reprinted with permission.

chapter 2

No Girl Stuff

t had been a great year! Many of the boys said it was their best school year thus far. As the boys at Twin Ridges Elementary School reflected on their first year of their school's pilot program of all-boys, fourth- and fifth-grade classes, they thought about many positive things—the friendly competition, the variety of exciting learning activities, and how for the first time in their school career they could learn in the ways they learned best (by moving around, doing hands-on activities, and experiencing things firsthand). They also remembered the close relationships they had developed with the other boys in their classes—the way they could be silly or gross together, the way they shared similar interests in their reading and writing, and the fun they had belonging to a team or tribe and working together as a group.

Unfortunately, there was also a very negative memory associated with this "closeness" with the other boys in the class. The memory of Valentine's Day was still very much on each boy's mind, even in June. As Valentine's Day had approached, some boys and girls in the mixed-gender classes had teased the boys in the all-boys classes. They teased them by asking who their Valentine was going to be. It was both implied and said by other students that the boys in the all-boys class were gay. Feelings were hurt, angry words were exchanged, and there was even a fight. Adults got involved. After a good deal of instruction, counseling, and mediation, it was assumed that the problems had been resolved. Four months later, at the end of the school year, the boys in the all-male class still remembered and were still upset by what had happened.

This vignette from Twin Ridges illustrates the power of boys' feelings as they relate to the classroom. Whether the issue is dealing with shame, fear, or anxiety as it relates to peers or teachers, emotions may interfere with academic progress. One of the most loaded classroom issues for boys may involve issues of gender identity, as illustrated in the vignette above. We want to emphasize that, as we discuss this issue, we are reporting a situation as it exists, not what we believe to be desirable. As we present solutions to both the academic and emotional issues facing boys, we will advocate for building tolerance and diversity and creating an environment where everyone is able to choose and experiment with a variety of activities.

> **The bottom line for many boys, in their own decision making about what activities they will participate in and choose, both inside and outside of school, is whether or not that choice or activity will make them appear unmasculine in the eyes of their peers.**

What is the situation as it currently exists? We don't often discuss it or pay much attention to it, but anyone who works with or is raising boys knows that the most powerful epithet that can be directed at almost any boy is to call him gay.

It speaks of nothing other than the fact that its target is inferior. Young children often have no clue as to its referent behavior, but they know that to call someone gay . . . is a curse of potent magnitude and . . . a crushing insult to their being. (Kerr & Cohn, 2001, p. 233)

The bottom line for many boys, in their own decision making about what activities they will participate in and choose, both inside and outside of school, is whether or not that choice or activity will make them appear unmasculine in the eyes of their peers. Another way of basically saying the same thing is for one boy to call another a "girl," an insult many school-aged boys use on one another. Again, boys constantly weigh whether or not their actions or activities will be seen as girlish activities. It is for this reason, some researchers believe, that boys stop enrolling in honors classes as the population of girls in these classes increases (Kerr & Cohn).

Numerous studies have found that homophobic language is mainstream and homophobia is indirectly reinforced in the school culture and curriculum (Thoneman, 1998). One study found that boys in elementary school hear the word *gay* used as a pejorative epithet an average of 25 times a day (Gay, Lesbian, Straight Education Network, 2000). Currently, in the minds of boys, "gay" or "girly" activities are to be avoided. If a boy is required to participate in one of these activities, he often does so in a less than wholehearted manner. These activities may include many reading and writing activities, especially those chosen by female teachers and administrators that reflect deep, sensitive emotions, or feminine characters and experiences. Boys often feel that these choices do not include their preferred male themes and styles (Newkirk, 2002).

Another way to examine this issue is to look at what happens when boys are in single-gender schools. Boys in all-boys schools are more than twice as likely to study subjects such as foreign languages, art, music, and drama than boys in mixed-gender schools (National Association for Single Sex Public Education, n.d.a). This supports the belief that boys may be even more concerned about what constitutes acceptable male activities when there are girls present.

THE BOY CODE

What do boys believe are acceptable male activities? An examination of the boy code, as discussed by Dr. William Pollack (1998), helps to illustrate the concept of appropriate maleness. This concept is learned at a very early age by most of our boys. Here are the rules of the boy code, as identified by Dr. Pollack (Pollack & Cushman, 2001):

1. Do not cry (no sissy stuff).
2. Do not cower, tremble, or shrink from danger.
3. Do not ask for help when you are unsure of yourself (observe the code of silence).
4. Do not reach for comfort or reassurance.
5. Do not sing or cry for joy.
6. Do not hug your dearest friends.
7. Do not use words to show tenderness and love. (p. 77)

Boys are taught that they are to be strong, silent, and self-reliant and that they should inhibit any feelings and desires that might be construed as feminine. Boys come to believe that to violate the boy code will make them seem girly or gay in the eyes of others. What is the price for observing the boy code in school? There are two parts to the price that boys pay for their adherence to this code—emotional and academic.

Emotionally, when faced with the stress of the academic environment, boys are unlikely to seek the help they may need or even to indicate, in a direct way, that they need help. In this way, adherence to the boy code plays into boys' natural tendency for fight or flight responses (Taylor et al., 2000). The result of this "male toughness" when dealing with the stresses of the school environment may provide one of the explanations as to why our boys are not achieving or demonstrating a positive attitude toward school. The combination of feeling stress and not being able to effectively deal with it leaves many boys feeling alienated and unconnected in the school environment.

Adherence to the boy code also makes boys less able to perform academically, especially in the language arts activities that are becoming a more and more pervasive part of the school day. With little or no practice in identifying and talking about their own emotions or the emotions of others, boys tend to be at a loss to discuss what a character in a story or book they read was feeling.

And, even if they were capable of doing so, boys will tend to avoid this discussion.

SHAME

Another powerful emotional factor that is at play in the classroom is boys' extreme sensitivity to shame. As William Pollack (1998) describes, "boys will do just about whatever it takes to avoid shame" (p. 33). At the same time, there is a widespread perception, on the part of adults, that boys' behavior in the classroom is toxic and needs to be changed or at least controlled (Pollack). One of the easiest and deadliest weapons in the disciplinary arsenal of teachers is the weapon of shaming students. This "weapon" may take on the form of direct aggression, the more veiled aggression of sarcasm, or the very subtle use of blaming language.

In a video of a presentation based on his book, *Learning Outside the Lines* (Mooney & Cole, 2000), Jonathan Mooney gives a powerful example of how, as a young boy, he was shamed and "learned" that there was something wrong with him. Jonathan was a young boy who needed to move his body in order to learn in the classroom. The classroom expectation was that 6-year-old boys should sit still at their desks and listen to the teacher. His teacher's approach to dealing with Jonathan's "behavior problem" was what we would call shaming by direct aggression. Jonathan's teacher attempted to control his behavior by yelling across the room, in one case shouting, "Jonathan, what's wrong with you?" (Golden, 2001). The result was that not only Jonathan, but his classmates, as well, concluded that there was, in fact, something wrong with him. Jonathan felt shamed and, in his case, over time his shame resulted in his both withdrawing from the life of the class and, at times, acting out.

Sarcasm is frequently used by adults to shame boys and thereby control them. While many teachers would defend their use of sarcasm as just "making a joke," their humor is often at the expense of a student whose behavior is somehow threatening the teacher's control of the class. This use of sarcasm is particularly seen as a way of subduing middle school and high school boys. Ironically, boys in the class may even admire the teacher who is demonstrating success in a game that the boys themselves play: putting each other down. We believe that this use of sarcasm is inappropriate when directed from an adult to a student, because of the adult's unequal position in the situation. Again, the effect of this type of behavior control is that the boy ends up feeling shamed and he at least temporarily withdraws from or rebels against the life of the classroom.

The subtlest type of shaming occurs when teachers use blaming language. Again, because of their position of power in the classroom, a teacher's statement about a boy's behavior or poor academic performance can be felt as shaming even when the teacher expresses the message in a calm tone that is not aggressive or sarcastic. Boys still experience criticism as shameful when they feel it is directed at them as a person, rather than at the specific behavior. Boys feel shamed when they are criticized personally. Furthermore, these messages are often spoken publicly, so there is the added layer of feeling ashamed in front of peers.

BULLYING

Bullying is also a huge issue that faces many students in our schools, but particularly boys. Whether they are in the role of the victim or the bully, there is an emotional price that certainly preoccupies the involved boys and makes them less available for instruction. We'll discuss bullying in more detail in Chapter 7.

CONCLUSION

Later in this book, we will provide detailed suggestions that lead to creating an effective classroom climate where boys can be successful. In summary, the strategies and methods we will present are all based on respecting and celebrating the individual. When this type of environment is promoted, what develops is a classroom climate that celebrates differences and teaches tolerance. Boys come into the classroom with attitudes and beliefs that shape how they respond to the emotional and academic life of school. Teachers and other school staff are in a unique position to either exacerbate this situation or to employ strategies that will help make the school environment a positive learning environment. Boys also come into the school environment looking for validation of who they are as learners. They quickly receive information about whether or not they will be a successful learner in school. In the next chapter, we will discuss the reason so many boys are currently seeing school as an academic environment in which they will not be successful. In the following chapters, we will present many solutions that can reverse this trend and help our boys to both achieve and feel connected in the school environment.

Boys come into the classroom with attitudes and beliefs that shape how they respond to the emotional and academic life of school. Teachers and other school staff are in a unique position to either exacerbate this situation or to employ strategies that will help make the school environment a positive learning environment.

CHAPTER 2 TOOLS

Gathering More Data

Discuss the following issues with your school PTA, administrators, and/or counselor.

1. How does my school currently deal with the issue of boys being teased or criticized as being "gay" or a "girl"?

2. What is my school currently doing to develop more tolerance, understanding, and appreciation of individual differences?

3. What is my school currently doing to help teachers become aware of boys' perception of certain lessons and activities as not being boy-friendly?

4. What is my school currently doing to help teachers become aware of how their behaviors may shame boys?

5. What is my school currently doing to help train teachers in ways of communicating with boys that don't result in feelings of shame?

6. What is my school currently doing to help boys feel more connected to staff and to programs?

chapter 3

What's Going on With the Schools?

"I hate math! I hate school!" Mrs. Johnson was shocked and saddened to hear these words being shouted by her 8-year-old son, Greg, as he threw his math test on the floor upon returning home from school. While any parent would be concerned to hear these statements, it was particularly shocking to hear them from this young man who had always amazed his family and friends by solving difficult math problems in his head. Hours of car trips had quickly passed as Greg asked for one problem after another and amazed his family with his quick and correct answers. How could that be the same student whose first math unit test of third grade was now laying crumpled on the floor with a big, red 55% on the top?

When Mr. and Mrs. Johnson had time to carefully analyze the test later that evening, Greg's new "math difficulties" became clear. Although he had answered all of the math calculation problems correctly in the beginning of the test, he had lost points for all of the short essays, where he was required to write about how he had solved the problems. His answers in this part of the test either had many points deducted, were emblazoned in red with the phrase "not enough details," or had received zeroes because he had left them totally blank. The Johnsons saw that he had then not even attempted the "challenge" calculation problems at the end of the test, which they knew he was capable of doing. He had either run out of time after the written portion of the test, or perhaps he had become so discouraged that he had quit.

Emphasizing Language Arts

There has been a growing emphasis on language arts instruction in our schools. Over the years, the standards movement in education has placed greater and greater emphasis on the need for all of our students to write more effectively. Few of us would argue with the value of writing well. It is clearly one of the skills that are important for many adults to possess in order to be successful in our society. For a variety of reasons, schools have gradually decided that students need to work on their writing abilities for a greater part of the school day, in every subject area during the school day, and to begin this focus at an earlier and earlier age. This rationale has two parts. Educators believe that if students get more practice in their writing, they will become better writers. Educators also believe that writing is a crucial part of all disciplines and that students must develop their writing expertise, regardless of the type of discipline that they may ultimately focus on in school and choose to pursue for their career. Many educators believe that being a strong writer is a crucial component of any career.

Standards-based education first gained momentum in 1983, during the Reagan era, with the federal educational goals and objectives highlighted in the report titled *A Nation at Risk*. This federal interest in reforming education lasted through the George H. W. Bush (America 2000) and Clinton eras (Goals 2000). In recent years, the No Child Left Behind (NCLB; 2001) legislation, mandated under current President George W. Bush, has brought this movement to our entire country. Student performance in skill areas is now tracked yearly and, in many school districts, high-stakes exams are in place that students must pass before graduating high school. Decisions have been made in line with this movement that writing must be emphasized across curricular areas.

The newest revision of the SAT exam further emphasizes the importance of writing in our schools. The new SAT exam, unveiled in 2005, now has a significant writing component. As all school districts strive to prepare students to successfully compete for college admission, the content of the SAT exam contributes to each school district's decision about where to place its emphasis. Many educators believe that we must emphasize writing throughout the curriculum, so that our students will have as much opportunity as possible to develop this skill, and thus be able to gain college admission.

Along with writing, the acquisition of reading skills has become part of the national focus. Just as with writing skills, reading has received a greater emphasis across curricular areas. More time than ever before is devoted to the instruction of reading as a separate content area and more time than ever before is devoted to teaching reading skills in all content areas. *The Washington Post* featured a front-page article about this phenomenon in May of 2004, focusing on one suburban elementary school that symbolized what is happening across our nation. The daily hour once devoted to science and social studies has been replaced by an extra hour of writing for second and third graders. Reading has been expanded to 90 minutes a day for all of the school's 770 students. Students who began the year behind their grade level in reading might get 3 hours a day of reading practice. "Once they learn the fundamentals of reading, writing and math, they can pick up science and social studies on the double-quick," Jerry D. Weast, superintendent of Montgomery County Public Schools told the newspaper. "You're not going to be a scientist if you can't read" (Perlstein, 2004).

As school systems have focused on how to improve student skills and raise their all-important test scores, they have searched for ways to increase the teaching time in these high-stakes areas. As described in the *Post* article (Perlstein, 2004), one way to increase the amount of time focused on these tasks is to change the priorities of the school day, directly allocating more time to the skill areas. Of course, this must come at the price of allocating less time to something else, or directly integrating the teaching of writing and reading into all of the content areas. In this way, every subject area becomes what Dr. Susan Baum (2005) describes as a "secret language arts lesson." School districts have found more time for language arts by beginning academic instruction in these areas earlier. Therefore, kindergarten is no longer a year to focus on social skills and acclimating to the school environment. It is now a year to learn the fundamentals of reading, writing, and math.

So, what is the impact on boys of this increasing focus on language arts skills? As described in detail in Chapter 1, a variety of statistics point to the fact that our boys are not doing as well as their female peers and that the gap is widening, rather than decreasing. As discussed in Chapter 2, school is becoming less and less a place that boys identify with and want to be part of. It is also a place in which boys are finding it increasingly hard to be successful.

As part of many psychological tests, students are asked to name three wishes. Typical wishes range from having lots of money and possessions, to world peace. One smart 8-year-old, who was not succeeding with the reading and writing demands of his school, made the following three wishes:

> I want my teachers to understand why I don't get my work done and to have them stop yelling at me as if I don't know anything.

> I want to make sure that none of my friends have the kind of problems that I have.

> I don't want to get in trouble any more.

Let's take a look at the impact on boys of each of the strategies schools are utilizing as they allocate more time to focus on writing and reading skills as a part of standards-based learning.

STRATEGY 1:
CHANGING THE PRIORITIES
OF THE SCHOOL DAY

As schools allocate longer time periods to work on writing and reading, something has to give. As described in the *Washington Post* article (Perlstein, 2004), this may result in less or no time allocated to a content area such as science or social studies or an area such as fine arts. The time may be taken away from instruction in technology, industrial education, physical education, or other movement activities like recess. "Despite mounting evidence that kids need an outlet to blow off steam, learn to interact with others and get the exercise they need, nearly 40 percent of American elementary schools have either eliminated or are considering eliminating recess" (National PTA, 2006, ¶ 2). Many of the areas that are being taken away or decreased are areas that boys have traditionally excelled in and been motivated by. There are considerable studies to show that when students have a chance to excel in areas, such as the sciences or arts, there is a carry-over effect on their performance in other academic areas.

With a decreasing focus on these nonfundamental areas, the result is that many boys are not having the opportunity to have their skills in these areas developed. They are also not finding school to be a place that they can identify with, a place that values their strengths. Educators may argue that there will be time to develop these other strengths later, after the students have mastered the fundamental skills. The evidence, however, points to the fact that more and more boys are not only performing poorly on these fundamental skills, but performing poorly in school in general. Rather than developing good readers who can later become scientists, as schools intend, we are losing future scientists who don't have a chance to focus on their

> Rather than developing good readers who can later become scientists, as schools intend, we are losing future scientists who don't have a chance to focus on their scientific talent and interest early in life and who quickly conclude that school is not a place where they can succeed.

scientific talent and interest early in life and who quickly conclude that school is not a place where they can succeed.

STRATEGY 2: INTEGRATING WRITING AND READING INTO OTHER CONTENT AREAS

The teaching of all subject areas, whether it is math, science, social studies, the arts, or physical education, has now become an opportunity for language arts instruction. Educators believe that this provides more time for students to develop the fundamental skills they need, as they apply them to the particular content area. For boys, this often means that their weakness is now a focus in the area that once would have been their strength.

As found in the vignette about Greg from the beginning of this chapter, a boy who is gifted in math may soon conclude that math is not for him, because it involves writing that is difficult and unmotivating for him. Instead of having an area of competence that gives him pride and may propel him toward a satisfying and successful career, Greg is discovering that he really isn't good in math after all. The red 55% on his math test confirms this very vividly. While boys used to have a consistent advantage over girls in math testing, this differential has virtually disappeared in recent years. And, like all decisions about time, if we are spending more time working on the areas of writing and reading, then time for something else has to give. That something else is often the time that was once allocated for hands-on activities, movement, experiential activities, and multisensory activities, all of which help engage boys and help them to learn successfully.

STRATEGY 3: TEACHING READING AND WRITING AS SOON AS STUDENTS ENTER SCHOOL

Some educators believe that the earlier we expect students to acquire necessary skills, the more years we will have to work with students and therefore, the more time we have for students to achieve positive results. Running counter to this argument is the evidence that many boys are not ready to learn how to read and write until a later age than their female counterparts (Sax, 2005). What then happens when we try to fit these square pegs into round holes? Some of the boys are ready and will learn some skills earlier than they otherwise would have done so. Many, however, will experience their first school years as frustrating, unsuccessful experiences. What they will learn in school, albeit about themselves, is that they are not smart and that school is not a place where they can be successful.

In the following two chapters, we will examine how to get boys involved successfully in acquiring reading and writing skills. Perhaps, even more importantly, we will discuss alternative ways to get information other than through reading and to demonstrate understanding besides writing. No one would argue that reading and writing are not important skills that we'd like everyone to develop to their fullest capability. However, the multiple intelligence approach to teaching and the advent of more technology have increased the possibilities for both learning information and for demonstrating understanding. We will explore how these alternatives can provide a variety of ways for boys to succeed in the classroom and beyond. These alternatives will allow for academic success, and they will allow boys to see school as a place that meets their needs, recognizes their strengths, and most importantly, see themselves as productive, capable individuals.

CHAPTER 3 TOOL

Continue Gathering Data

Discuss the following issues with school administrators, instructional specialists, and your school's PTA.

1. In what ways has the school increased the time allocated to writing and reading?

2. What subject areas have been decreased as a result of the additional time allocated to writing and reading?

3. In what ways have the teaching of writing been increasingly integrated into other content areas?

4. In what ways have the teaching of reading been increasingly integrated into other content areas?

5. In what ways have the expectations that students acquire writing skills in the early grades increased in recent years?

6. In what ways have the expectations that students acquire reading skills in the early grades increased in recent years?

chapter 4

Encouraging Boys' Interest in Reading

o one in his family had any doubt about how bright Phillip was. He could do puzzles that his older brother and sister could not do. He built intricate models with his many Lego kits. He could visualize anything in his mind. His kindergarten teacher had commented on his superior art abilities. This made it all the more surprising and disappointing when he quickly fell behind his classmates in reading. After initially approaching the reading instruction with a positive attitude, he gradually began to shut down and even to show oppositional behavior, as he would do anything to avoid having to read in class. By fourth grade he was getting many C's and even some D's on his report card and was seen as having a behavioral problem. Psychoeducational testing confirmed that he had very superior perceptual reasoning abilities. On the other hand, his language-related abilities were below average to average at best.

Gradually the school, in partnership with his parents, began to recognize both his needs and his strengths. He was given more opportunities to learn and to demonstrate understanding through the creation of projects, utilizing his incredible visual-spatial skills. He was given more opportunities to read in his areas of interest. He built a bridge that won the young engineers contest for his grade level. He also responded to the structured, multisensory approach that the special educator used for reading instruction. Now, in high school, Phillip is reading nearly on grade level. He uses Kurzweil text-to-speech software, which is loaded onto his laptop, for above-grade-level reading material. He is in an advanced technology program, he is an active member of the afterschool robotics club, and he is beginning to apply for colleges, where he hopes to pursue a degree in engineering.

For many boys, reading is one of the main obstacles to achieving school success. The statistics cited in the beginning of this book point to a downward trend in boys' achievement in this area. As described in the previous chapter, with the standards movement of the past two decades and more recently with the mandated testing that is required by the No Child Left Behind legislation, reading has become even more of a focus in school. As mentioned before, boys who could previously demonstrate competence in subjects that did not involve reading now find reading to be part of every subject. In addition to the difficulties that boys often face in acquiring the skill of reading, many boys, as described in Chapter 2, are not motivated to read. They may see reading as being a girly activity, or they may have little interest in the books that are chosen by their primarily female teachers and school administrators. They may have little ability or familiarity with exploring the feelings of the characters, as they are so often asked to do as part of their reading assignments.

How can we help boys to succeed in school in light of their problems with and attitudes toward reading? In this chapter, we will discuss two major ways of attacking the problem. One is to employ strategies that both encourage boys' interest and develop their reading skills. The other is to provide alternative ways for boys to get information, other than by reading. As we discuss these two ways of attacking the problem, we will be describing in detail the ideas and interventions contained in the checklists at the end of this chapter. It is crucial for teachers to think about their goals as they design a lesson. There will be times when improving reading skills is the goal of the lesson and it is essential that students work on developing these skills. More often, the goal of the lesson will be to understand some key social studies, math, or science concept. In these lessons, reading is one of several ways to gather the information that leads to mastery of the concept. Teachers can and should keep the same high expectations and goals for all of their students—that they acquire the key understandings related to the course content. It is important to remember, however that there are alternative ways for boys to gather the needed course content knowledge (Weinfeld et al., 2006). We will discuss these alternatives in detail below.

STRATEGIES THAT ENCOURAGE BOYS' INTEREST AND DEVELOP THEIR SKILLS IN READING

Ideally, we want all boys to be competent readers. Reading is a skill that we are called on to perform in many facets of both our jobs and our leisure activities. Although we will present strategies that help boys circumvent the need to read, the less we have to avoid, accommodate for, and circumvent problems, the more easily and effectively we can function as independent adults. The following strategies are aimed at building boys' desire and capacity to read effectively.

Continue to Systematically Improve Skills by Teaching Boys Reading

Improving boys' interest and motivation is clearly tied to their skill development. We all gravitate toward things we do well and try to avoid our areas of weakness. We owe it to all of our students to develop their skills as much as possible. Teaching boys reading in a structured, multisensory way has proven to be successful in many reading intervention and special education programs. Using structure feeds into boys' tendency to want to know what the rule is in any situation and then to attempt to prove it or disprove it. Teaching skills in a multisensory way allows boys to utilize their strengths to overcome a weakness, in this case, their poor reading skills. Examples of structured, multisensory reading instruction that focuses on improved decoding include the Wilson program and the Orton-Gillingham program. Examples of programs that improve reading fluency include Read Naturally and Great Leaps. Boys particularly like the feature of Read Naturally that calls on them to graph their progress. This competitive element is a good match for boys. There is, of course, a danger that older boys will see this reading instruction as a "babyish" activity. It is crucial to get "buy-in" for this and other skill development. In order for a boy to benefit from the instruction, he must see the value of participating and be motivated to do his best. The following are some important ways to get boys to buy-in or to commit to participate in this skill development:

> **When a boy sees that his teacher or parent knows who he is at his best, what he is capable of, and what he is interested in, the boy will be much more likely to be willing to work on developing his weaker areas.**

- *It must be part of balanced instruction, along with high-level, high-interest work.* When a boy sees that his teacher or parent knows who he is at his best, what he is capable of, and what he is interested in, the boy will be much more likely to be willing to work on developing his weaker areas.

- *There must be acknowledgment from teacher to student that this work may be tedious and not exciting, but it is necessary.* An honest acknowledgment that this skill development may not be the boy's favorite activity, but that it is very important, will open the way for the boy and adult to become partners in this endeavor.

- *There must be an adult-like approach—sharing the boy's strengths and needs; showing, sharing, and measuring his baseline and progress; and setting goals together.* Dr. Mel Levine (2003) refers to this as *demystification*, or the sharing of the student's strengths and needs so that he begins to truly understand who he is, which is the first step toward self-advocacy. Again, a partnership is formed when the teacher and student set and measure goals together. This approach capitalizes on boys' tendencies to want to set and achieve goals.

- *There needs to be challenge and competition, and there must be opportunities to infuse the instruction into high-level, high-interest reading.* Boys tend to be motivated by the excitement of challenge and competition. Skill development can take on these elements when boys are challenged to find examples of the type of word they have just learned to decode within their high-level, high-interest reading. Of course, allowing high-level, high-interest reading is much more motivating than the reading passage that may typically accompany skill development. For example, boys can practice finding a new vowel blend pattern as they read in an area of interest or in a new book that they are excited to explore.

Use Accommodations, Such as Books on CD or Tape and Speech-to-Text Software

Hearing books or portions of books read aloud is a powerful way to increase boys' interest in the written word, as well as being a crucial accommodation for students who can not access the printed word because of a learning challenge or disability. There are several options for using technology to access the printed word. Many public libraries and bookstores have large collections of audio books that are professionally produced, often read dramatically by the author or an actor. Some libraries are also beginning to offer an online service where their patrons can download audio books free of charge. The Recording for the Blind and Dyslexic (http://www.rfbd.org) organization offers a low-cost service that allows a student with a documented disability to order any print material on tape or CD.

There are also a number of text readers that allow the user to scan material into the computer program and then have the words read aloud to him or her. The Kurzweil 3000 is a particularly outstanding example of this text-to-speech software. Not only is print material read aloud, but words also are highlighted on the screen as they are read. This way, the student hears the information and has the opportunity to increase his reading fluency as he reads along, following the highlighted words. All of these technological options serve not only to help boys, but to motivate them, as well. Boys tend to enjoy these high tech "toys" and often forget that they are even involved in a reading activity.

Provide Outlines, Graphic Organizers, and Other Visuals

Many boys who have difficulties with reading have strengths in the visual area. The use of graphic organizers helps boys to literally see their background knowledge and see the key points that are part of the reading they are doing. This allows them to better comprehend the material they are reading. They are given the structure to organize their thoughts in their minds, and putting it on paper both helps them to organize their thoughts and to refer to it in order to overcome any memory issues. Because many of the boys who have difficulty with reading may also be poor writers, it is not necessary or desirable that they be required to write complete detailed sentences on these organizers or outlines. Instead, they may represent their ideas with a note, symbol, or drawing. Organizers may be created by parents or teachers and be as simple as just having a chart to record the names of characters and critical plot events. Boys can also be taught to create their own organizers. The software program Inspiration provides the opportunity for students to web their ideas in a wide variety of formats.

Provide Examples of Successful Men Who Have Struggled With Reading

It helps us all to know that we are not alone with our struggles. It's particularly helpful to know that someone who is highly respected by us and/or others has had the same issues. Historically, people such as Thomas Edison, Albert Einstein, and Leonardo da

Vinci are believed to have had a deficiency in some area of their academic abilities that coexisted with their incredible gifts. Some current examples of famous men who have experienced learning disabilities or differences include Charles Schwab, Tom Cruise, Danny Glover, Henry Winkler, Vince Vaughn, James Earl Jones, Patrick Dempsey, and Magic Johnson. It is important for boys to hear about these men, to learn about their struggles, and to learn how they were able to use their strengths in order to succeed.

Let Your Son See Males in His Family Reading

As male role models, we have a powerful influence over the boys in our family. Even if they don't acknowledge that they are doing so, boys are watching us to learn what is and isn't "appropriate" male behavior. Making a point of reading in front of the boys in our life sends a powerful message: Men can and do read for pleasure and necessity. And, yes, the sports page does count, as do comic books, magazines, and Web pages. Some families have had success by setting aside a specific reading time where all family members, including the adults, spend a period of time each evening reading.

> Making a point of reading in front of the boys in our life sends a powerful message: Men can and do read for pleasure and necessity.

Leave Books and Other Reading Material That Might Appeal to Your Son Lying Around

For many boys, at many ages, there is automatic opposition to anything that their parents may suggest. On the other hand, if they "discover" something on their own, they often are willing to read it. Magazines in the boy's area of interest, or books that require some hidden reading to solve problems or puzzles, are good examples of this. Similarly, while they may rebel against structured required reading time, they may read in their areas of interest without even thinking about it. We will talk more about topics and genres that may appeal to boys as we continue.

Encourage Reading Online (Web Pages)

There is not necessarily a greater value in reading a book than in reading online. Both have the potential to develop our reading skills, background knowledge, and thinking abilities. Many boys prefer reading Web pages to books. Perhaps it is the visual-spatial nature of this type of reading. Web pages typically have graphics and/or illustrations. They also invite interaction. They do not have to be read sequentially, and boys can follow their curiosity to move from one page to another linked page. Reading online has applications to many types of careers and the trend seems to be that most of us will be doing more and more of this type of reading in the future. Perhaps, most importantly, this is a type of reading that many of our boys are willing to do, that they enjoy, and that they may not even regard as reading. Reading online is a way to bring this generation's skills, interests, and attention span into the learning environment. *TIME* Magazine, in its cover story on Generation M (for multitasking; Wallis, 2006), reports that today's students tend to be extraordinarily good at finding and manipulating information online through Web pages.

Allow Reading to Be Private

Many boys are shy about reading aloud. Reading aloud may be one of the most painful experiences of school, potentially humiliating them in front of others. The bottom line is that for many boys, reading aloud should be voluntary, except in a safe environment where the boy and the adult have agreed that reading aloud is a skill that they are working on together. An alternative way to get boys engaged in reading aloud is to have them read aloud to a younger child. This activity is often an excellent way to motivate a reluctant boy to practice his reading without feeling judged by peers or adults. As we will discuss below, boys also need privacy when it comes to their choice of reading interest areas.

Subscribe to a Magazine About His Interests

Another way to encourage interest in reading is to buy your son magazine subscriptions in his area of interest. Boys who won't read otherwise will often read above their ability level in their area of interest. It is also thrilling to many children to have something delivered to their home or school that specifically has their name on it. Finally, the visual nature of most magazines is also motivating for most boys. Even if it seems that he is mainly looking at the pictures, he will probably become interested in some of the accompanying words, as well. And, remember, it's a process. Looking at pictures and reading a few words, without the pressure of having to read, can develop a pleasurable pattern that eventually includes more and more reading.

Give Books as a Present

Giving books as a present can be done alone or in combination with another present (such as a soccer ball and soccer book). Tie your son's interests into the books you give him. For instance, a boy who loves baseball might be given the book *Jackie and Me,* written by Dan Gutman, and some baseball trading cards. To top it all off, how about tickets to an upcoming game and, of course, a program to read at the game? When used to capitalize on boys' interests, to motivate them, and to provide them an opportunity for reading without the pressure of required reading, a book (or other reading material, like a baseball game program) that accompanies an object of interest is more likely to be read.

Let Him Choose

Let your son make reading choices at the library or bookstore. Don't criticize his interests. A common theme to all of these suggestions is to "make room for obsession" (Newkirk, 2002, p. 183), meaning that we should allow boys to read in their own areas of intense interest, even if this means waiting a little longer for them to read our chosen "classics." The theory here is that it is better for them to be reading in their area of choice and developing their skills and feelings of pleasure around reading, than for them to be resisting or opposing the choices that we think are important for them to read.

Don't Worry About the Reading Level If He's Interested in the Material

Let him pick books that are too hard or too easy. A book that is "too easy" may provide an opportunity for a boy to feel good about his reading ability. A book that is "too hard" may provide him with an opportunity to stretch his skills. And, once again, the reason he is picking the particular book should be because it is a real interest area for him, which will ultimately inspire him to read more, our main goal.

Lists, Facts, Action, Humor, Sciences, and Information

Look for books with lists, facts, action, humor, or those with information about the sciences. Recognize that reading for information is as legitimate as reading novels. Maybe it's more legitimate. Although there is a great deal of wonderful fiction to which we'd like to expose our boys, ultimately most of the reading that they do during their school, work, and leisure time will be nonfiction. This type of reading appeals more to most boys because it is logical and systematic and is not laced with all those difficult emotions. Finally, we come back to the issue of choice. If your boy's choice is nonfiction, this should be allowed as a means to keep him reading, knowing that he is more likely to later choose and enjoy novels. (See the recommended list of books for boys at the end of this chapter for some examples of nonfiction and fiction books boys like to read.)

Gross, Violent, and Silly = Engrossing for Boys

If the book grosses out a mom, then son (and dad) will probably find it engrossing. A mom should look for books that she finds boring, tedious, violent, silly, or gross. This recommendation comes from Kevin O'Malley, children's book author and advocate for improving boys' reading skills. It echoes the recommendations of Thomas Newkirk (2002) in his book *Misreading Masculinity*—that we must widen the circle of acceptable books for boys to read. It is OK for us to capitalize on boys' interests in gross bodily functions, if that's what they'd like to read about.

> If the book grosses out a mom, then son (and dad) will probably find it engrossing. A mom should look for books that she finds boring, tedious, violent, silly, or gross.

Regarding violence, all of us are concerned about keeping our boys and their schools safe. We certainly must be vigilant about what our boys are thinking and be aware of any disturbing preoccupations. Parents, it's always a good idea to monitor what your children are reading. If you feel that the material your son wants to read is too violent for his age and maturity level, then you should follow your instincts and replace that particular reading material with something more appropriate. On the other hand, it is clear that most boys love action. If they're not engaged in it, they are fantasizing about it. Allowing them to read about action, including some mildly violent themes, will encourage them to read more.

Seek Recommendations From Other Boys and Men

Encourage boys to read books that are recommended by other boys and men. There are more and more lists available lately of books that are specifically recommended for boys by other males. Two excellent sources can be found at http://www.guysread.com and by looking at the recommendations of the American Librarians Association at http://www.ala.org. Kathleen Odean (1998) has published a book of recommended books for boys called *Great Books for Boys*.

Teachers also can cultivate these types of recommendations from the boys in their classes. School librarians can do the same thing, by soliciting recommendations that can be posted on the bookshelves as "boys picks." Local bookstores can be encouraged to do the same thing, as well. At the end of this chapter, you will see our lists of top picks for boys of all ages. This list was developed by surveying boys, their parents, and their teachers. Warning: Be prepared to accept gross, silly, and violent themes.

Read Aloud to Your Son

Read aloud to your son on a topic that he wants to learn more about or read stories in which he is interested. Boys who may not yet have strong reading skills can be very stimulated by hearing information about topics for which they have a passionate interest. They may also be happy to hear a story that an adult reads to them. Hearing these stories can help to develop a love of the written word. Reading aloud allows time for discussion about what the author has written and also provides an opportunity to develop a connection between the adult and the boy. Again, this type of activity may be particularly powerful when the adult reader is a male, reinforcing that reading is an appropriate male activity.

Discuss the Ideas Presented in the Books Orally

It might be beneficial to engage in oral discussion about the ideas presented in a book using supporting text from the book before having boys read it. Although many boys are not avid readers, they tend to have strong ideas and interests. Engaging them in a discussion, particularly one for which they have some personal passion, can be an effective first step toward reading. Boys, and men for that matter, tend to want to reach conclusions, find information to support those conclusions, solve the problem, and give advice. Once they have done so, boys can then be asked to find written information in the book that supports their position and to share that information in an effort to support their opinion.

Begin With a Project or Experiment

Begin by giving boys an experiment, experience, or project to undertake, and then have them read to find out more information about the topic at hand. Traditionally, we have expected students to first read, and then write about a topic, and then we allow them to develop a project based on the topic. For boys, it is often useful to turn this process around. Once they are engaged in designing and implementing a project, boys will then have a motivation to read in order to gain information to utilize in the project.

Projects that are authentic, meaning that they are being done for a real-life purpose, are especially powerful. Reading about a rule or law that they want to have changed, or another hot current events topic is an example of reading for an authentic, real-life purpose. Using the methodology of the professionals who are working in a particular field is also particularly motivating. Reading online as they track the progress of present-day explorers through the Jason Project (sponsored by National Geographic) is highly motivating, even for boys with reading disabilities. Real-life experience that has bearing on what the boy may actually do in the world of work, after he has completed school, also gives school learning true meaning. Again, once he is involved in this authentic project, reading will have a real purpose, providing a great motivation for the boy to become involved in what he is reading.

STRATEGIES THAT PROVIDE ALTERNATIVE WAYS FOR BOYS TO GET INFORMATION

Despite our best attempts to help boys improve their reading skills, there will likely be some boys for whom reading continues to be an area in which they are not interested. Reading also will be an area for some boys in which they may not be competent, for a variety of reasons. Furthermore, as noted in Chapter 1, more and more students in this "wired" generation are not motivated, stimulated, and excited when information is presented only through reading. The following strategies provide alternative ways for boys to get information other than by reading the printed word.

Interview an Expert, View a Web Site, or Take a Field Trip

One of the most meaningful ways to gather information is to do so by hearing that information directly from an expert or by interacting with that information by participating in a field trip. The electronic age has made the world smaller, giving boys direct access to experts in all fields. Boys can be taught to use resources like the Internet to locate experts who they can then communicate with either via e-mail, Web sites, or phone. Although a Web site or e-mail will still involve some reading, this type of reading is generally briefer and tends to be the type of reading that more boys find motivating. Web sites will typically contain visual material that provides an alternative way of learning that may be a good match for the boy's particular area of strength.

It is also important to realize that as boys are interviewing an expert or searching a Web site, they are developing other skills that will serve them in similar situations as they progress in school and into careers. The self-esteem gained from being able to successfully interact with an expert in the field is invaluable. Experiential activities, such as expert interviews and field trips, also provide a powerful multisensory, real-life experience that results in information more readily becoming part of the boy's long-term memory.

Listen to a Guest Speaker

Bringing a guest speaker into the classroom can also provide a powerful alternative to reading about a topic. The guest speaker can provide firsthand information about the topic in a way that the printed page cannot usually provide. As with the expert interview, boys can be involved in choosing the speaker, making the arrangements for him or her to come to school, and developing questions for the speaker to answer. In this way, the boys are more actively involved in the event, and they are developing interpersonal skills that can continue to serve them in later years. When the guest speakers are male, there is also the opportunity for boys to see a powerful role model and perhaps even form a mentoring relationship.

View a Video

Viewing a video can be an effective way of gathering information, particularly for a student with visual strengths. Some boys will remember more and be more motivated by these visual images. A good teacher will provide a structure to watching the video that will make it more of an active than passive activity. As students watch the video, they should be looking for answers to specific questions. Videos do not have to be shown from start to finish. Anyone who has watched a boy (or a man, for that matter) flipping channels knows that a briefer viewing time, perhaps followed by some discussion, may be a more effective way to gain information from the video.

Listening to Books on Tape or CD and Viewing CD-ROMs

This alternative was discussed previously as a way to motivate boys to want to read, as well as a way to build their skills as they follow along with the text. It also is an effective way to gain information, particularly for the boys who may be primarily auditory learners, and they need not always be required to follow along with the text. Alternatively, the boy may be filling out a graphic organizer that allows him to highlight key points, drawing visual representations of what he is hearing, or just listening. There are also many excellent educational CD-ROMs that boys can both listen to and see. They are interactive, calling for the boys to respond to the information. Again, many boys who may not find print materials accessible or motivating will find using this multisensory computer software at their own individualized pace very motivating.

Incorporate Multiple Intelligence Activities

Having boys watch or participate in a multiple intelligence activity, such as a dramatization, musical production, or visual arts activity, is an excellent way for them to gain understanding of the key concepts of a lesson or unit. Boys, like their female counterparts, have a variety of different strengths. Based on these strengths, they learn information more readily depending on how it is presented. Presenting information in a variety of ways that utilize the eight areas of multiple intelligences first identified by Howard Gardner (linguistic, logical-mathematical, spatial, bodily-kinesthetic, musical, interpersonal, intrapersonal, naturalist) will help ensure that a variety of students are motivated, gain understanding, and will remember the information more readily (Armstrong, 2000). Parents and teachers should take the time to determine which areas of multiple intelligence are strengths for their boys. These strength areas can then be used as effective learning strategies in the classroom.

Many boys will respond to hands-on, experiential activities, which utilize their multiple intelligence strengths, such as dramatizations and creating musical or visual arts products that reflect the key concepts of the lesson or unit. While school has traditionally done a good job of focusing on the verbal-linguistic area, teachers will involve more boys when they emphasize other areas, particularly the visual-spatial and mathematical-logical area, as well. Thomas Armstrong's *Multiple Intelligences in the Classroom* (2000) provides excellent examples of how lessons can be adapted to focus on a variety of multiple intelligences.

Participate in a Simulation

There are a variety of excellent classroom simulations for many subjects and grade levels that provide boys with an active experience as a way of learning the course concepts. As they take part in these simulations, students play a role in a real-life enactment that illustrates and gets them involved in the concept that they are studying. A debriefing discussion helps the boys to process and summarize what they've learned. Project WILD's science simulations and Interact's social studies simulations are two excellent examples of these types of stimulated learning activities.

Use a Demonstration, Diagram, Graph, or Chart

While many educators recognize and believe in Gardner's theory of multiple intelligences, schools typically address only two of these intelligences: verbal-linguistic and, to a lesser extent, logical-mathematical intelligence. Using visual methodology, such as demonstrations, diagrams, graphs, and charts to teach concepts helps boys who may be primarily visual learners to acquire information that they may not successfully get from print materials.

CONCLUSION

As schools have become more and more focused on reading as both a skill in which all students must demonstrate competence, and as the primary way to learn all concepts, boys generally have become less motivated and have experienced less success. By providing strategies that encourage boys' interest in reading, as well as alternative ways for them to get information other than by reading, we increase the possibilities for boys to experience success in school and beyond.

> By providing strategies that encourage boys' interest in reading, as well as alternative ways for them to get information other than by reading, we increase the possibilities for boys to experience success in school and beyond.

CHAPTER 4 TOOLS

Literacy Strategies Checklist

Suggestions for encouraging boys' interest and developing their skills in reading at home and in school are presented below. Use the checklist to determine the strategies that you should employ with the boys in your life.

Strategies for Encouraging Boys' Interest and Developing Their Reading Skills

❏ Systematically improve skills by teaching boys reading skills.

❏ Use accommodations such as books on CD or tape and text-to-speech software.

❏ Provide outlines, advanced organizers, graphic organizers, and other visuals to aid in understanding.

❏ Provide examples of successful men throughout history and in today's world who have had difficulty with reading.

❏ Let your son see males in his own family reading.

❏ Leave books and other reading material that might appeal to your son lying around.

❏ Encourage reading online (Web pages).

❏ Allow reading to be private.

❏ Subscribe to a magazine that might interest him.

❏ Give books as present, alone or in combination with another present.

❏ Let him make choices at the library or bookstore. Don't criticize his interests.

❏ Let him pick books that are too hard or too easy.

❏ Look for books with lists, facts, action, humor, and information about the sciences.

❏ If the book grosses out a mom, then son (and dad) will probably find it engrossing. A mom should look for books that she finds boring, tedious, violent, silly, or gross.

❏ Encourage boys to read books that are recommended by other boys and men.

- ❏ Recognize that reading about information is as legitimate as reading novels.
- ❏ Read aloud to your boy about a topic that he wants to learn more about.
- ❏ Engage in oral discussion using supporting text.
- ❏ Begin with an experience or project and then read to find out more information about the topic.

Alternative Ways for Boys to Get Information Other Than by Reading

- ❏ Interview an expert, view a Web site, or participate in a field trip.
- ❏ Listen to a guest speaker.
- ❏ View a video.
- ❏ Listen to book on tape or CD or use a corresponding CD-ROM.
- ❏ Listen to print information that has been scanned into text-to-speech software.
- ❏ Watch or participate in a multiple intelligence activity, such as a dramatization, musical production, or visual arts activity.
- ❏ Participate in a simulation activity.
- ❏ Utilize a demonstration, diagram, graph, or chart.

Books Recommended for Boys by Boys

The following are book titles that the boys (and their parents) that we surveyed recommended for other boys. We have organized them into very general grade levels, but we encourage boys to ignore those grade levels and pick a book that interests them. These lists are only representative of many, many titles that were recommended by the boys we talked with. The titles listed here are the most popular, have been published fairly recently, and are easy to find at bookstores or online booksellers. Keep in mind that in narrowing down the list, we have eliminated some favorites that we believe that boys will already be asked to read in school.

If it's too hard for your boy to read on his own, read it aloud to him or get a copy on tape, CD, or on text-to-speech software on your computer. In addition to the following titles, many boys recommended nonfiction books. Favorite subjects included dinosaurs, machines, sharks, astronomy, and sports.

Grades 2–4
- Magic Tree House Series
- Goosebumps Series
- Bailey School Kids Series
- A–Z Mysteries
- Boxcar Children Series
- Encyclopedia Brown Series
- Cam Jansen Series
- Nate the Great Series
- Horrible Harry Series
- Magic School Bus Series
- Alien Series
- The True Story of the Three Little Pigs
- I Spy Series
- Frog and Toad Series
- The Stupids
- Henry and Mudge
- Knights of the Kitchen Table
- The Mouse and the Motorcycle
- Homer Price
- How to Eat Fried Worms

Grades 5–7
- Guinness Book of World Records
- Ripley's Believe it or Not
- Oh, Yuck!: The Encyclopedia of Everything Nasty
- The Mad Gross Book
- Artemis Fowl Series
- Harry Potter Series
- Lemony Snicket Series
- Hank Zipzer Series
- Mythbusters
- Animorphs
- Choose Your Own Adventure Books
- Red Wall Series
- Shiloh Trilogy
- Hoot
- The Phantom Tollbooth
- The Stinky Cheese Man and Other Fairly Stupid Tales
- Sideways Stories from Wayside School
- The Pushcart War
- Bud, Not Buddy
- Maniac Magee

Grade 8 and up
- Eragon
- Eldest
- Lord of the Rings Series
- Hatchet Series
- Down River
- River Thunder
- The Dark Materials Trilogy
- Hole in My Life
- The Book of Three
- Jake, Reinvented
- Ironman
- Extreme Elvin
- Slot Machine
- Starship Troopers
- Warriors Don't Cry
- Looking for Alaska
- Sanath
- Christine
- Slam
- Monster

chapter 5

Encouraging Boys' Interest in Writing

s the school IEP team began its discussion, everyone already knew that there was only one realistic solution for school placement for Andre. Although everyone felt sympathy when they thought of what he had been through, that didn't change the fact that he was making little or no academic progress and becoming more and more of a disruptive force in his fourth-grade classroom. Andre had come to live in this suburban school district when both of his parents had died within a matter of months and he was placed in a foster home.

In the classroom he was loud, distracting, and overly dramatic. He was very disorganized and produced little or no written work. In fact, during time when written production was expected, he was often out of his seat, taking on his role as "class clown." He generally seemed unmotivated, or as one teacher described him, "lazy."

As with so many other boys who were not being successful in the classroom, particularly minority boys, the only solution seemed to be placement in a program for emotionally disturbed students.

Fortunately, a special education supervisor present at the meeting asked the team to focus on Andre's strengths. There were many. Testing had revealed that he had very superior verbal abilities. On the other hand, it was not a surprise to anyone that his written language achievement scores were only in the low average range. One staff member also commented that although his "overly dramatic" behavior could be very disruptive, he excelled when given a chance to participate in plays in the classroom or in afterschool productions. Instead of implementing programming for him as an emotionally disturbed student, the team decided to focus on his strengths as a gifted student who had a learning disability in the area of writing.

Now, 4 years later, Andre is excelling in middle school. He has been successfully grouped with other gifted students, many of whom also have learning challenges or disabilities. He has become proficient on the computer, using either a portable Alpha Smart keyboard or a word processor for all of his writing assignments. He utilizes his exceptional verbal abilities by speaking his thoughts before writing them on the computer. Sometimes he even dictates to himself first on a tape recorder and then later transcribes and edits his own thoughts. He has begun to use Dragon Dictate, a software program that allows him to speak his thoughts directly into the computer and have the computer automatically write what he has said. When writing isn't the specific goal of the lesson, his teachers will also allow him to demonstrate his understanding in alternative ways. He may give a speech or create a brief dramatization (his favorite activity). Speaking of drama, he has continued to develop his dramatic talents, starring in last year's school play. His foster parents have now adopted him, and Andre's life seems to be headed in a very positive direction.

Of all the skill areas, written production seems to be the one area in school that creates the most problems for boys. Like reading, there are many pieces that have come together to make this area such a significant problem area. With the standards movement of the past two decades, writing has become a greater and greater focus in school. No longer just the domain of English class, writing is now part of every subject. It is no longer enough to solve the math problem—boys must now write about how they solved it.

Part of a boy's problem with writing may be skill related, while another part of the problem is attitude related, and these two parts are certainly interrelated. As discussed in Chapter 2, part of boys' attitude towards writing may be related to their view of language arts activities as not being activities for "real boys." The humorist Dave Barry commented on male attitudes toward writing in his 1995 book, *Dave Barry's Complete Guide to Guys.* Barry observed, "Very few guys write thank you notes or any other kind of note. Guys would probably commit a lot more kidnappings, if they weren't required to write ransom notes" (p. 16).

> No longer just the domain of English class, writing is now part of every subject. It is no longer enough to solve the math problem—boys must now write about how they solved it.

Analyzing all of the skill issues involved in written production reveals that this may be the most complex school activity that we ask boys to do. Some of the major obstacles that may interfere with boys being successful with the task of written production include:

- generating topics;
- combining words into meaningful sentences;
- formulating topic sentences;
- organizing sentences and incorporating details and support statements into organized paragraphs;
- revising and editing;
- using language mechanics effectively (grammar, punctuation, spelling);
- the physical act of putting words on paper; and
- handwriting. (Weinfeld et al., 2006, p. 75)

How can we help boys succeed in school in light of their problems with and attitudes toward writing? Similar to our approach to the problems faced with reading, we will discuss two major ways of attacking boys' problems with written production. One is to employ strategies that both encourage boys' interest and develop their skill in writing. The other is to provide alternative ways for boys to demonstrate understanding. As we discuss these two ways of attacking the problem, we will be describing in detail the ideas and interventions contained in the checklists at the end of this chapter. Again, we ask that teachers begin by thinking about their goals as they design a lesson. There will be times when developing writing skills is the goal of the lesson, and it is essential that students work on developing these skills. There will be more times, however, when the goal of the lesson is to understand some key social studies, math, or science concepts. In these lessons, writing is one of several ways to demonstrate understanding of the key concepts of the lesson or unit.

STRATEGIES THAT ENCOURAGE BOYS' INTEREST AND DEVELOP THEIR SKILLS IN WRITING

Ideally, we would like all boys to be competent writers. The skill of writing is one that we are called on to perform in most of our jobs and for many of us, in our private lives, as well. We will present strategies that help boys to circumvent the need to write, allowing them to demonstrate understanding in alternative ways, when possible. However, we do believe that the less we have to avoid, accommodate for, and circumvent the need to write, the more easily and effectively we can function as independent adults. The following strategies are aimed at building boys' desire and capacity to write effectively.

Utilize Assistive Technology

Today's boys are fortunate to be in school in an age when a variety of computer hardware and software can make the writing process easier and more exciting for them. Parents and educators have a responsibility to make sure that assistive technology is available to their boys. For many boys, this technology will make the difference in their being able to write effectively and therefore succeed in school. It is also important for us to realize that as we prepare boys for their future careers, that we are preparing them for a world where, not only will they be able to use technology, but the more comfort they have with a variety of technology, the more successful they are likely to be. The following are some current technology that we have found to be especially helpful to boys as they tackle the writing process.

Computers or word processors allow boys to write without the physical effort of putting pencil on paper and forming the letters correctly. They allow boys easy access to spell checkers and even grammar checkers. Perhaps most importantly, they allow an easy opportunity for editing and revision. Most of our schools and classrooms now have one or more computers available. Unfortunately, many of these computers go unused much of the day and are only used occasionally for the final part of the writing process. It is crucial that our boys have access to word processing hardware throughout the writing process.

Portable keyboards are a lightweight, low-cost, durable alternative to stand alone computers. Brands such as Alpha Smart allow boys to use a keyboard at their desk, save information from multiple files, and easily print or download the information. For some boys, the fact that only a few lines are visible on the screen at a time is a negative aspect to using this form of technology. For many others, this technology makes keyboarding easily and effectively accessible to them.

Presentation software, such as Microsoft PowerPoint, allows boys to create a demonstration of their understanding of a topic using a variety of computer graphics and visual effects. While this may be utilized as an alternative to writing, there is a certain amount of writing that is part of most computer-generated presentations. In this way, boys are still working on their writing within the context of a very stimulating program that may use other strengths, particularly those in the visual area.

Some boys may have difficulty with the writing process but may not yet have the typing skills to utilize a keyboard effectively. Word prediction software, such as Co-writer, allows the boy to type the first few letters of the word and then have the program give them choices of the words that they may be trying to type. For boys who also have a reading problem, this program may be paired with a program that reads the printed words aloud so that boys can hear the choices that the computer has generated. As the boy continues to write the sentence, the word predictive software will predict the third, fourth, or fifth word of the sentence based on what he has written for the first two or three words. As the boy's keyboarding skills improve, this word predictive program will no longer be necessary. On the contrary, it may actually slow him down.

Organizational software programs such as Inspiration and Kidspiration allow a boy to web his own ideas, using the graphics and design of his choice. After he is satisfied that he has created a web showing all of his ideas about a topic and how those ideas are interrelated, the boy can press a button and the web will automatically become an outline, taking him the next step on his way to writing. These programs are especially beneficial for students who have difficulties with writing and simultaneously have visual strengths. Draft Builder is another program that allows students to move sequentially from ideas, to sentences, to paragraphs.

Voice-recognition software or speech-to-text software allows a boy to speak his ideas into the computer and have the computer transcribe his speech. This tool especially shows promise for older boys whose voice quality is consistent and who will take the time to patiently train the software program. In the future, as this technology continues to develop, this alternative will likely be used more often with boys, particularly those who have poor writing skills but strong verbal skills.

A handheld electronic speller can support a boy who has good writing skills, but has problems with spelling. These spellers, including the very popular Franklin Speller, allow the boy to type the word as he thinks it is spelled and then see the correct spelling. One type of these spellers allows the boy to hear the choices, so that his selection of the correct word is not dependent on his reading the choices correctly. The definition of the word is also available, so that the boy can check to see that he has indeed found the word for which he was searching.

Programs that allow for audio spell check, grammar check, and homophone distinction, including software programs such as Text Help, are useful to boys who struggle with writing. Text Help allows students to hear what they've written and cues them to look at grammar errors and possible misuse of homophones, a frequent area of difficulty for boys, particularly those who may have learning challenges or disabilities.

Although just being given the opportunity to use any one of these gadgets will be very motivating for most boys, it is important to note that simply giving a boy one or more of these tools is not enough. Boys must be taught how to use the technology and have a chance to become comfortable with its use. The more that this is an option for all students in the class, the more the individual boy is likely to be comfortable in choosing to use it, and unlikely to feel embarrassed in front of his peers for being different.

Provide Rubrics, Model Papers, and Motivating Story Starters

For many boys, getting started on writing is a large problem. Again, because boys are more likely to be dependent on rules and systems, it helps to give them a lot of information about what is expected. A clear rubric that specifies what the teacher is looking for and may even differentiate what would be necessary to achieve different grades will be very helpful to most boys. Seeing a model paper, particularly one that was written by a boy, will help boys to see exactly what is expected of them. Seeing that another boy has done the model paper will be especially helpful in showing them that this is not only an activity of which they are capable, but also one that is OK for them to participate in. Finally, having some story or writing starters that are particular to the assignment in question will help boys to get over the hump and get involved in the assignment.

Systematically Improve Skills by Teaching Writing Skills

Improving boys' interest and motivation is intertwined with their skill development. When we have a greater comfort level and experience success with a skill, we gravitate more toward performing that task. Conversely, we all tend to avoid performing tasks that involve our areas of weakness. We owe it to all of our students to develop each of their skills as much as possible. Teaching boys writing in a structured, multisensory way has proven to be successful in many school settings. Using a structured approach feeds into boys' tendency to want to know the rule and then to try to prove it or disprove it as they are asked to apply it. Teaching skills in a multisensory way allows boys to utilize their strengths to overcome a weakness (in this case, their writing).

Just as with reading instruction, there is, of course, a danger that older boys will see writing instruction as babyish or as a girly activity. It is crucial to get boys' commitment to this and other skill development. For more information on helping boys commit to skill development, see Chapter 4.

Provide Examples of Successful Men Who Have Had Difficulty With Writing

As described in Chapter 4, it helps us all to know that we are not alone with our struggles and it is particularly helpful to know that someone who is highly respected by us and/or others has had the same issues. Again, reference to historical figures who have had learning problems, such as Thomas Edison, Albert Einstein, and Leonardo da Vinci, or to modern-day celebrities, such as Woody Harrelson, actor; Terry Bradshaw, former NFL player and TV host; Jay Leno, comedian and TV host; Orlando Bloom, actor; Jim Shea, Jr., Olympic Gold Medalist; Gavin Newsom, Mayor of San Francisco; and Stephan Jenkins, singer for the rock group Third Eye Blind, will help boys to be inspired to tackle their own issues.

Expand on Writing in Preferred Styles, Including More Narrative Forms

We must widen the circle to allow and encourage boys to write in their preferred styles. Our experience and the research of others tells us that boys prefer to write in alternative forms that include cinematic style, joke books, sports pages, and Web pages (Goldberg & Roswell, 2002; Newkirk, 2002). It is crucial that we make these styles part of what we accept and encourage in school. Boys quickly learn whether or not their interests and talents have a place in school. If we accept the styles of writing that boys prefer, we will have a chance to help them develop their talents and skills while they are writing in these styles of interest. Later, after we have cultivated their interest and they have experienced this success, they will be more willing and capable of taking on other styles. Thomas Newkirk found that boys particularly like to write in certain youth genres—wish fulfillment, stories that include their friends as characters, and, of course, exaggerated and extreme situations.

> Boys quickly learn whether or not their interests and talents have a place in school. If we accept the styles of writing that boys prefer, we will have a chance to help them develop their talents and skills . . .

Encourage Writing on Preferred Topics

Certain topics have a greater appeal for many boys. Again, violent, silly, and gross seem to head up most of their lists. Allowing and even encouraging boys to write on these preferred topics will get them writing and let them see that their thoughts are included in what school is about. Violence is an especially touchy subject. In the light of the increased school violence that has occurred over the past decade, it is understandable that schools would want to be especially vigilant about what students are writing. While a written plan to actually harm one's self or another person should continue to be cause for an immediate response, violent creative writing should be seen as what it truly is for most boys, an opportunity to fantasize about movement and action.

Also, allow boys to write about their obsessions. Whether it's action, violence, or another topic, many boys will want to write again and again about the same topic. Our tendency as adults is to want our students to branch out. However, allowing boys to focus on one seemingly obsessive topic may be the best way to keep their interest involved in the process of writing and may still provide educators the opportunity to teach them different written language skills, albeit, around the same topic.

Allow for Critical or Negative Writing

When Goldberg and Roswell (2002) blindly analyzed the writing of hundreds of students for the book *Reading, Writing, and Gender*, they were able to blindly guess the gender of the writer and be correct almost all of the time. One of the ways they separated the boys from the girls was that the boys, when asked to give an opinion about something they had read, almost always responded negatively. Goldberg wisely realized this was something not to be stamped out, but to capitalize upon. She encourages teachers to have boys write "boo reviews," telling what was wrong with the book or story that they had read. Again, the idea is to accept boys as they are, not try to change them into something more acceptable. The idea is to use what they already are inclined to do to motivate them and increase their skills.

Start With the Generalization and Then Allow Boys to Prove It

While it has been observed that girls like to gather information and gradually come to a conclusion, boys are more likely to want to form a quick generalization and then prove or disprove it. Educators can use this to help involve boys in their writing. Boys can be encouraged to do what they seem to do naturally—start with the generalization and then find and write about the details that support what they have stated.

Allow Boys to Write After Expressing Their Thoughts Orally, Visually, or Kinesthetically

In order to get boys involved in writing, it is crucial to capitalize on and use their strengths as a way to enter the writing process. Thinking in terms of the multiple intelligence approach (Gardner, 1983), some boys may have strengths in thinking about things through discussion and in presenting their understanding verbally. It is crucial to let these boys talk with another person or dictate their own thoughts into a tape recorder as the first step toward writing.

Other boys may have great strengths in the visual-spatial area. For these boys, creating a storyboard, where they draw each scene they will be writing about, may be the crucial first step toward writing. For other students, organizing their ideas on a graphic organizer or through a visual program such as Inspiration may provide that crucial entry into the writing process. For still others, whose strength may also include the bodily-kinesthetic area, having the opportunity to make a diagram or model or act out their ideas may provide the crucial motivation and stimulation that will provide them with the ideas and words that will ultimately translate onto paper.

Begin With the Experience or Project, Writing for an Authentic Purpose

Often, educators use the experience or project as the culminating activity, after the students have done the work of writing. For many boys, participating in the experience or project first will provide the motivation and the development of ideas and words that will then easily translate into writing. These experiences or projects are especially powerful when there is a real-life purpose. A project that involves improving something in the community, changing a rule or law, or writing to a famous person or expert provides another level of motivation that involves boys in writing without them even thinking about the skills that they are acquiring and practicing.

Grade Ideas and Mechanics Separately

Grades provide valuable feedback about each boy's performance. Because writing involves so many distinct skills, it is crucial that the feedback that boys receive is specific to the varied and distinct skills that they are using. There is no doubt that grades can also encourage or kill motivation. By separating out grades for ideas and mechanics, boys can see that although they may need to improve on specific mechanics, their wonderful ideas are being valued.

Strategies That Provide Alternative Ways for Boys to Demonstrate Their Understanding

Despite our best attempts to help boys improve their writing skills, there likely will be some boys for whom writing continues to be an area in which they are not interested. Writing will also be an area in which some boys are not competent for a variety of reasons. Finally, as effective adult communicators, we want boys to have a repertoire of different ways that they can demonstrate understanding, including, but not limited to, writing. The following strategies provide alternative ways for boys to demonstrate understanding other than by writing.

Use the Multiple Intelligences Approach

Utilize the multiple intelligences approach with boys, allowing them to demonstrate their understanding in a variety of alternative ways, other than through the verbal-linguistic area. Some of these ways include utilizing the arts, building models, creating a dramatization, writing a musical composition, or making a chart or diagram.

Schools primarily utilize the verbal-linguistic intelligence, and to a lesser extent, the logical-mathematical intelligence. There are six other identified intelligences (Gardner, 1983), and teachers can encourage students to demonstrate their understanding using a wide variety of options that result in products that are in line with their area of strength (Armstrong, 2000). Whether the student is building a model or developing a dramatic presentation, musical composition, chart, or diagram, it is crucial that his or her product be measured in the same way it would be if he or she had developed a written product. All of these different products should be measured in terms of whether they demonstrated understanding of the key concepts of the lesson or unit.

Allow Boys to Present Information Orally

Teachers should give boys the alternative of demonstrating their understanding orally, rather than in writing. Whether it is considered a learning disability or a learning difference, many boys have difficulty with putting their thoughts into writing. Some of these boys are strong verbally, while others have greater strengths in the visual-spatial area. For the boys with verbal strengths, they should be encouraged to use these strengths to demonstrate their understanding orally. This oral presentation may be done as a speech, a dramatization, a tape-recorded presentation, or as a one-on-one interview or test.

More Hands-On, Experiential, and Project-Based Learning

When teachers conduct hands-on, experiential, project-based learning activities, they have the opportunity to evaluate boys' understanding of concepts as they participate in the activity, rather than waiting for a written evaluation at the end of the learning experience. These hands-on experiences tend to be more motivating and allow boys to succeed without the possible limitations of their writing abilities.

Participate in Simulations

When boys participate in educational simulations, they typically are not only more motivated but they also have the opportunity to demonstrate their understanding as they take on a realistic role and interact with others in a realistic way. Teachers can evaluate understanding based on the quality of these interactions as the simulation progresses. Educational simulations are available in most subject areas. Project WILD is an outstanding example of a group of simulations that focus on attainment of the understanding of key concepts in the area of science. The Interact simulations are equally outstanding in the area of social studies.

Allow Cartooning/Storyboarding as the Final Product

As described in the first part of this chapter, drawing visual scenes may be the first step toward writing for many boys. At other times, a boy who has visual strengths may demonstrate his understanding of key concepts through the scenes that he draws and use this final product as an alternative to a written product. It is important with this, as with all of the other alternatives we've discussed, that the goal of the lesson and the understandings that these boys are demonstrating are the same as those for the students who are writing. Their cartooning or storyboarding must clearly contain the key understandings that are the goals of the lesson or the drawing may be paired with an opportunity for the boy to provide an oral explanation that meets the goals of the lesson.

Utilize Assistive Technology

As an alternative to writing, a boy may demonstrate his understanding through the creation of a Web page, a PowerPoint presentation, or an Inspiration web that shows he has acquired the knowledge that meets the teacher's goals of understanding the key concepts of the lesson or unit. When we allow a boy to use one of these alternatives to demonstrate his understanding of the key concepts of the lesson or unit, it is crucial that this be done in a respectful way. The teacher must communicate that the alternative option that has been chosen is just as valuable as the other options that other students may have used. The most powerful way to communicate this message is to allow all students to choose among alternative ways of demonstrating their understanding. As stated above, the expectation for understanding the key concepts of the lesson should not be watered down. The key concepts that the boy is learning have not changed. The only thing that may have changed is that there are now ways other than writing for a boy to demonstrate his understanding of a concept.

CONCLUSION

As schools have become more and more focused on writing as both a skill in which all students must demonstrate competence and as the primary way to demonstrate understanding of all concepts, boys have generally become less motivated and have experienced less success. By providing strategies that encourage boys' interest in writing, as well as alternative ways for them to demonstrate understanding, we increase the possibilities for boys to experience success in school and beyond.

Chapter 5 Tools

Writing Strategies Checklist

Suggestions for encouraging boys' interest and developing their skills in writing at home and in school are presented below. Use the checklist to determine the strategies that are employed with the boys in your life.

❑ Utilize assistive technology, including:
  - word processors,
  - portable keyboards,
  - presentation software,
  - word predictive software,
  - programs that allow writing to be read aloud,
  - organizational software,
  - voice recognition software,
  - electronic spellers, and
  - programs that provide for audio spell check, grammar check, and homophone distinction.
❑ Provide rubrics and model papers.
❑ Utilize motivating story starters.
❑ Allow for writing after students have expressed their thoughts orally (dictating into tape recorder or to another person), visually (storyboarding, cartooning, hands-on projects, or graphic organizers), or kinesthetically.
❑ Begin with an experience or project and then write about the topic.
❑ Write for an authentic purpose (e.g., community project, changing a rule or law, writing to a famous person or expert).
❑ Continue to systematically teach how to improve writing.
❑ Provide examples of successful men throughout history and today's world who had difficulty with writing.
❑ Expand on writing in preferred styles.
❑ Allow writing on preferred topics. Allow action-filled writing.
❑ Include more forms of narrative (e.g., jokes, Web pages, sports page).

- ❏ Accept youth genres (e.g., wish fulfillment, quick cinematic narrative, exaggerated, extreme, silly).
- ❏ Make room for obsession (i.e., fixating on certain topics and wanting to write about them repeatedly).
- ❏ Allow for critical or negative writing (i.e., boo reviews).
- ❏ Start with the generalization and then prove it.
- ❏ Grade separately for ideas and mechanics.

Suggestions for alternative ways for boys to demonstrate understanding other than in writing are provided below. Use this checklist to determine the strategies that you should employ with the boys in your life.

- ❏ Multiple intelligences approach (include drama, music, models, visual arts).
- ❏ Present information orally.
- ❏ More hands-on, experiential, project-based learning.
- ❏ Participate in simulations.
- ❏ Provide alternative ways to demonstrate mastery of concepts—portfolios, projects, oral presentations.
- ❏ Assistive technology—create a web of ideas or a PowerPoint™ presentation.
- ❏ Allow cartooning/storyboarding as the final product.

Alternative Educational Programs That Empower Boys to Succeed

enjamin Wright, principal of Thurgood Marshall Elementary School in Seattle, WA, was upset as he looked at the results of his test scores in 1998. As the leader of this elementary school in a primarily low-income area of the city, he believed he had done what he could to improve his students' education, but the test scores were still low. An analysis of the test scores showed that it was the boys' scores (in the 10th percentile) that were dragging the scores of the school down. In addition, he and his staff were spending a great deal of their time dealing with the inappropriate behavior of the boys in the school, particularly the bullying. There were no additional funds coming from the state or local school district. He decided on a very unusual course of action, particularly for a public elementary school. All of the classes were changed to single gender. In May of 2002, he reflected on the dramatic changes. The staff was no longer attending to one behavioral crisis after another and the scores of the boys on the Washington Assessment of Student

Learning had gone from the 10th percentile to the 73rd percentile (National Association for Single Sex Public Education, n.d.b).

The results are in from the first year of the fourth- and fifth-grade all-boys classes at Twin Ridge Elementary School in Maryland. They show the beginning of the same trend that was seen at Thurgood Marshall Elementary School in Washington. The boys have made dramatic increases on the Maryland State Assessment, particularly in the area of reading. One has to wonder if this can be attributed to the fact that the boys are reading and writing more on topics of their own choosing and in ways that they choose, that they are demonstrating an improved attitude to spending their school days in their teams and tribes, that they are more motivated because they are allowed to frequently engage in friendly competition, that they are more alert for learning because brain breaks are a regular part of the day, and perhaps that they are willing to take more risks with emotional content without the presence of girls in the classroom.

Not every boy can and will succeed in the regular education classroom. We have seen individual boys that have succeeded through a variety of alternative academic programs. The descriptions of single-sex groupings mentioned are proving to be successful and are one very powerful example of what the regular education system can do to support the educational needs of boys. There are other options beyond those traditionally provided by school districts and, in some cases, these programs can provide the avenue for success for boys that are struggling.

We believe that public schools have four major choices when considering the alternatives for programming to help boys succeed in the regular classroom setting. The choices range from the least intrusive to the most radical. First, schools can incorporate the boy-friendly academic strategies that are described in Chapters 4 and 5 of this book, as well as the social/emotional strategies that will be described in the second part of this book. In other words, schools can choose to not change the way they group students, but instead focus on implementing the boy-friendly strategies into the coeducational classes that currently exist in their buildings. A second alternative is on the other end of the spectrum. Schools can restructure some or all of their classes so that the boys assigned to these classes spend the entire school day in single-gender classes, as described in both of the vignettes above. The third alternative is to have some single-gender groupings in the context of a school day where all students also participate in coeducational classes. The fourth possibility may be based on the services available outside the local school. This avenue would explore programming beyond the traditional classroom. We will look at each of these possible alternatives in this chapter.

INCORPORATING BOY-FRIENDLY ACADEMIC STRATEGIES INTO EXISTING STRUCTURES

Some schools will want to follow Thurgood Marshall's example and establish a full-day, single-gender system for their entire school. Other schools will want to follow the example of Twin Ridge and establish a partial school program of single-gender classes that will involve some, but not all, of their classes. Even though there has been, relatively speaking, a good deal of movement in the direction of single-gender programs, there are currently only 42 public schools in the United States with full-day single-gender programs and 151 schools that offer some single-gender classrooms for all or part of the day (National Association for Single Sex Public Education, n.d.a). That, of course, is a small fraction of all of the public schools in our country. There are, of course, private single-gender options available, as well, but a majority of our boys will likely continue to find themselves attending schools that do not offer single-gender educational options. We believe it much more realistic to expect that schools incorporate boy-friendly strategies into their existing structures. Not only do we have a great deal of anecdotal evidence to suggest the benefit of these strategies, we also are beginning to see the empirical data.

In the report *Raising Boys' Achievement* (Younger & Warrington, 2005), the authors describe the results of a 4-year study of gender differences in education. Working with more than 50 primary, secondary, and special schools in England, the authors worked to identify strategies that appear to make a difference to boys learning, motivation, and engagement with their schooling, while consequently raising levels of achievement. Their research concludes that gains can be made in the areas of reading and writing with targeted strategies that include:

- the use of speaking and listening as part of the writing process;
- bringing more creativity and variety to reading and writing;
- greater use of technology;
- greater use of active learning;
- utilizing the arts;
- incorporating an understanding among teachers and students that individuals have different preferred modes and styles of learning, including a focus on the multiple intelligences;
- creating lessons that incorporate more learning styles and a greater variety of intelligences;
- using mentors to mediate and negotiate for their students and at the same time challenging their students to do more and better;
- targeting boys who have the greatest capacity to influence others and seeking to give them greater positive involvement in school; and
- providing leadership opportunities for all boys. (pp. 10–14)

While some of the results are not conclusive, the research reported in the Cambridge study supports the suggestions that are put forth in this book. There is clear evidence to support the continued incorporation of these strategies into the mixed-gender classrooms, targeting the achievement of our boys. And, as the Cambridge study also made clear, girls also will benefit from many of these strategies.

SINGLE-GENDER CLASSES

There are many advantages to incorporating boy-friendly strategies into those classes that are still gender integrated, but there may, for some boys in these coeducational classes, remain an additional deterrent to successful learning. The Cambridge study reports the need that many boys feel to play a role, to show off, and to act in stereotypical ways when girls are present (Younger & Warrington, 2005). Single-gender classes may provide an opportunity for boys to relax, focus on learning in ways that are more comfortable for them, and take more chances with things that are not comfortable for them.

A variety of studies have reported the effects of this level of comfort (National Association for Single Sex Public Education, n.d.a). Boys in all-boys schools are more than twice as likely to study subjects such as foreign languages, art, music, and drama. Girls in all-girls schools are more likely to study subjects such as advanced math, computer science, and physics. It is not just that they participate, but they also have high achievement in these courses. The Cambridge study (Younger & Warrington, 2005) revealed that participation in the single-gender classroom resulted in improved performance for boys, particularly in English and foreign languages, as well as for improvement in the performance of girls in math and science.

> **Boys in all-boys schools are more than twice as likely to study subjects such as foreign languages, art, music, and drama. . . . It is not just that they participate, but they also have high achievement in these courses.**

One danger of the boys-only classes, as reported in the Cambridge study, may be that they will produce an environment that is macho and unfriendly to some of the boys in the class. The authors point out the need to go beyond just placing students and their teachers in these single-gender situations, but emphasize the importance of providing training that will allow teachers to create the optimal learning climates. We believe that these climates will celebrate who boys are while also allowing boys to expand their repertoire of skills and behaviors and to develop the all-important trait of tolerance for individual differences. The Cambridge study authors (Younger & Warrington, 2005) talk about compelling evidence:

> Freed from concerns about the need to perform to role, boys and girls have repeatedly described the advantages of single sex classes: a willingness to engage more in discussion and

questioning, being prepared to discuss feelings, a readiness to participate without fear of scorn or discomfort. (p. 144)

Although the advantages of single-gender classes are seen for both girls and boys in the study, it is clear, as we look at the current achievement of our boys, that we may have the most to learn from the ways boys are responding to these opportunities.

SINGLE-GENDER GROUPINGS ALONGSIDE COEDUCATIONAL CLASSES

This third alternative, setting up some single-gender classes in the context of a school day where all students also participate in mixed-gender classes, may encompass the best of both worlds while maintaining the advantages of each. This alternative is simpler than it sounds: It breaks up students into single-gender classes for some subjects, but keeps them in coeducational classes for the remainder of the day. In this alternative, all students take part in both the single-gender and coeducational classrooms.

Despite all of the advantages of single-gender education reported in the Cambridge study, the majority of boys and girls questioned by the researchers said that they would prefer to be in at least some mixed-gender classes (Younger & Warrington, 2005). We believe that there is always a danger in any type of segregation, a danger of separate and unequal opportunities. Furthermore, we believe that in order to prepare our students for the diverse world that they will live and work in, we must give them structured and supported experiences in dealing with that diversity. Clearly, however, there are advantages in creating boy-friendly classes that focus on improving the achievement of boys while providing them with an environment that both celebrates their differences and encourages them to take chances. We do believe that we can maintain the advantage of these single-gender classes while giving boys experiences in dealing with the diversity that will always be part of their lives.

Language arts clearly have shown to be an area where boys have experienced great difficulties. We believe it would make sense to have boys participate in single-gender classes in reading and writing in elementary school and to participate in single-gender classes wherever English and reading are taught as separate subjects in secondary school. English was one of the areas where boys clearly demonstrated benefit in the Cambridge study (Younger & Warrington, 2005). This is the area where we believe the teaching of reading and writing should be the focus and, as we have discussed, this is an area of challenge for many boys. All-boys classes in these areas would allow teachers to focus on boy-friendly strategies and to create an environment that would allow more boys to take risks.

We believe that having all-boys language arts classes would help create school awareness and focus on boy-friendly teaching strategies that would penetrate the mixed-gender classes, as well. Our hope is that, in schools that contained single-gender classes, the staff of the mixed-gender classes would be more likely to receive training in the strategies that will help boys to be successful throughout their school day. This carry-over effect has been one of the successes of the Twin Ridge program. Teachers in the mixed-gender classes have been included in training on best practices for working with boys, and so the boys in their classes have benefited.

EDUCATIONAL ALTERNATIVES BEYOND THE REGULAR CLASSROOM

Many of the young men that we have worked with over the years did not find success for a variety of reasons in the regular classroom environment. Instead they, their parents, and in some cases, the school district, sought out specialized programs beyond the regular system to meet their education needs. The following case studies demonstrate a variety of educational alternatives that may be considered. It is important to remember that these programs do include the boy-friendly points mentioned earlier (see p.

78), including the use of speaking and listening as part of the writing process, greater use of technology, greater use of active learning, a focus on the multiple intelligences, and providing leadership opportunities for all boys.

Early Graduation or Acceleration

Dave wanted a life beyond his rural southern school district. He was a dreamer who had decided at an early age he wanted to design buildings. Dave took all of the advanced-level classes he could at his school but still pursued more challenge. His local school was willing to provide advanced courses and even negotiated with a local university for Dave to begin taking college-level courses. It was in the beginning of his junior year of high school that a guidance counselor mentioned an international education program in Arizona that allowed students to complete a high school diploma and begin work on college coursework in a challenging, multiethnic learning community. After discussing his options with his mother and the high school principal (whom Dave had a good relationship with), Dave chose to skip his senior year and enter the program. According to Dave, this was the best decision of his young life and it launched him into a new world of opportunity.

The program Dave entered focused on boy-friendly educational principles for all of its students. What Dave found was a group of young men with similar interests and advanced-level abilities that he had not found in his home school district. He gained an in-depth understanding of the skills and the real-world problems faced by engineers from working with mentors in the field. Dave grew from the leadership opportunities he was presented with by overcoming his fear of public speaking and his self-confidence was increased by realizing that his creative ideas were valued and that other people wanted to hear his ideas. Dave also found an advanced level of technology that was far beyond what his former school could offer. In essence, Dave had made a choice that benefited his educational needs and propelled him into a career that he really had a passion for.

Acceleration and early college entry has been much maligned since the release of the movie *Little Man Tate*, in which the main character enters a college physics course as a 10-year-old. For many years, parents and educators have expressed and discussed their concerns over the social and emotional development of students who accelerate their education. The argument against acceleration typically presents two specific concerns: how will the acceleration affect the social aspect of the student's life and will the student bypass "normal" experiences of growing up due to the acceleration?

Many people worry how a cognitively advanced boy will deal with being with older, more mature students in a learning environment. In other words, the argument is made that students should be with their own age group to encourage "normal" socialization. In Dave's case, he clearly states that he felt the chronologically older students were his peers on every level. He also states he had much more in common with these peers because they were on the same intellectual level. In fact, Dave said he learned valuable social lessons from his older classmates that he feels helped him to understand the process of moving from a teenage boy to becoming a man. Instead of growing up too fast, Dave feels he grew up at the rate he was intended to.

The second concern deals with those milestones that many consider part of "normal" teenage experiences, such as the school prom. Dave also had comments on this. Simply stated, Dave asked, "What is a normal life?" He had no interest in going to the high school prom. That was not a priority for him. In fact, Dave said he had a life changing social event in college that totally negated any thoughts of loss of teenage socialization. He met his future wife at a dance; she was also an accelerated student. While events of "normal" teenage progression can be important to some students, we must remember that not all boys place a value on them. High school graduation was another event that Dave had no regrets missing. He found his early college graduation and later his master's degree graduation much more fulfilling.

We must recognize that there are drawbacks to acceleration and that it might not be appropriate for all high-ability boys. On

> On the other hand, many young men are being held back from receiving an appropriate education by a lack of acceleration and may be just as much at risk of social and emotional difficulty by "being tethered to an unrewarding educational program" (Gross, 1994, p. 28).

the other hand, many young men are being held back from receiving an appropriate education by a lack of acceleration and may be just as much at risk of social and emotional difficulty by "being tethered to an unrewarding educational program" (Gross, 1994, p. 28).

The recent report, *A Nation Deceived: How Schools Hold Back America's Brightest Students* (Colangelo, Assouline, & Gross, 2004), states six points of contention that may be preventing schools from using acceleration on a regular basis. These include:

- limited familiarity with the research on acceleration,
- philosophy that children must be kept with their age group,
- belief that acceleration hurries children out of childhood,
- fear that acceleration hurts children socially,
- political concerns about equity, and
- worry that other students will be offended if one child is accelerated. (p. 53)

In fact, current research is indicating that these concerns are negligible and the benefits of acceleration can far outweigh the concerns. There are many forms of acceleration and a full discussion of acceleration is beyond this chapter. It should suffice that this avenue can be a lifesaver for many young men that demonstrate above-average ability and maturity.

Alternative or Last Chance Schools

This category of schooling may go by several different names, with the same goal in mind: to provide an educational setting for students that are at risk of dropping out of the regular educational setting. They may be called schools within schools, continuation schools, opportunity schools, dropout prevention/recovery schools, and so on. Interestingly enough, the participants of these programs are majority male (Kelly, 1993; Neu, 1993). This is not a surprise in light of the problems boys are having in the traditional classroom.

This type of educational environment tends to be more open, and student behaviors that would have them removed from the regular education class are tolerated in this setting. There are rules and expectations, and the students are aware of this and abide by them in this educational environment that is much more open and accepting.

Kelly (1993) warns in her study of California schools that some schools are using this kind of placement as a staging point for students the school system has determined are in the final stages of dropping out. She also suggests that high schools are using these alternative schools to shield the true number of dropouts in a school district. These boys have very different reasons for dropping out of the regular school system, many of which are typical issues that could have been alleviated by implementing boy-friendly educational principles (Kelly; Neu, 1993).

Despite some of the misuses of these alternative schools by some school districts, in many cases these schools allow boys to succeed who could not do so in the regular classroom. Let's look at two examples of boys who have entered alternative school programs and found success there.

Eric found himself in his district's alternative school. His school district did not identify him with a special education need, but did recognize he was at risk for dropping out. He did not complete homework, had very few interactions with other students, and withdrew socially from peers and teachers, with one exception: Eric did enjoy studying classic literature and writing poems. His only positive and open interactions came with literature or creative writing teachers. In addition, Eric had always been on the social fringe in school. He was large for his age at 6'4" and 220 pounds. Eric's passion was Goth/Industrial music. While his frequent clothing choice of black leather pants and jacket with various metal studs and a brass skull for a belt buckle took many teachers aback and even caused some disruption when he went down the main hallway of the high school, Eric was at home in his alternative school classroom. No one gawked or sought confrontation with him. He was also encouraged to develop his poetry there.

Sam, on the other hand, was classified as being socially and emotionally maladjusted. His school performance was puzzling, because he demonstrated above-average ability in specific academic areas and scored well on state standardized tests. Sam was an interesting case in which the school district was at its wit's end. Even if Sam did show up for school, there was no guarantee that he would show up for class. When Sam did show up for class, he either could be actively involved in a debate or sound asleep in the back of the room. He refused to attend a special education class in high school. Sam was quick to point out that "The entire school knows who [is] in special education and I don't intend to be identified with that group of losers" (Personal communication, October 17, 2003).

These two students were placed in their district's alternative school program as a last resort. The goal for both of these young men was to provide a specialized educational environment that would meet their educational needs and encourage them to complete their high school diploma. Both of these young men had a special bonus working for them in the alternative school setting: They were going to be working with teachers and mentors who practiced a multiple intelligences approach to education and were trained in and very aware of the educational and emotional needs of struggling boys.

The alternative education program these young men attended followed boy-friendly suggestions. They kept the teacher-to-student ratio low, with one teacher for every four students. Instruction was differentiated and allowed for both young men to produce a variety of products using a multiple intelligences approach. Their learning style preferences were integrated into the instructional model. The multiple intelligences approach will be discussed in more detail in Chapter 10.

Both Sam and Eric had core subjects to complete in order to meet school graduation requirements. Sam was in danger of losing academic credits due to his excessive absences. The school agreed to allow him to compact some of his coursework and to accelerate other courses in order for him to complete graduation requirements on the same timetable as his peers. (Compacting is a research-based educational technique that allows a student to pre-test out of specific areas of core subject matter.) Sam would come into the alternative setting on Monday and take a series of pretests. If he scored more than 90% on the tests, this would be considered mastery of the subject and he could move on to other material. For Sam, this approach was a lifesaver. He was bright and could easily learn the material on his own and then demonstrate his under-standing on the pretests.

Sam also benefited from his teacher bringing more creativity and variety to reading and writing. One of his alternative school teachers was constantly bringing in new and challenging books that went beyond the regular social studies curriculum and engaged Sam in discussion and debate on the ideas presented. Sam was also a big fan of technology and used the computer and Internet in most of his assignments.

Eric had a unique opportunity that would not have been afforded other young men had he not been in the alternative school setting. Eric found a mentor in one of the high school English teachers. Bob was a self-proclaimed frustrated rocker from the 1970s and although he no connection to the Goth/Industrial genre of music that Eric preferred, he did understand the need to communicate a message through lyrics, and he had a knack for putting words to music. Bob and Eric met 3 days a week during Bob's planning period and worked on setting Eric's words to music. Eric was quick to point out that besides the accepting environment of the alterna-tive school setting, it was his relationship with Bob that kept him in school. More information about the importance of mentors will be discussed in Chapter 9.

Both of these young men are now attending local junior col-leges and are succeeding. Eric has gained acceptance into a theatre arts program at a major university and will be attending there in the fall of 2006. While the journey of these young men is far from over, the boy-friendly education environment provided by the alternative school of their home district encouraged them to stay in school and earn a diploma.

Magnet Schools

The magnet school system is common across the United States. Many districts around the country have magnet or specialized schools that address the specific academic interests or recognized talents of students. Typically, two major advantages are cited by proponents of magnet schools: These schools are designed to desegregate urban schools and provide a variety of educational opportunities for a diverse population of students, and they provide a specialized focus of study for students, typically in the arts or sciences, that goes beyond the regular curriculum being offered in a home district. Typically, these programs are supported by either grant money or contribution of local school districts. In 2001, 1,372 magnet schools were operating in the United States (National Research and Development Center on School Choice, 2006). Let's look at the story of one boy who entered a magnet school system.

Ron was frustrated with his local public school. He had taken all the art electives that his school offered and excelled in the visual arts. He had created award-winning sculptures of metal, but had no further outlet to develop his arts ability at his local school. While a good student, Ron was slowly losing interest in the regular education program that he was being offered. Ron really desired an opportunity to experience the arts. In the summer following his sophomore year, he learned about the audition process for a magnet school for the arts. Ron discussed this opportunity with his parents and then began the audition process.

In Ron's case, the arts-related magnet school he attended was located 24 miles away in a different school district. His school did have a tuition agreement so that if a student was accepted into the program the home district would pay the tuition; however, the student's parents would have to pay for the special bus system that would pick up identified students at their home school to transport them to the magnet school each day. Ron decided on a program in which he would complete core courses at his home district and then take the bus ride to the magnet school to focus on classes that would help him develop the skills of the practicing artisan.

For Ron, the opportunity to work in the practicing arts was a huge motivating factor. The teachers at the magnet school knew exactly how to use the arts to draw out the strengths and interests of their students. Each class presented a concept important to arts and utilized active learning. For every class when a lecture was used, the following class would focus on the production of the concept in an art form. Perhaps most unique to this educational environment was the fact that the educators at the magnet school were not only trained in learning styles and in using a multiple intelligences approach, but the educators themselves learned using these different styles and intelligences. Ron was amazed at the difference this made in his teachers' ability to create lesson plans that were meaningful.

Depending on which state and which school district you live in, there are a variety of magnet school choices across the United States. Urban areas have found the magnet school concept to be successful in retaining male students (Metz, 2003). The magnet school concept has benefited many boys by allowing them to pursue their interests and abilities in way that their local schools could not.

Homeschooling

An option that an increasing number of parents are turning to is to remove their children from the public education system and provide homeschooling. While this is not an option for all parents, it is an avenue that some parents choose for a variety of reasons. Whether it is chosen for purposes of religion, a general philosophical disagreement with public education, or a negative public school experience, many boys are flourishing in a homeschooling environment.

Whether it is chosen for purposes of religion, a general philosophical disagreement with public education, or a negative public school experience, many boys are flourishing in a homeschooling environment.

Kerry's parents were highly trained professionals that were disillusioned with the public school setting and especially their district's lack of differentiation for students with individual differences. Kerry was an active child, but did not have Attention Deficit/ Hyperactivity Disorder (ADHD), as his public school system hinted at. Kerry's parents took the unusual step of taking him out of the public school and providing a homeschooling experience for him for 8 years. Kerry did thrive in this environment and demonstrated a love of reading on an advanced level. His father was a practicing psychologist and kept abreast of research in learning styles, especially the special educational needs of boys. Speaking and listening were vital parts of the writing process, and his mother provided an incredible array of creative activities in reading, writing, and math.

Kerry did have another area that he worked at diligently. Kerry was a nationally ranked mountain biker. When many of his friends were in school, Kerry was riding long hours over trails or pumping away on the indoor trainer. His homeschooling experience allowed for the training time he needed to compete on the national level. Kerry is still involved in cycling and has nothing but praise for his homeschooling experience.

Homeschooling is a radical departure and is an option that should not be considered lightly. While the number of students who are being homeschooled continues to grow, data on the effectiveness of this educational provision is inconclusive. At this time, we are working with many young boys who are being homeschooled and carefully monitoring their progress, but have not yet been able to come to conclusive results. Keep in mind that many states now have regulations regarding the registration and testing of homeschooled students.

The advantage many parents find with the homeschooling system is the freedom to develop an educational program that meets the needs of their son as an individual and unique learner. In the case of Kerry, his parents educated themselves on learning styles and learning modality (processing of information into memory). They felt that the public school system was overtaxing otherwise talented and concerned teachers by having too many students in each classroom. The teacher did not have the time or opportunity to alter instruction and differentiate to a degree that individual learners needed. Kerry's parents point to his active kinesthetic learning modality as being misinterpreted by teachers as ADHD. They felt strongly that this misunderstanding is a prime example of a teacher's inability to differentiate for different learners in a crowded classroom.

The list of learning opportunities is wide open for boys when they are homeschooled. Parent who choose homeschooling also make extensive use of field trips and local museums. Several of the boys with homeschooling experience who we have worked with have had a variety of unique educational experiences and are entering or have completed their university studies.

Social opportunities are a common concern for parents that homeschool. The lack of socialization with same-age peers for their boy can be easily overcome. Many parents enroll their homeschooled children in group activities such as Boy Scouts of America or organized sports to provide contacts with peers. Kerry found peers in the mountain biking community who became his lifelong friends.

There is a large group of homeschooling parents who are very concerned with today's school systems being based on a factory model. In other words, they see that schools emphasize that everyone needs to keep up and move along at the pace determined by the curriculum. Homeschooling parents tend to educate boys at their own pace based upon the child's interests. This does require dedication and hard work for the parent. However, materials are now much easier to obtain and the Internet allows for unique educational opportunities. Parents can move a boy through the material at his own pace. The boy may move quickly or even choose an area to study extensively. This opportunity is rarely available in public schools.

Homeschooling is now a highly developed and accepted education option. There are a variety of support organizations and state organizations dedicated to the advancement of homeschooling. Many of these can be found using a simple Web search online.

Special Schools

For some boys with specific learning disabilities, specialized schools may be in order. In Bart's case, his parents were able to advocate for a well-known school in New England that specialized in the education of students with dyslexia. His local school system agreed to pay the tuition at this special school. Bart's reading scores improved in this setting and he returned to his local school system to graduate. When reflecting on this experience, Bart was certain that the special reading strategies he learned and the fact that he was in an environment in which being learning disabled was OK were the keys to his success.

Once again, Bart was very fortunate to attend a school that used boy-friendly strategies. In this school's case, it was not just to benefit the needs of boys, but it was sound educational pedagogy for students with learning disabilities. Bart was very aware that his teachers were creating lessons that incorporated different learning styles. In fact, when Bart began his studies at the University of Connecticut, he was exceptionally aware of his learning needs and able to convey them to others. Bart went on to graduate from the University of Connecticut with a degree in engineering.

Special schools can have a variety of purposes and services available. For instance, in New England there are several well-known private schools that have developed educational programs for student with learning disabilities. The Eagle Hill School, for example, has developed an individualized student-driven program to provide instruction in deficit areas for students with learning disabilities. The instructors are sensitive to all aspects of learning disabilities and have received extensive training in a variety of educational techniques especially designed for students with learning disabilities. The environment in this educational setting is different in that all the students are there because of learning problems. Many boys find that going to a special school for students with learning disabilities is difficult at first, but when they realize that there are others with similar learning problems and that they can learn using different techniques, they report that the experience was worthwhile and gave them the tools they need to succeed.

If parents can make a case for it, many home districts will pay for the tuition in these out-of-district placements. Out-of-district placements are not impossible, but do require extensive parental education and advocacy. Essentially, parents must demonstrate that the services provided by the special school are far superior to the local school. On occasion, parents have been known to demonstrate that the local school has not been able to document educational improvement and that continuing in the current school placement will be detrimental to the boy. In our experience, parents that succeed at obtaining an out-of-district placement in a special school for a boy usually have a long history of confrontations with the local school system, understand special education law, and are tenacious. These parents believe that a special school placement is the least restrictive environment and will afford their child the best educational opportunities.

Special schools differ from magnet schools in two ways: educational programming and goals. The special school typically constructs its programming around an educational need or special education category, while magnet schools develop programming based on a specific discipline or fine art. The special school focuses on goals that will help the boy achieve despite his learning problems. The emphasis is always on the academic attainment of compensation strategies. The end result is that the boy can return to his academic environment with mastery of the skills (often organization, reading, and writing) that previously were eluding him due to his learning disability. The magnet school promotes goals of the discipline and prepares students to learn advanced skills of certain professions and subjects. Upon completion of the magnet school program, these students are capable of stepping into advanced programs in the sciences or arts at the university level.

The disadvantages described by some boys are sometimes related to the special schools' strengths. Although small size gives an increased attention from faculty members, it also means that the smaller student population may limit extracurricular activities. Parents describe the greatest disadvantages as cost and the distance traveled to special schools. A quick search on the Internet will show that many special schools do have expensive tuitions, and it is not uncommon for some boys to have a 45-minute bus ride to the special school.

The decision to place a boy in a special school should be thought out very carefully. We recommend that parents have open discussions with their son about the nature of the program and weigh the advantages and disadvantages these schools present.

Vocational Education

Will loved the kitchen. Several times a year he would treat his parents to full course meals. When he went to neighborhood social events, he always brought elaborate cookies. While Will had friends, he did have some noticeable social skill deficits and was a victim of taunting by some of his peers in middle school. But, Will had a passion for cooking. In his district, the local vocational school had a culinary arts program. Will could not wait to enter high school so that he could attend the vocational school and study his passion.

The history of vocational education can be traced back to the Middle Ages. The basic premise was to develop the skill of a trade under the watchful eye and guidance of a mentor. For many modern boys, this pathway is providing opportunities based on their strengths and interests that they could not obtain in the regular academic track.

Eddie always valued education, but realized that what he wanted to learn was not being offered in the regular school curriculum. He was also very quick to realize that some of his teachers did not even speak the same language he did. Eddie was a self-proclaimed "motor head." He could listen to the sound of a motor and begin to diagnosis potential problems. Eddie sought out the vocational education system to fulfill his educational needs.

Traditionally, technical education programs attempt to provide for both the academic success of students in core subject areas and trade/technology mastery. The ultimate goal is to instill life-long learning in a specific trade or area of technology in students. The vocational/technology path prepares students for postsecondary education, including apprenticeships and immediate productive employment. The trade curriculum responds to employers' and industries' current and emerging and changing global workforce needs and expectations through business and school partnerships.

In Will's case, his vocational school gave him the cooking skills he needed to enter the food industry. Will was able to pursue an apprenticeship with a major resort chain in Florida and is on his way to becoming a dessert chef. This opportunity would never have presented itself if Will did not have the specific vocational training afforded in the culinary school he attended.

Eddie still loves to learn. He has earned master mechanic status and oversees a large automotive repair center. In this role, Eddie seeks out young men with a similar passion and educational background to work in his shop. He is convinced his vocational education has led him to a successful and rewarding career.

The vocational/technical school system is widespread across the U.S. The advantages that these schools have are student choice, specific and advanced training, instruction that is experiential, and the opportunity for mentorships and apprenticeships.

Student choice is a powerful motivator. In Will's case, he knew the regular education program did not offer the choices he was interested in. The vocational system offered a choice of topics that excited him, and Will earned straight A's in these self-chosen classes, while in his academic courses he only attained B's and C's. When asked about the difference in the amount of time he spent on these two type of classes, Will quickly responded that his cooking classes were interesting and he knew how he was going to be able to use those lessons in his everyday life. The importance of student choice is discussed more in Chapter 10.

The vocational/technical school systems provide an opportunity for students to receive specific and advanced training in specific trade domains that the regular education and academic programs do not have the resources to offer. For instance, in Will's school, the culinary department had a variety of ovens that represented the diverse appliances used in the industry. Eddie's automotive technical school had the complete and modern equipment of any well-equipped dealer's shop. In fact, Eddie's training in computer diagnostics in his high school program gave him a distinct advantage as he entered the job market. Again, the advantages of vocational and technical schools include receiving advanced training and having the experiences of the practicing professional.

The nature of the fields of vocational and technical education necessitates instruction that is experiential. Likewise, the students that are drawn to these programs have learning styles that respond best to experiential educational experiences. Numerous researchers have found that students with visual and spatial abilities and difficulty in regular classroom learning styles gravitate to hands-on fields of endeavor (Cooper, Baum, & Neu, 2003; Dixon, 1983; Neu, 1993; West, 1997). It would seem intuitive that an electrician requires a hands-on application of electrical concepts, so the vocational school would provide experiential workshops in which students actually rewire electrical boxes. Will and Eddie report that the experiential training they received at the high school level reflected their later career experiences.

The development of mentorships and apprenticeships in the vocational/technical educational system is reminiscent of the apprenticeships of ancient times. Many of the trade areas still require mandatory supervised journeyman experiences for students of the trade. Smaller class sizes and the creation of mentorships in local businesses are definite advantages over the regular education paths. Here, the student makes a connection with a practicing professional in the field that will guide him as he learns workplace skills. Will was placed in an internship with a chef in a local restaurant who spent the extra time to impart his "secrets" of the pastry chef. Eddie benefited from his internships, but went a step further. Eddie learned so well from expert mentors that he recognized this type of learning suited his style. He began to actively seek out mentors in specific areas of expertise beyond the scope of vocational training.

There are some disadvantages to the vocational/technical educational path. Many schools are struggling at this time to correct these issues. Testing and state diploma requirements are some of the current areas that are under investigation. With testing becoming a major emphasis across the nation, vocational/technical schools are acutely aware that their curriculum is skill based and not representative or accurately measured by state testing instruments. In 2000, 74% of Massachusetts's vocational/technical school students failed the math section of the state exam, as compared to 36% of their peers in regular education programs (Massachusetts Association of Vocational Administrators, 2003). The typical vocational/technical student spends only half of his or her school day taking academic courses, which puts him or her at a disadvantage when taking standardized tests.

Increasingly, states and school systems are tying test scores to graduation requirements. In some cases, passing a state exam is required to earn a diploma. In other states, minimum academic requirements must be met. Again, in the vocational/technical system the emphasis is on mastery of the skills of a profession, which means the student might not be taking as many language arts, social studies, science, or math classes as his peers are required to take. Check with your local school district or state board of education, as many states have adopted alternative graduation requirements for vocational/technical school students.

CONCLUSION

We have described six major choices to be considered when deciding upon educational programming for boys. In our experience, among these six approaches the educational needs of many boys can be met effectively. Some of these alternative educational options are quite fundamental and easy to implement in the regular classroom. As we have seen, some are also very complex and take extensive commitment from school districts and parents to actually to meet the needs of certain boys. The one universal theme that runs throughout all of these alternatives is our recommendations for a boy-friendly education that benefits young men in a variety of educational settings. The second part of this book will build on the educational strategies discussed in the first section as we focus on the social and emotional strategies and programs that help boys succeed in school.

CHAPTER 6 TOOLS

Raising Boys' Achievement in Your School

Evaluate the effectiveness of your school or another school, using the key findings from the Cambridge University study, *Raising Boys' Achievement* (Younger & Warrington, 2005). Look at what's being done now (current status) and what needs to be done.

The use of speaking and listening as part of the writing process.
Current status:
What needs to be done:

Teachers bringing more creativity and variety to reading and writing.
Current status:
What needs to be done:

Greater use of technology.
Current status:
What needs to be done:

Greater use of active learning.
Current status:
What needs to be done:

Utilizing the arts.
Current status:
What needs to be done:

Incorporating an understanding among teacher and student that individuals have different preferred modes and styles of learning.
Current status:
What needs to be done:

Including a focus on the multiple intelligences.
Current status:
What needs to be done:

Teachers creating lessons that incorporate more learning styles and a greater variety of intelligences.
Current status:
What needs to be done:

Using mentors to mediate and negotiate for their students and at the same time challenging their students to do more and better.
Current status:
What needs to be done:

Targeting boys who have the greatest capacity to influence others and seeking to give them greater positive involvement in school.
Current status:
What needs to be done:

Providing leadership opportunities for all boys.
Current status:
What needs to be done:

Program and Service Options Checklist

The following services and/or programs are examples of those that may be available in schools:

Local Public Schools

(Sources: school system Web site, school principal, school counselor, GT specialist)

The school in consideration offers:
- ❏   Talent development programs
- ❏   GT/LD services
- ❏   GT services
- ❏   LD services

Evidence of:
- ❏   instruction in the student's area of strength
- ❏   opportunities for the instruction of skills and strategies in academic areas that are affected by the student's challenges
- ❏   an appropriately differentiated program, including individualized instructional adaptations and accommodations systematically provided to students
- ❏   comprehensive case management to coordinate all aspects of the student's Individual Educational Plan
- ❏   rigorous instruction
- ❏   clear roles and responsibilities
- ❏   attention to social/emotional issues

Other Public Schools

(Sources: state department of education Web site, state GT coordinator, special education coordinator, private advocates)

Does the school in consideration offer:
- ❏   Talent development programs
- ❏   GT/LD services
- ❏   GT services
- ❏   LD services

Evidence of:
- ❏ instruction in the student's area of strength
- ❏ opportunities for the instruction of skills and strategies in academic areas that are affected by the student's challenges
- ❏ an appropriately differentiated program, including individualized instructional adaptations and accommodations systematically provided to students
- ❏ comprehensive case management to coordinate all aspects of the student's Individual Educational Plan
- ❏ rigorous instruction
- ❏ clear roles and responsibilities
- ❏ attention to social/emotional issues

Private Sector
(Sources: private school Web sites, local colleges and universities, private advocates)

Does the school/program in consideration offer:
- ❏ Talent development programs
- ❏ GT/LD services
- ❏ GT services
- ❏ LD services

Evidence of:
- ❏ instruction in the student's area of strength
- ❏ opportunities for the instruction of skills and strategies in academic areas that are affected by the student's challenges
- ❏ an appropriately differentiated program, including individualized instructional adaptations and accommodations systematically provided to students
- ❏ comprehensive case management to coordinate all aspects of the student's Individual Educational Plan
- ❏ rigorous instruction
- ❏ clear roles and responsibilities
- ❏ attention to social/emotional issues

Note. From *Smart Kids With Learning Difficulties: Overcoming Obstacles and Realizing Potential* (pp. 147–148), by R. Weinfeld et al., 2006, Waco, TX: Prufrock Press. Copyright ©2006 by Prufrock Press. Reprinted with permission.

Bullying

ordan is an enthusiastic boy who's almost 4 years old. He enjoys physical games, has above-average hand-eye coordination, and interacts well socially. He is not generally prone to possessiveness, as is demonstrated by his willingness to share with other children. He tends to be sensitive, and will seek comfort or privacy if he is hurt or embarrassed.

Recently, Jordan went with his family to a local mall. While his parents were shopping, his grandfather took him to an indoor play area. The highlight of the play area was a foam rubber slide shaped like a rock cave with wide steps leading to a small observation area at the top. Twenty-four children were in the play area, ranging in age from 2–10 years old.

Jordan waited patiently for an opportunity to climb the steps of the slide, smiling and hopping from foot to foot in anticipation. He didn't seem overly interested in the other children, instead focusing on his grandfather watching him play. Upon reaching the top of the slide, he was immediately shoved aside by five older children who came scrambling up the steps and then slid down the slide in a tangle of flying knees and elbows. Jordan looked upset by the aggressiveness of the older children, but seemed determined to have fun on the slide. The slide was only about 3 feet in length, so Jordan quickly reached the bottom. Immediately, the group of older children, having circled and descended for a second time, piled into Jordan, knocking him around before running off toward the steps to continue their game.

Jordan was visibly upset as he came over to his grandfather, telling him that the children were pushing him around and he didn't like it. Jordan's grandfather began thinking about the different methods he could employ to handle the situation.

He was relatively sure that the children were unaware that they were being inconsiderate. Their nationality and the fact that they seemed related to each other led him to believe that they had a different concept of personal space than Jordan, who was an only child. Reprimanding the older children would probably have little impact and would most likely lead to a conflict with the children's parents, as would addressing said parents directly. He could tell Jordan to stand up for himself, and be more physical, only he was outnumbered and outsized. He also didn't want to send the wrong message by encouraging Jordan to respond to bullying behavior by becoming a bully himself.

He sat Jordan down, and explained to him that this was how these children wanted to play. He voiced the fact that it wasn't fair to Jordan, but they would have to find a way for Jordan to have fun anyway. He suggested that Jordan play in another area until the older children got bored with the slide, then Jordan could take a turn. He cautioned Jordan to try to be quick in case the older children decided to come back. Jordan agreed, and his grandfather sat back to observe the outcome.

Jordan moved around the play area, stopping briefly, then moving on, all the while keeping an eye on the slide. Eventually the older children moved on to other things, and Jordan ran over to the slide, climbed the steps, and quickly slid down the other side. He jumped up at the bottom, a huge grin on his face, gave his grandfather a thumbs up, and ran off to continue playing.

The topic of bullying is an extremely broad subject, with so many factors that it becomes challenging to provide generic solutions that can be used to alleviate the problem. The above story illustrates how bullying issues can begin to surface at a young age, and how the actions of each individual involved can change the outcome of the situation. We will periodically refer back to this story to discuss in what way each person involved influenced how the situation was resolved.

Acts that are considered bullying cover an extremely wide range of behaviors and responses. The challenge is in first finding some commonality present throughout the range of bullying acts. By interviewing boys, the following definition of bullying was derived, "the act of *manipulating* another into an emotional or physical state not of their choosing, thereby causing them to *respond* in a manner not of their choosing" (Caputo & Neu, 2006; Neu & Caputo, 2005). In addition, bullying is generally thought of to occur "when a child or group of children take advantage of the power they have to hurt or reject someone else" (Trautman, 2003, p. 243). Using these definitions, we can create a platform from which to first identify, then combat, bullying in its many facets.

This chapter will focus on identifying the different classifications of bullies, as well as different classifications of victims. By addressing possible resolutions for both parties, we effectively double the opportunities for disrupting the victim to bully cycle. By holding the victim, as well as the bully, accountable for his role in the situation, the bully could experience less resentment toward his victim and vice versa, because both parties are required to follow a prescribed course of action.

By holding the victim, as well as the bully, accountable for his role in the situation, the bully could experience less resentment toward his victim and vice versa, because both parties are required to follow a prescribed course of action.

BULLY TYPES

Bullying comes in a variety forms, and there exists a danger of ignoring its more subtle forms and instead focusing on the more obvious cases. Determining how best to deal with a situation must first start with an attempt to classify the type of bullying present. Next, we must determine if one or both sides involved are engaging in bullying behavior.

The types of bullying behavior that children are most likely to encounter include (a) verbal and written bullying, such as name-calling, intimidation, and threatening notes or statements; (b) physical bullying, such as kicking, hitting, and derogatory or offensive gestures; and (c) social/relational bullying, such as gossiping, telling lies about others, or excluding others from group activities (Gray, 2000).

For example, a parent of two male siblings, ages 10 and 7, is trying to mediate between a physical confrontation that has just occurred. The older child pushed the younger to the ground while playing with his friends outside. The younger sibling runs inside crying to tell the parent what his older brother did.

The obvious solution would be to reprimand the older child for physically abusing his brother. However, the parent knows that the younger child has been bothering his brother all day, and has not respected his older sibling's desire to be left alone. The younger child has been engaging in a passive form of bullying, trying to manipulate both his brother and his parent into giving him what he wants. He continued this behavior while the older child, who had been attempting to ignore him, was trying to play with his friends. The older brother eventually became frustrated enough to tell his younger brother to "get lost" and to push him to the ground.

This is a situation where both parties involved are being bullies. The older child should be told not to resort to physical means, and also to try to include his younger brother in some of his activities. The younger brother should be told to respect the fact that his older brother is not required to include him all of the time. By holding both children responsible for their roles in the situation, you are less likely to generate the boys' resentment toward each other.

Understanding how the individual bullies, and also under what circumstances he or she bullies, is essential to choosing a successful form of intervention. Below are listed some common bully types, as well as a brief description and example. Please note that some categories will be linked, such as a child who acts like a passive bully when he is alone and as a casual bully when he is with a group.

Characteristics of Bullies

Researchers sought to determine which of 70 characteristics were seen by an international group of experts as being most applicable to bullies and victims (Hazler, Carney, Green, Powell, & Jolly, 1997). There was strong agreement among the 14 experts on the following 18 characteristics for bullies:

- *Control others through verbal threats and physical actions.* Common behaviors include: threatening to tell on another child if he or she doesn't follow the bully's direction, grabbing or shoving to gain compliance, threatening to break toys or hurt a third child, and threatening not to be his or her friend anymore.
- *Quick to anger and sooner to use force than others.* Common behaviors include: throwing a pencil because their homework is difficult, slamming doors, aggressive behavior when playing video games, and knocking over a board game when losing.
- *Tend to have little empathy for the problems of the other person in the victim/bully relationship.* Common behaviors include: finding the victim's reactions funny, stating that the victim deserved what happened, and assigning blame to the victim.
- *Chronically repeat aggressive behaviors.* Common behaviors include: pinching or aggressive tickling, breaking toys, throwing objects, and crowding others' personal space.
- *Inappropriately perceive hostile intent in the actions of others.* Common behaviors include: stating that no one understands or likes them, feeling falsely accused, and always being

involved in altercations that were started by the other individuals involved.

- *Angry, revengeful.* Common behaviors include: fixating on the idea of getting back at other kids and becoming bitter about other children's accomplishments or possessions.
- *Have more family problems than usual.* May experience the following: broken family, aggressive parent, or financial hardship.
- *Parents are poor role models for getting along with others.* Parental behaviors include: being argumentative with neighbors, critical of others in public, or having trouble with the police.
- *Parents are poor role models for constructively solving problems.* Parental behaviors include: continually blaming others for their situation, yelling and punishing their children repeatedly, and being unresponsive to the explanations their children provide.
- *Inconsistent discipline procedures at home.* May experience the following: different children being punished differently for similar situations and having privileges or toys taken away for vague and confusing reasons.
- *Parents often do not know child's whereabouts.* May experience the following: child doesn't get picked up after an event or parents show up at wrong time or in wrong place.
- *Suffer physical and emotional abuse at home.* Common behaviors and signs include: unexplained marks or bruises, shies away from physical contact, unexplained emotional outbursts, and a reluctance to be at home.
- *Are likely to have contact with aggressive groups.* Common behaviors include: hanging out with other children in an unsupervised area, interacting with kids who commit acts of vandalism, and engaging in hazing rituals (often among athletes and social organization members).
- *See aggression as the only way to preserve their self-image.* Common behaviors include: a fascination with weapons and violent movies, using swear words repeatedly, and intimidating others with words and actions.
- *Perceived physical image is important for maintaining a feeling of power and control.* Common behaviors include: wearing cloth-

ing that emphasizes their physique, choosing aggressive jewelry, wearing shirts with angry or violent pictures or phrases, and scowling or making angry facial expressions.

- *Focus on angry thoughts.* Common behaviors include: talking about people they dislike, being critical of authority figures, complaining about their home or school situation, showing resistance to having fun, and acting demeaning toward positive role models.
- *Create resentment and frustration in peer group.* Common behaviors include: seeking out targets for the group to pick on, spreading rumors between their peers, and disrupting events where their peers are having fun as a group.
- *Exhibit obsessive or rigid actions.* Common behaviors include: wearing the same type of clothes regularly, showing resistance to try something new, having aggressive behavior toward new acquaintances, showing extreme possessiveness, and being resistant to allowing anyone to see or enter their room, especially parents.

These characteristics (Hazler et al., 1997) will in some part be present regardless of how we categorize the type of bullying behavior that is being exhibited.

Casual Bullying

This form of bullying surrounds us every day, and rarely is it addressed appropriately, if it is addressed at all. This type of bullying is almost impossible to control when it happens, because the encounter is usually brief, and there is a lack of awareness that this behavior is indeed bullying (Caputo & Neu, 2006; Neu & Caputo, 2005). Sometimes the person being bullied may not even be aware that that is what just occurred. Some examples of casual bullying include: an overweight child called "fatso" by another child riding by on his bike, a student pinched by another in the hallway between classes, or two children pointing and laughing together at the expense of a third.

Often times, these subtle forms of bullying have been committed repeatedly, and begin to build up, eventually culminating in a more aggressive confrontation. Every parent and teacher has had to attempt to mediate a situation where the parties involved are throwing accusations back and forth: "He called me a . . . ," "Well, he told me . . . ," "But, yesterday he said . . . ."

Attempting to control these behaviors as they occur would be fruitless. Children learn quickly how to engage in these casual bullying behaviors without getting caught. The only hope lies in educating them to the fact that these actions are hurtful, and differentiating this with having fun and good-natured teasing between close friends. The situation is further complicated by adults who engage in similar behaviors, which removes any credibility when they tell their children it is wrong. When an adult is heard ridiculing a neighbor, the child will see that as permission to do the same.

Passive Bullying

> When children are asked to describe a bully, most of the descriptions involve mean or aggressive behavior. They rarely connect the fact that displaying weakness or neediness can also lead to manipulative behavior that can be considered bullying.

When children are asked to describe a bully, most of the descriptions involve mean or aggressive behavior. They rarely connect the fact that displaying weakness or neediness can also lead to manipulative behavior that can be considered bullying. Passive bullying behavior usually stems from the individual learning that by playing on the sympathies of others, he can get what he wants. The main tool in this form of bullying is emotional, rather than physical. The response may be physical, but these bullies generally will not initiate a confrontation in a physical manner. Examples of this would include crying or tantrums to get one's way and voicing emotional or physical distress to gain sympathy and compliance (Caputo & Neu, 2006; Neu & Caputo, 2005). When faced with two children, one of whom appears upset and one of whom appears angry, the tendency would be to side with the apparently hurt child. By gathering more information, we find that this can be untrue. We do need to subcategorize this type of behavior into intentional verses unintentional passive bullying.

Unintentional passive bullying often can be resolved by simply explaining to the individual that he is in fact being a bully. Creating this shift will cause him to reexamine his behavior and give him a new perspective as to what it truly means to be a bully (Caputo & Neu, 2006; Neu & Caputo, 2005).

Intentional passive bullying can be more difficult to deal with. A child who has learned that he can manipulate an outcome by appearing to be victimized is going to use that to his advantage (Caputo & Neu, 2006; Neu & Caputo, 2005). Here is an example:

> Chris was in the middle of a verbal altercation with another student. The teacher came over to intervene, and Chris stated that the other child was calling him names. The teacher questioned the other child on what he had said, and the response was that he had told Chris that he was tall. Chris promptly announced that he thinks if someone tells him he is tall, they are really saying that he is skinny, and that bothers him. Obviously, the issue is with Chris, not the other boy. When Chris's behavior was called into question, he began explaining how he is always being picked on, and how he is not at fault. The teacher firmly explained that Chris's behavior would not be tolerated, and Chris ceased the behavior in this class. He continued to do similar things in other classes, however. Obviously these behaviors were intentional, and would only stop if Chris felt unable to manipulate the adult mediator.

With a little bit of observation and a knowledge of the histories of those involved, many conflicts will take on a new light, and the passive bully will be recognized and held responsible for his role in the situation. When the more aggressive member of the situation is removed or disciplined, a passive bully who is not also disciplined will simply find a new person to generate conflict with.

Passive bullies are also sometimes considered to be those bullies who are associated with aggressive bullies, but rarely provoke others or take the initiative when bullying. The passive bully, often identified as a member of a bully group (see group bully section below), will simply support the more aggressive bully and begin to participate once the bullying has actually begun (Coy, 2001).

Aggressive Bully (Predator)

Aggressive behavior is what people traditionally associate with a bully. An aggressive bully

> is seen as an individual who is belligerent, fearless, coercive, confident, tough, and impulsive. This type of behavior typically comes from individuals who have a low tolerance for frustration coupled with a stronger inclination toward violence than that of children in general. (Coy, 2001, p. 2)

These bully types tend to seek out someone weaker than them and exert authority over them. These bullies can feel superior in a number of ways. The most obvious is physical, but they may also feel smarter or more talented in some way (e.g., the A student making fun of a "dumb jock," or an athlete ridiculing a "band geek"; To be clear, these terms are labels used by kids and are listed to remind you of the importance of knowing the cultural language your children use to categorize themselves and others socially.).

Aggressive bullying can be exhibited in a number of ways besides the well-known physical method. Constant verbal attacks can be just as damaging. Working to isolate the victim by manipulating social circles can be devastating, especially at the confusing time at and around the onset of puberty. When a child feels that he is being excluded and cannot interact with his preferred group of peers, he can quickly retreat inward and get labeled as "weird" or a "loner," which can lead to either bullying or victimizing behaviors (Caputo & Neu, 2006; Neu & Caputo, 2005).

Simply acting in a physically imposing fashion, without actual contact, can be frustrating and humiliating (such as blocking doorways or hallways). Often times, aggressive bullies think they are being funny, and they are reinforced by positive feedback from their peers. Sometimes convincing the bully that his actions are hurtful can change this behavior (Neu & Caputo, 2005).

Group Bully

These individuals become a different person when with certain groups of peers. When finding a constructive outlet as an intervention for bullying behavior, it is important to know if there is a specific environment that encourages a bully's behavior. Getting a group bully involved in a team sport (such as baseball or basketball) could potentially provide him with a means to take control and continue picking on weaker teammates. An individual activity (such as track or swimming) could cause him to focus his energy on self-improvement. There are two subcategories for this type of bully: the pack leader and the follower (Caputo & Neu, 2006; Neu & Caputo, 2005).

The *pack leader* would naturally take charge and direct the group in how they interact with those both inside and outside of their clique. He will hold court, determining who is in or out of favor, as well as who is included or excluded from the group.

The *follower* does exactly that, allowing his behavior to be dictated by others so that he can feel a sense of acceptance. He usually will not be the initiator of bullying behavior, but will either join in to avoid becoming a target or will allow himself to be manipulated into bullying behaviors to gain further acceptance.

The pack leader and follower also can be identified as being aggressive and passive bullies, respectively, with the aggressive pack leader initiating the bullying and the more passive follower supporting his actions and joining in later (Coy, 2001).

Individual Bully (Loner)

These individuals tend to keep to themselves, and will look for opportunities to isolate their victims, usually out of fear of being caught. They may have difficulties interacting socially, and may lash out at those they feel are to blame (Caputo & Neu, 2006; Neu

& Caputo, 2005). An example might be pushing around or stealing from a child who is seen as a rich kid, if the bully is less fortunate financially than the victim.

When these bullies are in a group environment, they may be very quiet in an attempt to blend in and may not show any outward signs of what could be inner turmoil.

High Self-Esteem Bully

Many people assume that a bully naturally suffers from low self-esteem. This is not always the case. Although the stereotype remains that bullies have low self-esteem, many are actually quite self-confident, popular with their peers, and make friends easily (Cohen-Posey, 1995, as cited in Scarpaci, 2006). Some children feel strong and confident, and have little or no tolerance or understanding for those whom they see as weak. They may become aggressive out of a sense of frustration for the victim's inability to perform well. A good example of this is when a bully verbally attacks a teammate who causes the team to lose the game. Bullies with high self-esteem also have been observed striking out at those who can't fight back if they feel slighted or excluded by other popular, self-confident peers.

Low Self-Esteem Bully

Most people associate low self-esteem with bullying behavior. These individuals feel weak or inadequate in some way, and therefore build themselves up at the expense of others. This type of bullying can be linked to what we will call the food chain effect.

In the food chain effect, a child who is being picked on finds someone weaker than himself for him to pick on, so that he feels better about himself. By breaking one link in this chain, the behaviors of those lower in the chain may stop. Obviously the higher up in the chain the intervention occurs, the more beneficial it will be (Neu & Caputo, 2005).

Cyberbullying

The Internet has created a whole new set of opportunities to inflict emotional harm in the world of preteens and teens. Cyberbullying refers to when bullying occurs via electronic communication tools (Li, 2005). A survey of 177 seventh-grade students conducted by Li showed that more than a quarter of the students had been cyberbullied. Almost 15% of the students reported that they had bullied others via electronic communication, and 52.4% said that they knew someone who was being or had been cyberbullied (Li).

The level of anonymity provided by a computer can embolden otherwise timid children to make aggressive and hurtful statements or spread rumors over Instant Messenger (IM) and e-mail programs. Unfortunately, at some point, the parties involved may have person-to-person contact and the situation can escalate rapidly. Many children have computers in their rooms, and have confessed to staying up late talking to their friends and peers through instant messaging and chat rooms. The latest in teenage communication is a Web service called MySpace, which allows them to post pictures, as well as comments. The majority of students in Li's (2005) study who said they had engaged in cyberbullying reported that they had used more than one type of electronic communication to bully others, including e-mail, chat rooms, cell phone messaging, and IM.

There is great difficulty in parents monitoring their son's use of IM, text messaging, and blogs. Today, young men have an entire computer language that has been developed to avoid adult detection (e.g., sending the acronym PLOS means that one has a parent looking over his shoulder). The best avenue for parents is to keep lines of communication open with boys, encourage them to talk about their online experiences, and have high expectations for computer use. Parents also need to set guidelines and consequences for proper use.

VICTIM TYPES

Now that we have identified the different types of bullies, we should look at the various types of victims. Various studies of bullying have found victimization to be prevalent. For example, in their study of 432 eighth graders in 16 school districts across 11 states, Peterson and Ray (2006) found that 67% of all students (and 73% of males) in the study reported being bullied at some point from kindergarten to eighth grade. Focusing on just the bully only offers half the solution. As we discovered in the opening story about Jordan, we can also resolve issues by helping victims learn how not to be a victim. By approaching the problem consistently from both sides, we potentially double the likelihood of a resolution (Neu & Caputo, 2005). Let's look at the main victim types: physical, verbal, and social victims.

Physical victims are being manipulated physically. Actions like pushing, punching, pinching, and even tickling can become abusive. These victims could be subjected to an invasion of personal space, abuse of their possessions (such as knocking down books or breaking toys), or a bully stealing their possessions.

Verbal abuse can be just as damaging as physical abuse. Victims of verbal abuse might experience name calling, racial or familial insults, or identification of embarrassing physical or personality characteristics. Peterson and Ray (2006) found name-calling to be the most prevalent type of bullying reported by the students in their study.

The *social* victim is placed in embarrassing situations or manipulated into unhealthy acts by others. These individuals desire attention by their peers and unwillingly fall into a social trap designed by the bully. For example, social victimization may occur when one student is invited to a party and told it is to be a costume party. The social victim arrives to find that he is the only one dressed up and that he was misinformed purely for the amusement of the social group. The difference between a prank and bullying is that a prank typically occurs between friends and/or social equals. Retaliation is expected on a friendly basis. The social victim has been preyed upon because he was seeking social acceptance and the act of bullying is used to reject him from the social group (Caputo & Neu, 2006; Neu & Caputo, 2005).

A report on bullying and school crime from the U.S. Department of Education's National Center for Education Statistics (DeVoe & Kaffenberger, 2005) lists two other types of victims: passive and provocative. *Passive* victims signal to the bully that they will not react or retaliate his actions. This may occur through crying, withdrawal, or becoming quiet. *Provocative* victims are likely to respond aggressively, providing a counterattack to the bully (DeVoe & Kaffenberger).

There are warning signs to watch for in children that you feel may be a victim of bullying. Victims are likely to (Dake, Price, & Telljohann, 2003; DeVoe & Kaffenberger, 2005; Sheras & Tippin, 2002; Trautman, 2003):

- have low self-esteem;
- show symptoms of depression;
- express feelings of loneliness;
- spend a lot of time alone;
- show reluctance to go to school;
- skip classes or be truant from school;
- cease participation in extracurricular activities;
- have a sudden drop in grades;
- show fear at meeting new people or trying new things;
- have physical markings, such as bruises or cuts, related to bullying; and
- be involved in physical fights.

Causes of Victimization

There are many potential causes of victimization and identifying these may bring you to the root of the problem, allowing for the elimination of the victim as a viable target. Unfortunately, some of the causes of victimization are difficult to identify. A bully may be heard to say "I don't know why, I just don't like her." We don't always know why we respond to different people differently, and encouraging positive interaction may simply be impossible. There are two basic categories under which the various causes will reside: victim-based causes or environment-based causes.

Victim-Based Causes

SOCIAL

Some children lack the "coolness factor." They have difficulty interacting with others in a way that generates a positive response. There may not be anything specific they can do to change this, although organized group activities can help build confidence and increase camaraderie.

Parents can also help by letting their children have some say in the types of clothes they wear, as well as allowing boys to explain what toys, movies, music, and activities are popular. These things are constantly changing, so listen to your kids when they try to tell you what is currently popular with their peers.

SITUATIONAL

Sometimes certain situations can lead to ridicule and embarrassment. Most parents know that day will come when their child will not want to give them a kiss goodbye or say "I love you" in front of their peers. The pressures of trying to fit in can cause even non-bully types to jump on the bandwagon and ridicule another child. They will operate under the premise of "Better him than me."

PHYSICAL

The media kids are exposed to create a physical ideal that they try to emulate and also seek out in others. Unfortunately, the vast majority of us fall considerably short of the images portrayed on MTV or in magazines. The kid who looks "goofy" or "weird" will have to work much harder to gain acceptance, and will often become the target of bullying attacks. Clothes, hairstyle, body type, and even one's complexion can add to the difficulties of navigating the social minefield both in and out of school.

EMOTIONAL

Children who are prone to emotional outbursts or are non-demonstrative can become easy targets. Examples of this include a boy labeled a "spaz" due to his hyperactivity or a boy labeled as a "wimp" because he is overly sensitive. The lack of response to social cues is taken as a sign that the boy is an "airhead" or is "not with it." In either case, it is the emotional response or the lack of response that attracts the bully.

Environment-Based Causes

A NONRESPONSIVE SCHOOL ENVIRONMENT

Bullying is closely related to school and school functions. Randall (1996) points out that is not the social nature of school that causes bullying, rather it is the lack of diligence by educators who allow it to continue. Schools must be aware and become an active agent to prevent bullying. Common contributing factors that allow bullying to occur in a school environment are:

- the lack of a comprehensive antibullying policy in the school,
- no established line of communication for students to communicate concerns or reports of bullying occurring,
- unsupervised areas of the school or playground, and
- the absence of teacher training in identifying and addressing bullying.

UNSUPERVISED COMMUNITY LOCATIONS

The community environment itself may have locations that foster bullying situations. Common locations in the community where bullying is most often reported include the walk from the bus to the student's home, local hangouts, and public playgrounds. These environments sometimes offer bullies the opportunities to victimize a boy that may not be available in a supervised setting.

THE SPECIFIC CLASSROOM ENVIRONMENT

As educators, we have seen a variety of individual classroom environments that provide opportunities for bullying to take place. Although a schoolwide antibullying approach is important, we have found that bullying may be occurring most often in specific educators' classrooms. Elements of a specific classroom environment associated with bullying include:

- an ineffective or inexperienced teacher,
- a teacher who is struggling with classroom management in general, and
- a classroom environment in which the teacher does not value differences and may even inadvertently encourage bullying due to his or her own biases.

The Home Environment

Of the all the environmental influences, this one is the most pervasive and difficult to counter. Rigby (2002) points out a close relationship between the home environment and the relationship of both bullies' and victims' behaviors in school settings. Characteristics of home environments that may be promoting bullying include:

- family members with low tolerance for differences,
- prominent display of prejudice,
- a history of violent behaviors,
- tendency to tease or verbally abuse,
- lack of open lines of communication with children, and
- apparent lack of concern for children.

Suckling and Temple (2001) stress that educators need to be prepared to both support parents who have children who are being bullied, as well as to confront parents whose child is involved in bullying. These authors recommend a multifaceted support system involving school and counseling professionals to support parents.

ADULT INTERVENTION

The importance of the adults who are in a position to mediate in these situations cannot be overlooked. Bullying behaviors can follow us into adulthood, and then create a filter through which we view a situation. An adult who was picked on as a child may identify with certain victim types, just as an adult who was very confident and well liked as a child may not be as sympathetic to the same victim type. Below are a couple of stereotypical examples of how casual bullying can be influenced by an adult mediator. We will use two male teachers of differing backgrounds, then a third, impartial teacher, and place them all in similar situations.

Situation A:

The subject is English, and the teacher was not athletic as a child, and had some difficulties with "jocks" as a student. Aaron, who reminds this teacher of his younger self, comes into class late and drops his books all over the floor. Steve, a football player, laughs out loud and audibly calls Aaron a "geek." The English teacher promptly reprimands Steve, and makes him get up to help Aaron pick up his books before returning to his seat

Situation B:

The subject is math, and the teacher was athletic as a child, playing both football and baseball. He was well liked as a student, and handled himself with confidence. Aaron, who is nothing like this teacher was in his school years, comes into class late and drops his books all over the floor. Steve, a football player, laughs out loud and audibly calls Aaron a "geek." The math teacher tells the whole class to quiet down, then in a gruff tone commands Aaron to hurry up, collect his things, and get to his seat.

Situation C:

The subject is science, and the teacher's childhood history is unknown. Aaron, who he knows is not very popular and struggles socially, comes into class late and drops his books all over the floor. Steve, a football player, laughs out loud and audibly calls Aaron a "geek." The science teacher informs Steve that his comments are unnecessary, tells the whole class to quiet down, then politely asks Aaron to retrieve his books, and be on time for class in the future.

Situations A and B will probably lead to future difficulties between the two students. Situation A will probably cause the bully to harbor resentment toward the other student for "getting him in trouble." The teacher singled out and embarrassed Steve, while defending a student who was not only late, but also disrupted the class. Most likely, Steve will seek out Aaron for further abuse when there are no authority figures present.

Situation B will probably lead to the bully feeling that the teacher validates his actions. The teacher did not reprimand the bully, but instead made a general statement to the class. He then made it clear that he had little tolerance or sympathy toward Aaron's feelings, who will feel belittled and may end up retreating further inward, causing him to be a continual target.

The impartial adult mediator of Situation C diffused the situation by reprimanding Steve for his comment, but then extending it to the group, as well. He also held Aaron accountable for his actions without further embarrassing him.

A lack of impartiality could seriously impair the ability to find a resolution that is fair and long lasting. A victim who repeatedly complains can come to be viewed as annoying. A bully who has been involved in several altercations may be viewed as guilty until proven innocent.

Impartial mediation, especially in regards to casual bullying, could be key to reducing the amount of conflicts that escalate to an uncontrollable level. In addition, the mediator will find that the effectiveness of the solution will increase based on the amount of information at hand. Jordan's grandfather, in the opening example, assessed the personality of the child being bullied, the possible background of the other children involved, and the environment they were interacting within to determine how to instruct his grandson to best deal with the bullies.

The greater the understanding of the individuals involved, the more likely it becomes that a solution will present itself. In addition, the adult mediator can play an extremely important role by developing awareness within the parties involved that they are in fact either being a bully or being victimized. Often, as children are developing socially, they are unaware of the result of their behavior, and its impact on others. Learning that their actions were inappropriate, especially from an adult they respect, could lead to dramatic behavioral changes.

PRESENT COURSES OF ACTION TO PREVENT BULLYING OR VICTIMIZATION

Schools use many different interventions to help prevent bullying. Some of these will be discussed in this section. Some schools designate a safe area, with an adult who is trusted by the students being an available advocate for victims to report problems and to talk to. Other schools hold workshops with questionnaires that help both adults and students become aware of the extent of the problem, help to justify intervention efforts, and serve as a benchmark to measure the impact of improvements in school climate once other intervention components are in place. In addition, a parental awareness campaign can be conducted during parent-teacher conference days, through parent newsletters, and at PTA meetings. The goal is to increase parental awareness of the problem, point out the importance of parental involvement for program success, and encourage parental support of program goals.

In some schools, teachers work with students at the classroom level to develop class rules against bullying. Many programs engage students in a series of formal role-playing exercises and related assignments that can teach those students directly involved in bullying alternative methods of interaction. These programs also can show other students how they can assist victims and how everyone can work together to create a school climate where bullying is not tolerated (Sjostrom & Stein, 1996).

There are effective training programs that school districts are using to develop schoolwide antibullying interventions. One

> Often, as children are developing socially, they are unaware of the result of their behavior, and its impact on others. Learning that their actions were inappropriate, especially from an adult they respect, could lead to dramatic behavioral changes.

highly recommended program is the Olweus Bullying Prevention Program. This program provides facilitation to schools to plan and implement procedures and training for teachers and help with building a schoolwide support system.

Other components of antibullying programs include individualized interventions with the bullies and victims, the implementation of cooperative learning activities to reduce social isolation, and increasing adult supervision at key times (e.g., recess or lunch). Schools that have implemented the Olweus program have reported a 50% reduction in bullying by providing intensive counseling for bullies and victims during the school day (Olweus Bullying Prevention Program, 2003).

Proposed Course of Action

We are going to discuss three primary methods of breaking the bully to victim cycle. Although we are speaking in general terms, it should be remembered that each child is an individual, and we can only provide guidelines that have proven to be helpful. The more information that is gathered about the individuals involved, the greater the likelihood of successfully resolving the conflict.

Resolving bullying issues most likely will not be a quick process. Separation and punishment will only cause resentment, and the conflict will resume at the earliest opportunity. The visible expression of the incident is merely a symptom, and we need to focus on the root of the problem. Think of it like taking antibiotics; they take a little time to work, then you keep taking them after the symptoms have disappeared to prevent a relapse.

The victim and the bully should both be required to take responsibility for their part in the conflict. The victim may be totally blameless, but based on the information discussed above, there may be something preventative that can be done to avoid future incidents.

Activity

One method that is very helpful is to find some type of activity that will occupy and challenge the child and allow him to build confidence and self-esteem. For example, if you were to go to the local mall on a Tuesday evening, you would discover dozens of 12- to 15-year-olds hanging around, basically unsupervised, engaging in loud and disruptive behavior. Why? Because there is nothing for them to *do*. There is no constructive outlet for all of that pent up energy and hormones, so they circle around like predators, preying on both groups and individuals who do not share their attitudes, styles, and interests. The amazing thing is how they will turn on each other if they do not have any targets from outside their group.

Across town, at the same time, more than likely there is a group of children, ages 12–15, practicing and training in a martial arts studio. They are interacting physically, mentally, and socially under the supervision of an instructor. This group of children has direction and a positive and safe place to develop skills and abilities, which also keep them away from the places and situations that inevitably lead to trouble.

Finding an appropriate activity should involve some research and exploration on the part of the parent and educator. Let's look at some situations and activities that would provide a constructive influence on the individual involved.

Situation 1:
John is an aggressive boy of 15 who has a group of friends who look to him as their undisputed leader. He is strong and athletic, and seems to move through his social circles with ease. He is very disdaining toward anyone weaker than him, and seems to find a way to ridicule and verbally abuse the "geeks" in school. He always gets a laugh from his friends whenever he has the opportunity to publicly humiliate another boy. When you get him alone, he seems personable and holds up his end of a conversation well.

John will probably gravitate toward team-related sports, which may encourage a continuation of the type of behaviors he is exhibiting. He may end up as the captain of the football team, and then engage in hazing behaviors directed at lower class members or less athletic team members.

If John were to get involved in an individual sport, such as track or swimming, it may cause him to focus his energy inward, and gain a sense of satisfaction through individual accomplishment. This could help guide him away from the desire to gain authority and popularity at the expense of others. A nonathletic activity, such as peer mediation or tutoring, could also help change his views toward his weaker peers and allow him to develop a sense of satisfaction by helping others.

Situation 2:
Douglas is a loner who has difficulty interacting with others. He is intolerant of his peers, and will lash out both physically and verbally when approached. He likes video games and computers, and becomes more social and animated when discussing these topics. He is critical of jocks, and detests physical education.

Getting Douglas to participate in team sports would probably be difficult, even though it would seem like an obvious solution. He would more likely respond to a group forum, such as a computer or gaming club, which would allow him to interact socially with individuals who share his interests.

Situation 3:
Andrew is small for his age, and has various health issues that limit him physically. He has difficulty socially, and has learned to use health problems to demand preferential treatment. His peers find him annoying, and Andrew gets picked on frequently by several of his classmates. He keeps

trying to be friendly toward them, but this just seems to aggravate the situation.

The solution for Andrew will probably involve noncompetitive individual athletics. Team sports will just aggravate his existing problems, and competition will just lend itself to his desire to make excuses for himself. Gymnastics or martial arts would allow him to challenge himself as an individual, but he can avoid competing until he is ready.

Finding an appropriate activity for each child will hinge upon understanding first what the child will enjoy and then considering other factors, such as finances and transportation. Experimentation is good, and the child should not feel forced to "make it work." Let him explore several options, but make it known that he must settle on something.

Intervention

Sometimes the best way to avoid a conflict between two parties is to simply limit the amount of opportunities they have to interact. Intervention involves an adult mediator defining clear boundaries for the children to follow. Often times, the parties involved are separated and punished. This just aggravates the problem, and most likely as soon as they are released, the conflict will resume.

Here is an example where the adult mediator describes a boundary that addresses the problem, and offers a solution that doesn't make the victim totally happy, but does diffuse the situation.

Trey went to his teacher about a bully on his bus. The teacher asked what happened, and Trey explained: A boy would push or throw things at him when he tried to sit down toward the back of the bus. The teacher asked him what would happen if Trey were to sit toward the front instead. Trey replied that he had occasionally sat toward the front when there were no back seats available, and the bully left him alone. He then stated that he is a fifth grader, and fifth graders were allowed to sit in the back. He complained about how unfair it was that he couldn't sit in the back because of the bully.

The teacher proceeded to explain that sometimes situations occur that are unfair. The bully's parents were unresponsive, and the bus driver was not helpful either. The best thing to do was to sit in front and avoid the situation. Trey replied that he was a fifth grader, and he could sit in the back of the bus. The bully was wrong, not him.

The teacher proceeded with a situation for Trey to consider. He asked him what he would suggest to his mother if she was going to walk out alone into a dark parking lot where a mugger was waiting to attack her. Trey had numerous suggestions to help his mother avoid the mugger. The teacher asked him if it was fair that his mother would have to behave differently because of the mugger. Trey said it was unfair, but it was more important that his mom stayed safe.

The teacher then explained that the bully was like the mugger, and the important thing was that Trey remained safe. The teacher told him that, unfair or not, he was to sit in the front to avoid further conflict with the bully.

Sometimes violence is the only answer still available. We are not condoning a violent course of action, but no one should feel that he is not allowed to defend himself against unwanted aggression. By not fighting back, an aggressive bully will take that as encouragement that the victim is an easy target. This could have a ripple effect that will encourage others to also bully the victim. Violence should not be considered until all other options have been explored, and the parents of the victim should discuss the repercussions of the action first. It will be up to the family to decide what is acceptable.

For example, David was a freshman in high school who was getting bullied by a junior at lunch. The junior would lean over the lunch table and spray a mouthful of milk into David's face. The teachers seemed unable to resolve the issue, and the bully was adept at not getting caught. Sometimes he would lean in, and if a teacher saw him, he would act as if he were talking to David. David was starting to talk about dropping out of school or transferring, so his parents decided it was time for an extreme measure. They decided that David would hit the bully in the mouth when he tried his trick next. They were willing to accept a suspension from the school if it resolved the problem. When the bully next leaned in, David struck him in the mouth, and the bully jerked back, choking and spraying milk around. David was suspended for 2 days, and so was the bully, who couldn't explain why he was covered in milk. David did not have any difficulties with the bully after that incident.

The adult mediator may need to take a hard line approach, and require one or both parties to adjust the way they interact to limit the opportunity for conflict.

Adaptation

Our opening story about Jordan and his grandfather is an example of educating the child to operate in a way that acknowledges the environment in which he finds himself. An adult mediator may not be present to intervene in a bullying situation. If the victim is trained to observe the situation surrounding him, he may be able to make decisions that will allow him to avoid conflict.

We first must understand that things are not always fair. The antelope may not like the fact that they have to be vigilant against the lion in the forest, but the lion is not about to change its behavior.

To successfully adapt to a situation, we have to move beyond what should be and focus on what is. Looking at the situations that are causing the bullying behavior and having the victim take responsibility for what he can do to change is key. For example, a young boy thinks it is funny to make farting noises in the hallway between classes every day. At first, some students think it is funny, but then others who are being exposed to his antics are becoming intolerant, including one aggressive peer. When this peer starts calling the boy names and threatens to kick him the next time he makes that noise, the boy making the

> To successfully adapt to a situation, we have to move beyond what should be and focus on what is. Looking at the situations that are causing the bullying behavior and having the victim take responsibility for what he can do to change is key.

noise now feels intimidated and bullied. But, by learning to refrain from acting out in public, the individuals bothering him may stop. We are not excusing the actions of the bully, but showing that the victim may play a role in the bullying, as well.

The victim should learn to operate in such a manner that he does not present bullies with opportunities to manipulate him. He needs to target what changes can be made to reduce his role as a victim.

Lines of Communication

Being bullied can lead to a variety of complicated emotions that make it difficult for children to communicate what they are experiencing. Many children think their parents won't understand and that the generation gap is too great an obstacle to overcome.

Parents need to try to keep up with what is popular with their children, and the best way to find out is to simply ask. By expressing an interest in their culture without criticizing or passing judgment on it, your children will start to open up and share more with you. Remember: They are much more likely to come to you with a problem if you speak their language.

Pay special attention to what your children are doing on the Internet. Many children are bullied online, and do not say anything out of fear of losing their online privileges. The impersonal nature of interacting through a computer screen has emboldened many kids to behave and say things they would not normally consider.

Chapter 7 Tools
Opening Lines of Communication About Bullying

One of the best defenses against bullying and the path to supporting victims is to have an avenue for communication. The following is a list of questions to open up dialogue with boys concerning their world. To a victim of bullying, knowing that an adult cares about all aspects of his life will give him the approval needed to discuss the bullying.

1. What activities do you enjoy?

2. What programs do you watch?

3. What books, music, or video games do you like?

4. List your immediate family (parents, siblings, other)

5. What is your favorite subject? Is it the topic or the teacher that you like?

6. Who is the most popular kid in school/neighborhood and why?

7. Who is the least popular kid in school/neighborhood and why?

8. When you are upset, do you prefer to be alone or with others?

9. What emotion do you feel most of the time (happy, depressed, angry, etc.)?

10. Do you look forward to school, how often, and why or why not?

11. Who picks on you?

12. Where and why?

13. Is he your friend some of the time?

Boys in Athletics

he night air is crisp and the crowd has gathered under the lights to watch the boys play. Anxious fathers wait for their sons to take the field resplendent in their team's colors. Boys stretch their muscles and go through their favorite drill to steady their concentration before the upcoming contest. As Ryan stretched, he looked in the stands to see waves of the two opposing teams' colors worn by their supportive fans as cheers begin to encourage the participants. Ryan was more aware of performing to the best of his ability in this game. Coach T realized that Ryan was a little distracted and moved over to give him some words of encouragement. There were scouts from large universities in those stands and they had come to tonight's game to watch Ryan. Ryan had two coaches on his team who had been there for him and motivated him to succeed in the sport and in the classroom. These two coaches had given Ryan a respect for education and the discipline to practice academic skills. Coach T's words helped Ryan relax and his focus returned to the

game at hand. Coach T's simple words of encouragement meant so much to Ryan.

This scene could be the beginning of any number of settings in communities around the world. It could be North American football in Texas, soccer in Nigeria, baseball in Japan, or hockey in Canada. Athletics provides a connection between the biological need for movement in conjunction with the competitive nature of a boy's neurological hard wiring and the community support and expectations of these important exhibitions. Athletics also provides many boys like Ryan with an outlet for motivation and discipline for success.

This chapter will explore the positive and negative aspects of organized athletic competition in the United States and perhaps give some insight into this phenomenon. The individuals mentioned in this chapter are a mixture of adult athletes reflecting back on their sports career, current collegiate athletes, and young men still in the public school sports system. We have coached boys and young men in both the public school system and in the Little League arena for several years, so some of the information in this chapter reflects our direct experiences.

Athletics provides an opportunity for many boys to develop physically, release their energy, and develop their talent. At the same time, as First Lady Laura Bush has pointed out, coaches enjoy a unique relationship with boys. They have an opportunity to teach boys life lessons that can impact their academics and their entire way of life. Self-efficacy, self-esteem, perseverance, and organization are just a few of the personal traits that can be promoted by athletic coaches. Athletics and coaches, both the amateur and the professional, have the opportunity to impact boys' lives.

> There is a biological need for boys to express themselves through motion and to find an outlet for competition.

Boys' Need for Movement

There is a biological need for boys to express themselves through motion and to find an outlet for competition. These hard-wired needs have been mentioned in earlier chapters. Neurology tells us that the nervous system's connections to boys' brains are exclusively designed for motor function response.

Pollack (1998) has suggested that we can use this movement function to help boys open up and express their feelings. "Action talk" frees a boy to open up and express his feelings when words tend to elude him. For instance, boys tend to open up and talk while engaged in an active, hands-on task. It could occur in the context of a fast-paced game or slower-paced activity like fishing, but many of our boys need movement of some sort to be able to express their feelings (Pollack, 1998). To support the emphasis on movement in boys' lives, Sax (2005) has found that the optical systems of boys are far superior at tracking moving objects than similar aged girls. This optical tracking ability may be a major advantage in many common athletic endeavors.

Time and again the boys we interviewed constantly described the need for more movement in the school day. Among athletes, this was discussed often, however all boys expressed the need for some form of movement to relieve their stress.

In Project HIGH HOPES (Baum, Neu, Cooper, & Owen, 1997), allowing for movement was key to all of the classroom instructional activities. Researchers found a reduction of classroom disruptions and a general improvement in behavior when movement was incorporated in the learning environment.

Competition in the 21st century has many individuals questioning its importance and challenging its relevance to modern society. Yet, for thousands of years, across many cultures, boys have been competitive. In recent years, psychologists have questioned whether competition is actually a societal expectation learned by boys that could be conditioned away. They propose if we create noncompetitive environments, then boys will follow suit and lose interest in competition. Again, the field of neurology has combated this idea, noting that the brain of the male fetus is bathed in testosterone that could contribute to a competitive drive (Tyre, 2006). Thompson and Kindlon (2000) note that competition is necessary to a boy's understanding of himself. In order for boys to understand their own abilities, they test them in a series of competitions to measure what they can do. Thompson and Kindlon also say that teenage boys crave a competitive situation, yet will shy away if they believe that the task is one in which they will not be successful. Again, a function of competition is to give a boy a measure of what he can do and a knowledge of when he does not have a developed set of skills and runs the chance of losing. Competition forms the measuring stick for boys to understand their abilities.

Joseph's story presents an interesting case study of how important movement and competition is to a boy who chooses not to participate in team sports, but who is an avid sports fan. Joseph is large for his age, but has never expressed an interest in participating in organized sports. He gets good grades in school and participates in extracurricular activities, but does not consider himself a teacher's pet or one of the in-crowd at his high school. In the past, Joseph has been singled out in class for his need for motion. In middle school, he would create little dance steps in class when he was bored with the subject matter. Joseph is also a percussionist in the school marching band, as well as the stage band. There have been occasions when Joseph has caught himself performing drum solos on his desktop, only to be reminded by the classroom teacher that he is math class, not band rehearsal.

Joseph demonstrates his need for movement in two areas. In marching band, he says that he can learn a new piece much more quickly if there is a marching piece to go with it. He has expressed on several occasions that the worst part of school is that he must sit still; so to counteract this, he often puts the teacher's lecture to choreographed moves. Joseph has very modern way to use movement to unwind: He plays an unusual interactive video game called Dance Dance Revolution (DDR). This video game requires players to watch a brightly colored screen and replicate dance steps shown on the screen on a corresponding dance floor wired to recognize the pressure of the player's feet while corresponding music is being played.

This is where Joseph gets very competitive. He is recognized at his high school as a top-notch DDR player and will take on all challengers in the timed competitions. As two players literally dance off, the computer plays music and shows dance steps to be replicated on the electronic floor sensors. These dance steps represent points and deductions are scored for steps missed or lack of timing to the tempo. Joseph, who says he is not a competitive person, admits that he loves to compete at DDR.

Joseph also has an interesting goal. He wants to play in the pep band of a Big East Division university. Although he never plays basketball, he knows the names of every player on the university team. The pep band will allow him to connect movement to the team's competition, even though Joseph is not an athlete, just a very supportive fan.

Joseph does not consider himself an athlete, but he loves competition and movement. He is not alone, for many boys follow professional or collegiate sports for the competitive connection, yet they do not participate in organized sports. Joseph is an excellent representative of those boys who crave movement as an outlet and seek some sort of competition in their lives other than athletics.

THE BENEFITS OF ATHLETICS

Although boys can find outlets to express their needs for movement in competition other than organized sports, many still opt to join an athletic team or club at some point in their lives. However, athletics has many more benefits than just allowing a boy to release his energy. In Randy's case, athletics allowed him to express himself physically and competitively, while giving him a means of finding male mentors who encouraged him to succeed on and off the football field.

Randy looked like a stereotypical football player. At 6'3" and 245 pounds, he was an imposing figure. By his own admission, he credits football with saving his life, and he would add the word *literally* to that admission. Randy was a typical boy with academic difficulties, but he found civics and government fascinating. Many of his other academic subjects had little meaning for him. Randy had a tough home life and again, freely admitted to us that he needed an outlet for his aggression and anger toward his abusive father. In high school, Randy was recognized for his athletic abilities on the football field as a middle linebacker. In the classroom, Randy was recognized as unmotivated, yet capable of doing the academic work. Teachers reported that he was either constantly moving or not moving at all.

Randy was highly competitive in everything he did, with the possible exception of his academic work early in his high school career. Although he enjoyed demonstrating what he could do athletically, Randy also had a sense of the importance of teamwork. He was known for setting up competitive challenges for his teammates, such as mini agility and endurance contests. For Randy, this was not an exhibition of his strength; it was a method to motivate his teammates to train a little harder.

Two of his coaches were not just instructors in the game, but also confidants and mentors off the field. Randy is very clear that these two men became his role models and surrogate fathers. These older men specifically reminded Randy that school is crucial to life; the head coach was also Randy's American government teacher, while the assistant coach taught health. The role of older men as a guidance toward continuing education is a common finding (Gurian, 2005). Randy made a commitment to work to his fullest ability. This included making the academic grade to attract college recruiters. (Many of the athletes interviewed for this chapter reported a similar realization: In order to continue in their athletic passions, they would also have to make sacrifices that ensured their academic success.)

Randy was recruited to play for a major college football powerhouse in Texas. After a distinguished football career, he returned to coach at his former high school. As a coach, he excelled in teaching techniques using movement. As a classroom teacher, Randy used competition and movement to involve students in his American government classes, incorporating simulations and role-plays.

So, what are the benefits of athletics to a boy's life? There are several personal qualities and life lessons that the boys and men we interviewed said they have learned as a direct result of their chosen sport, including self-efficacy, resiliency, perseverance, self-regulation, goal-setting, self-esteem, coachability, and teamwork.

Self-Efficacy

Sports have a dramatic effect on some boys' belief in their own abilities to achieve on and off the field. The development of competence in a sport can increase a boy's self-efficacy. According to Bandura (1994), self-efficacy is a boy's belief in his capacity to accomplish specific tasks. Self-efficacy can be affected by cognitive perceptions of the boy, as well as environmental influences such as an instructor's method of teaching. Changing classroom instructional strategies to match a student's ability has resulted in improved self-efficacy in students who struggle in a regular academic setting (Baum et al., 1997).

Sports have a dramatic effect on some boys' belief in their own abilities to achieve on and off the field. The development of competence in a sport can increase a boy's self-efficacy.

Randy, the football player we mentioned earlier, made a connection to the acquisition of new academic information and the incorporation of new and more complex playbooks for university-level football. This connection to learning new plays gave him confidence and a strategy to implement in the university academic setting. With success in his early university courses, Randy developed the self-efficacy to be able to approach more challenging courses with confidence that he could study accurately and write effectively.

Resiliency

Resiliency can be described as a person's ability to recover from and adapt to adversity. Boys who have their resiliency nurtured in sports have been able to face crises, trauma, stress, and challenges to experience success in life. In other words, boys who are confronted with continual challenges in athletics can also face life problems and find success. Trulson (1986) also suggested that boys with active athletic lives are more adept to resist adversity in the form of gang-related delinquency.

Todd competed on the collegiate level in track and field. He was very clear that the ups and down of track competition was the best training imaginable for his high-pressure job in the business world. The long hours of training did not always pay off for Todd in the way he wanted. In two different seasons, he improved his time, but was replaced by another athlete who had better times in the event. Instead of giving up, Todd adapted and tried new training techniques. Todd credits track for helping him develop the resiliency he has exhibited in life.

Perseverance

Perseverance has been referred to in the business world as "stick-to-itiveness," or continuing to try until you succeed. This includes commitment, hard work, enduring hardships, and having the patience to continue to do the mundane on the road to excellence. Participation in sports requires perseverance in continued training and self-discipline. One key element to success in sports is not giving up despite facing stiff opposition and overwhelming odds.

Evan is an All-American hockey player at a private university in New England. In elementary school, he soon realized that he could not read at the level of his peers and was diagnosed with dyslexia in third grade. Hockey was Evan's outlet, but even there his learning disability affected his ability to play the game. When presented with a new skill or a drill, Evan took twice as long to master it than his teammates. Luckily, his coaches understood this and allowed Evan more time to incorporate the task. Evan doggedly repeated the skill on his own time at home. He reports having very little free time some nights, because it took him twice as long to do his homework, and then he'd be out in the garage working on the new technique that others seemed to pick up easily.

Evan has developed perseverance in sports. Because his learning disability inhibited the acquisition of new information or a new sport skill at the same rate as his nondisabled peers, he had to repeat the drill several times to be able to understand and reproduce the intended skill. Evan describes how once he understood that he had

to work on skills differently than his teammates, he felt successful and understood that perseverance actually paid off. Evan later
realized he also needed to persevere in academics. In high school
when he realized that his low reading level was holding him back
from acquiring new knowledge, Evan applied his perseverance in
his sport to the acquisition of reading and study skills. He began
to practice study strategies with the same diligence as he practiced
his slap shot. The end result of his perseverance was being named
an Academic All-American, a payoff that was a fitting capstone to
his former academic struggles. Evan says that he was only able to
overcome his academic struggles by looking to the perseverance he
developed in the sport of hockey.

Self-Regulation

The ability to influence one's own motivation, thought processes, emotional state, and controlling patterns of behavior can
be described as self-regulation. Behncke (2002) suggests that athletes use self-regulation and self-monitoring and actually build
confidence in their ability to achieve specific tasks. Several of the
athletes we interviewed said that the motivation and awareness
of their own behavior developed in their sport has proven to be
highly beneficial to their academic success.

Jay competes in archery and the martial arts. When confronted
by his parents that he needed to earn good grades in order to have
the privilege of driving, Jay decided to get "serious" about school.
He describes it as " . . . a major breakthrough in studying," when he
realized he could use the same powers of concentration he used in
archery and karate in his Advanced Placement literature class. Jay
began to schedule and monitor his study times. He was actually
able to see the effect of regulating his study times by the improvement in his grades, and as an added bonus, he earned the good
student discount with his insurance company.

Evan, the hockey player, agrees that the self-monitoring of
sports behaviors has helped him to be more aware of his academic
behaviors. Evan uses a laptop computer to record class notes,
which he finds helps him to stay focused during the lecture. He

also finds that time management is less of a problem when he can motivate himself to stick to a practice and study schedule.

Goal Setting

The ability to set a specific goal and take the necessary steps over a period of time to achieve it can be more difficult than it seems. Season goals are commonly posted in locker rooms around the country. Athletics teaches boys to set appropriate goals and work until they achieve them.

Todd relates the story that each year he set a goal to improve his time in the 440-yard race. Each year he did improve, dropping seconds off his time. Todd was careful to set realistic goals that he could build off of subsequently. Todd now shares with younger athletes how they can set small goals over short periods of time and build to long-term goals that take years to accomplish.

Landen, a shot putter, calculated the changes he would need to make to his workout to extend his throwing distance. He also set goals for weightlifting and conditioning. When he met these, he reevaluated his goals and set new ones. Landen's yearly, goal-driven improvement got the attention of college recruiters, resulting in several full ride scholarships for him to choose from. His athletic goals in the shot put led him to a new set of goals, including earning a university degree.

Self-Esteem

Self-esteem is the collection of beliefs or feelings that we have about ourselves. Self-esteem can also influence our motivation, attitudes, and behaviors. Several studies have connected self-esteem and its effect on emotional adjustment. Bailey, Moulton, and Moulton (1999) found a definite connection between participation in sports and healthy levels of self-esteem. Paluska and Schwenk (2000) found sport participation had a direct effect on individual self-esteem that transferred to other areas of the athlete's life. Participation in sports develops a boy's sense of success.

The long hours of practice and seeing gradual improvement gives boys a positive sense that they can succeed at a variety of tasks. This positive sense of self can sustain them through many challenges and confrontations, whether they are sport oriented or in the academic arena.

Tony claims that success in high school football changed his poor self-esteem into a positive sense of self and motivated him to succeed in academics. Tony was from a broken home and his mother depended on government programs to make ends meet. He did not feel accepted by others and he was unmotivated to attempt any academic task. When his mother found a job in different town, Tony felt like he had a chance to start over. He did just that. When he made the football team at his new school, Tony felt he had accomplished something for the first time in his life. His next 4 years of high school saw a dramatic change in Tony. He developed a new circle of friends. Tony found with his growing success in sports that instead of being ignored or put down, other students sought him out as a friend. Tony now saw himself as an individual who was worthwhile and as a young man who had something to offer. The same is true for his academic challenges. With a new positive and growing self-esteem, Tony began to participate in class. He admits that it wasn't until his sophomore year that he began to seek out the tutors supplied by the athletic department. Tony realized the more work he put into academic studies the better he felt and the more he succeeded.

Manuel looks back on his middle school days as a disaster. Manuel credits his participation in the martial arts with helping him to develop a strong sense of self-esteem. Manuel admits his social skills in middle school were not the best and at times he just tried desperately to get attention. He had very low self-esteem and the local school was observing him for possible social and emotional maladjustment. After Manuel went to a school assembly that featured the martial arts, he wanted desperately to take lessons. His father was surprised that the martial arts instructor allowed Manuel to return to class after being quite disruptive in class one week. After this incident, the instructor pulled Manuel aside and set some very clear rules for interaction in the workout area. Over time, Manuel progressed and was promoted. With each new belt he celebrated a newfound success. The next 5 years saw that the influence of the self-discipline aspect of martial arts had begun a progress of positive increase in his self-esteem. Manuel transformed into a successful, confident young man who now is interested in special education and wants to be involved in advocacy work.

Coachability

The attribute of being able to listen to and receive constructive feedback, and then demonstrate a change in behavior due to instruction sums up the notion of coachability. This characteristic is so sought after that a search on the Internet returns a large number of business programs to access and develop coachability. Athletics has valued this vital attribute for years.

Any individual who has coached a young man has a sense of this characteristic. The former boy athletes who we interviewed who now serve as coaches of young men could not stress the importance of coachability enough. Interestingly enough, there seems to be a connection between those with a coachable disposition and the ability to coach others.

This characteristic also has a powerful relationship to school success. Newman (2005) found a high correlation to the number of successful athletes and their achievements in academic endeavors. The coachability characteristic allows boys to take instruction on or off the field and apply it to other situations to improve their performance. David is a good example of a boy who possesses the coachability factor.

David had been introduced to tumbling at an early age. He had the unique quality of listening to what the instructor said and watching intently. David was also an excellent mimic; he worked intently on copying the moves his coaches showed him "muscle by muscle." When David was given the opportunity to join a gymnastics team, he was thrilled. He went on to earn a reputation among his coaches for ability to work at implementing coaching suggestions. David was truly coachable. He was eager to learn and took suggestions as a challenge. In high school, he decided to enter the sport of diving, a field that used his gymnastics skills. David competed on the collegiate level, where again, his coaches noted his intensity as he tried to constantly improve his skill by following coaching suggestions.

Teamwork

Teamwork is another characteristic that was repeatedly mentioned in our interviews with former and current student-athletes as being highly valued in the corporate world. Team spirit and cooperation is vital in any workplace, and many boys will develop these characteristics through sports. The ability to work with others to complete a common goal is necessary not only to win sporting championships, but it also is the basis for much of mankind's success.

Teamwork sometimes requires self-sacrifice and putting aside personal goals for the good of a team. C. J. was an excellent basketball player. Unfortunately, his entire team consisted of exceptional athletes. He realized very quickly that if he wanted to play on the varsity team he would have to alter his personal desire to score more points, and instead concentrate on being a point guard that would set up the plays that would lead to his team's success. C. J. altered his playing style and became a team leader, making the passes to his teammates that helped the team win games. Although two of his teammates were recruited to play college ball for big name universities, and C. J. only received offers from junior colleges, C. J. had developed an essential life skill when he decided to become a team player. He now has a brilliant career in the corporate world as a teamwork troubleshooter for a major corporation.

> **Team spirit and cooperation is vital in any workplace, and many boys will develop these characteristics through sports. The ability to work with others to complete a common goal is necessary not only to win sporting championships, but it also is the basis for much of mankind's success.**

AN ATHLETIC COACH'S ROLE IN A BOY'S LIFE

The coach has a unique influence on the development of boys. A coach may or may not be a lifelong mentor, but his or her impact is undeniable. A common theme among the boys we have worked with and interviewed is the impact a coach has on his or her players. The coach directs, instructs, and challenges the players on a daily basis. The style the coach embodies has a major influence on the receptivity of the athlete. How a coach motivates his players can make or break a young man's dedication to a sport. Many athletes find that their coach can be both a friend, giving guidance on and off the playing field, and a nemesis, driving the boy to push his body to new levels of strenuous activity in practices and major games. Among the young men we talked with, the level of respect a coach develops among his athletes is key to the athlete-coach relationship.

Coaching Styles Do Matter

One of the authors of this book decided to reflect back on the coaches that he had played sports under to formulate some questions to ask boys on their perceptions of coaches. He also decided to interview some of the former athletes he himself had coached. He notes, "I did receive somewhat of a surprise when interviewing some of the athletes that I had coached years ago. My former athletes were very candid and shared both positive and negative aspects of my performance as a coach." In further interviews with college-level athletes, this author found a similar collection of positive and negative tendencies in coaches. The following are discussions of the six most prominent coaching styles: leader, dictator, intellect, motivator, specialist, and manager. Young men and boys have discussed that many coaches actually have a combination of these styles.

COACHING STYLE #1: LEADER

The leader coach leads by example and gains the trust and dedication of his players. Martin, Jackson, Richardson, and Weiller

(1999) indicate that boys favor a coach who demonstrates a concern for the welfare of individual athletes, promotes a positive group atmosphere, and has warm interpersonal relationships with athletes. This style may mean that the development of a successful athletic program turns into a longer process, but among our interviews with athletes, this style was preferred for the lessons learned beyond the sport.

The leader coach actively encourages his athletes on and off the field—he leads by example. The leader coach demands academic excellence in addition to athletic excellence, because his chief goal is for his athletes to succeed in life.

COACHING STYLE #2: DICTATOR

"My way or the highway" would be a common philosophy associated with the dictator type of coach. This coaching style can be domineering and rigid in its programming. Martin et al. (1999) found that many boys do tend to prefer a directive coaching style that is clear on expectations. The dictator style gets things accomplished, can be very demanding, and may be the easiest style for coaches to employ. In order to be successful, a dictator coach normally surrounds himself with assistants who tend to be more personable toward athletes.

COACHING STYLE #3: INTELLECT

Some coaches have the ability to see all the factors, angles, and different possibilities and turn coaching into an intellectual pursuit of sport. The intellect coaching style concentrates heavily on the statistical aspect of the game. Some of these coaches have been accused by athletes of being more concerned about the numbers or the stats surrounding the game than the individual players. In several cases, coaches with the intellect style surround themselves with coaches of the motivator style, a combination that many athletes find very successful.

COACHING STYLE #4: MOTIVATOR

People can tell this coaching style as soon as the team gets off the bus. The motivator style coach is constantly encouraging his or her players. These coaches tend to pace the sidelines and are not afraid to jump with joy and yell at the success of their team. The motivator style coach generally develops good relationships with his players. This style is great for boys' self-esteem, as the constant feedback and praise give boys guidelines and goals to attain.

COACHING STYLE #5: SPECIALIST

The specialist is a technician of sorts. This style of coach may develop a specific set of skills in his players that helps them to achieve above-standards play. An example of this would be a basketball coach with a mediocre winning average, but whose players lead the conference or district in free throw shooting. Specialists can teach and coach a specific skill sometimes at a loss to the overall game. Specialist coaches are great for learning skills but may lack the big picture of the game.

COACHING STYLE #6: MANAGER

This is the individual who seems to hold the team together sometimes for the pure love of the sport. Many volunteer coaches have a manager style. They are there to ensure that the boys have fun and learn a few skills. The manager style is also common in the public schools with coaches who consider sports to be an opportunity and are not necessarily concerned about winning seasons. Normally, the reward for this coach is just seeing boys participate.

Characteristics of Successful Coaches

No matter what combination of styles a coach employs, there are four characteristics that are shared by all successful coaches: knowledge of the sport, enthusiasm and motivation, understanding of the individual players, and the ability to communicate effectively.

Knowledge of the sport is not as obvious as it seems. A successful coach must be a student of the sport and keep abreast of new techniques or strategies. Knowledge of the sport includes being able to adapt to an opponent's game plan and to be able to innovatively manipulate his players' abilities to counter unforeseen challenges.

Enthusiasm and motivation is contagious. Athletes on different levels of sports competition describe the importance of the enthusiasm of the coach. For instance, Randy and Tony both related that an enthusiastic comment went a long way in fueling their motivation to succeed on the high school football field.

Being able to understand the individual player is critical for all levels of sport. The younger the boy, the more vital this skill is to a coach's success. Coaches must be able to understand what drives young boys to succeed and provide appropriate instruction based on their needs. This includes keeping the sport fun and fulfilling to the young athlete.

The ability to communicate may be the "make or break" characteristic for most coaches. It is not enough to be able conceptualize a game plan, it must be clearly communicated to the players through drills and clear expectations. Several boys noted that communication breakdowns between coaches and players were a leading cause of their team's losses.

THE ROLE OF ADVERSITY IN ATHLETICS

When Nietzsche said "that which does not kill us only makes us stronger," he could have been talking about one very important role of the coach. It needs to be understood that the coach is the person who constantly must confront our boys with a new challenge to push them to new limits. The coach monitors the skill level, conditioning level, and motivation of young male athletes. When a weakness is found, the coach will prescribe an intervention to challenge the athlete to improve. Boys who succeed in sports understand this and accept the new challenge, even as they may be badmouthing the coach under their breath as they run the drill for the 20th time.

This experience of overcoming a challenge can be transferred to school and academic challenges. Many of the young men we interviewed who participated in university-level sports related that the postsecondary coursework is a step above what they experienced in high school. They were confronted with greater demands for academic standards. In response to this challenge, they attended academic help sessions to acquire the study skills and strategies they need. Evan said, "If you need to change your skating technique for hockey, you do it. If you need to alter your study strategies, you make the same adjustment to meet the academic challenge."

After working with boys over many years, the benefits of athletics in a boy's life have become apparent. There are several personal qualities and life lessons that the boys and men we interviewed said they have learned as a direct result of their chosen sport, including those mentioned previously: self-efficacy, resiliency, perseverance, self-regulation, goal-setting, self-esteem, coachability, and teamwork. These same characteristics are highly valued by career areas beyond sports. In essence, these characteristics can be developed in sports and later applied to life endeavors to improve one's self and his surroundings.

Coaches attempt to foster the development of these characteristics not only for success in sport but for the benefit of the athlete in his later careers. The importance of the role of the coach is echoed by the countless young men we have interviewed who point to specific relationships with coaches who have influenced their lives. One coach may have given them skills, while another impressed upon them the importance of education, but each coach had different impact on these young men on and off the field.

CHAPTER 8 TOOLS

Common Sports in the U.S.

The following tables present a brief overview of some of the most common sports for boys in the United States. These descriptions are not comprehensive, rather they are intended as a guide for parents to consider in the decision-making process. These concise overviews were derived from the interviews with male athletes and coaches from different sports.

TRACK AND FIELD

Orientation:	individual sport
Level of Aggression:	unaggressive (toward others)
Ideal Body Type:	all types; depends on the individual event
Pace:	very high intensity for short periods of time
Physical Demands:	very high physical demands on the body's performance
Skill Requirements:	specific skill requirements for each track and field event
Equipment Costs:	very low relative equipment costs
Pressure on the Individual:	high to moderate
Level of Motivation for Success:	high to moderate; intrinsic to extrinsic
Note:	The boys and men we talked to described track and field as one of the loneliest of all sports. (Archery had the second most responses in reference to individuality and loneliness.) Yet, this sport is commonly found in some format in the majority of school systems. The events vary from fast, short sprints, to long-distance running, to field events like javelin and shot put throwing.

WRESTLING

Orientation:	individual sport
Level of Aggression:	aggressive (toward others)
Ideal Body Type:	all types; divided into weight divisions
Pace:	very high intensity for short periods of time
Physical Demands:	very high physical demands on the body's performance
Skill Requirements:	does have specific skills and moves that must be learned
Equipment Costs:	very low relative equipment costs
Pressure on the Individual:	high to moderate
Level of Motivation for Success:	high to moderate; intrinsic to extrinsic
Note:	This ancient sport does have a team component, as individual participants wins are tallied to total a team score. The primary aim is to pin or hold down your opponent on the mat. This sport does teach balance and manipulation of the participant's body, as well as how to control the opponent's body. Several of the boys we interviewed said wrestling's attraction is the one-on-one competition it entails. Some boys stated that wrestling was "cool," because participants were matched against an opponent according to weight. These boys related that they felt this gave everyone an equal chance of winning.

MARTIAL ARTS	
Orientation:	individual sport
Level of Aggression:	aggressive to semi-aggressive
Ideal Body Type:	varies; may have weight classes for some events
Pace:	short, high intensity bursts or slow, initially repetitive movements
Physical Demands:	very high physical demands on the body's performance in flexibility and certain core body muscle systems
Skill Requirements:	does have specific skills and requirements for each form of the art
Equipment Costs:	very low equipment costs, but training costs can vary
Pressure on the Individual:	high to moderate
Level of Motivation for Success:	high to moderate; tends to be intrinsic
Note:	Soldiers in the 1940s were introduced to a form of hand-to-hand combat from Asia that took them by surprise. The East had practiced a form of exercise that could be used to disable or immobilize an opponent. The poor also practiced the martial arts as a means of protecting themselves without the use of weapons. In many cases, these fighting styles were concealed as movement exercise. Today, martial arts schools are a common site in strip malls around the country. Many boys discussed being attracted to the martial arts after watching the Teenage Mutant Ninja Turtles cartoons and movies. Five of the college athletes we interviewed took various forms of the martial arts for a short period of time and then moved on to focus almost exclusively on their sport. Those still participating ranged from 10-year-old boys to college students. The theme of their comments suggests that the martial arts' attraction is that it allows for movement and it can be as competitive as the participants want it to be. Several boys said that they did not enjoy team sports but would not miss a karate workout for anything.

FOOTBALL	
Orientation:	team sport (11 players on the field at one time)
Level of Aggression:	aggressive (although a less aggressive form of flag football is becoming popular for young boys)
Ideal Body Type:	varies by position, but the older the age group the greater the need for well-developed physiques and specialized training
Pace:	high intensity with breaks to regroup
Physical Demands:	very high physical demands on the body's performance
Skill Requirements:	does have specific skills and requirements for each position
Equipment Costs:	very high equipment costs
Pressure on the Individual:	high to moderate

Level of Motivation for Success:	the level of motivation increases significantly with the age, with motivation moving from extrinsic to very intrinsic
Note:	With 11 different positions requiring different duties, responsibilities, and skill areas, this team sport can be very complex. Football can be very culturally relevant for the community and can be demanding of the participants. The player must ask himself, "Why are you here? What are you willing to do on a physical level to accomplish a task?" Of all the team sports, North American football requires the most in capital for equipment, insurance, and support fees. As a result, many school districts have dropped this athletic program in favor of less costly endeavors.
	Not all boys should play this game. Many parents have channeled their sons into other sports areas. Many of the athletes we interviewed had a fascination with football, but size requirements limited their participation. There were many opportunities for one of this book's authors to pursue other less aggressive sporting activities, yet North American football was a calling that kept him in school. In a recent discussion with his son, he has found that for some men, there is something about participating in a physical, contact sport with another male that is quite liberating. It also seems that there is a continual market for this sport, gauging by the amounts of money TV networks are willing to pay to broadcast football games. This in turn is an attractive lure for many boys who do not understand the level of commitment and sacrifice needed to succeed in this sport.
SOCCER	
Orientation:	team oriented (usually 11 players, but can be played with fewer)
Level of Aggression:	semi-aggressive
Ideal Body Type:	typically a slim body; this sport requires extensive prolonged running and well-developed coordination with the feet.
Pace:	very fast paced
Physical Demands:	very physically demanding
Skill Requirements:	general specific skills to be attained by all players, and some positions require advanced skills
Equipment Costs:	very low equipment costs
Pressure on the Individual:	high to moderate
Level of Motivation for Success:	varies; local programs require low motivation; however, traveling teams are much more demanding
Note:	Among world sporting events this one ranks the highest. We have watched soccer games from Canada to Columbia, Germany to Nigeria. In other countries, soccer stars are as recognizable as any NFL or NBA player is in the United States. As the number of youth programs for soccer continues to increase in this country, we are seeing an increased number of boys playing this sport for at least 2–4 years. Several of the athletes that we interviewed had played soccer on some level of competition. Like baseball, skill levels and commitment to the sport dictate the number of years a young man can play the sport.

BASKETBALL	
Orientation:	highly team oriented (only 5 players)
Level of Aggression:	low level of aggression
Ideal Body Type:	tall players definitely have an advantage
Pace:	very fast paced
Physical Demands:	very physically demanding
Skill Requirements:	general specific skills to be attained by all players, although some players may specialize in certain skills such as 3-point shooting
Equipment Costs:	low equipment costs
Pressure on the Individual:	high to moderate
Level of Motivation for Success:	this sport can be enjoyed throughout life; however, to truly succeed, a high level of motivation must be maintained
Note:	This sport is one of universal appeal and can be played from the driveway, to the inner-city court. Like soccer, all that is needed is a few players, a ball, and a goal. Basketball is played by many boys because of its simple organization and availability. This is a great game for developing teamwork and self-regulation skills. It has also become more popular in recent years due to broadcasts of professional games and the NCAA's Final Four tournament on network television.

BASEBALL	
Orientation:	team sport (9 players)
Level of Aggression:	low levels of aggression
Ideal Body Type:	varies; can accommodate a variety of body types depending on position.
Pace:	positions often determine pace; outfielders may have long periods of low movement
Physical Demands:	low physical demands in certain parts of the game, high physical demands in others
Skill Requirements:	general specific skills to be attained by all players, and some positions require advanced skills
Equipment Costs:	low equipment costs
Pressure on the Individual:	high for infielders, moderate for outfielders; often depends on the specific game's level of intensity
Level of Motivation for Success:	as the age and level of competition increases, so does the level of motivation required
Note:	Sometimes called America's pastime, baseball is definitely a favorite in North America. Most of the athletes we interviewed had played on organized city or recreational teams as a boy. By the age of 13 or 14, boys without a serious passion for this sport begin to drop out. However, many retain a love of watching the game.

HOCKEY	
Orientation:	team sport
Level of Aggression:	highly aggressive
Ideal Body Type:	general athleticism with good depth perception
Pace:	very high intensity
Physical Demands:	very high physical demands on the body's performance
Skill Requirements:	general specific skills to be attained by all players; some positions require advanced skills
Equipment Costs:	very high equipment costs
Pressure on the Individual:	high to moderate
Level of Motivation for Success:	high level of motivation is required
Note:	While few of the athletes we interviewed had actually played this winter sport, many found it fascinating and enjoyed watching hockey games. Known for the speed and aggression of play, hockey is spreading across the nation and is attracting younger participants. Again, this is a sport that is not for every boy.

A Guide for Parents:
What to Look for in a Coach

Has the coach been certified by an agency?

Check with the town or city league. Many Little League organizations are now requiring some form of training for all coaches.

How does the coach react to winning or losing?

There is nothing wrong with getting excited with the outcome of a game. However, avoid coaches who demonstrate and or allow poor sportsmanship following the outcome of a game. Observe the coach giving feedback to players after a win and again, after a loss.

Is there use of sarcasms or insults?

Some degree of "smack" talk and sarcasm is expected in the sporting arena. In fact, many boys, regardless of the sport, point to a coach's motivational speeches as a prime reason they stayed with a particular sport. There is a fine line between comments to encourage a young athlete, such as "My grandmother can block better than you guys. I want to see you block that defense like I have seen you do on so many other occasions. Remember to stay low and drive," versus a comment that is insulting with no corrective or instructional purpose, such as, "My grandmother can block better than you guys. We are losing because of you. You just wait until next week's practice."

How well does the coach organize practice?

Observe a practice session, watching closely to answer the following questions: Is there appropriate time for stretching and conditioning? How much time is allotted to skill development? Does the practice run smoothly? Did your boy feel like he learned something today?

How well does the coach explain the goals of the team to the athletes and to the parents?

Depending on the age of the boy, communication about the goals of the team can vary. For younger boys, the coach may emphasize the fun of the game and development of skills. For older boys, look for a coach who involves his athletes in discussions of what they want out of this experience.

Does the coach demonstrate an understanding of boys' learning styles?
The coach should be able to model some expected skills. The coach should also have a realistic expectation of the boys' attention spans and be able to explain the game to boys.

Does the coach have expectations for all players?
Especially among young boys, skill levels are going to vary widely. See if the coach works effectively with all of the players and if the players are valued as part of the team.

How does the coach handle negative situations on and off the field?
When a parent or player gets out of line and insults a referee or another player, how does the coach handle the situation? Can the coach handle parent pressure? What is the coach's stand on academics and drug and alcohol use by players?

chapter 9

Mentoring Boys

"A mentor is a creatively productive person who teaches, counsels, and inspires a student with similar interests. The relationship is characterized by mutual caring, depth, and response."
E. P. Torrance (1984, p. 2)

A young man discusses what's on his mind in front of a group of nine teenaged boys and four men who are in their 40s. Sean has come to this group looking for male support in his life. The only male who has had an important impact on his life is his grandfather, who is currently in the hospital with a heart problem. Emotionally, Sean shares with the group his feelings about his grandfather. He then asks advice from the group concerning a bully who rides his school bus. Other boys in the group know the bully in question and an open discussion on how to handle the situation ensues. Luis suggests "punching the sucker out," but does caution that such actions can have consequences with the school and possibly the law. Luis should know, as he was suspended from his school three times last year for fighting. His social worker suggested this group, hoping that Luis would connect with a mentor who would listen to him and provide guidance for this troubled teen.

At the end of the meeting, Sean stands and expresses his respect for each member of the group. He also shares that the group is his second family. Sean then thanks the men of the group for listening to him and supporting him when he needed it. The group is called Boys to Men and it is funded by a state grant. This group fulfills a specific need of boys: to be heard and seen by older men and to feel that there are men in their lives who can mentor them. Sean, like many other young men, was searching for a mentor, and this program offered an opportunity for him to find a mentor who could provide guidance when he had no other male role model to turn to. A certified therapist runs the group, and the men are volunteers who feel like their life experiences can benefit the growth of young men. These adult males know the importance of a mentor in their lives and are willing to give back to the next generation of boys.

So, what is a mentor? There are several definitions and distinctions that need to be made. A mentor is an experienced and trusted advisor. The mentor provides a trusting relationship and safe environment and is known for being available to answer life's difficult questions. They are good listeners and are willing and able to spend time with the mentee. Mentors are probably best distinguished for their ability to share ideas and help a boy develop values and successful practices.

> **Mentors are probably best distinguished for their ability to share ideas and help a boy develop values and successful practices.**

Coaches and teachers have similar roles in the development of boys. However, not all coaches and teachers are mentors. Both coaches and teachers are concerned with developing specific skills sometimes within the context of a limited time period. However, to truly be a mentor, the coach or teacher has to go beyond just teaching skills in order to develop a relationship with the boy.

Historically, Mentor was the trusted friend of Odysseus, and his name has been associated with the idea of a faithful and wise advisor. Throughout history, great leaders and artists had mentors who instructed and supported them as they pursued their craft. Freedman (1993) notes that the traditional concept of mentoring consisted of young boys learning a trade or skill under the guidance of an older man. Bronfenbrenner (as cited in Freedman) defines a mentor as "a one-to-one relationship between a pair of unrelated individuals, usually of different ages and is developmental in nature . . . a mentor is an older, more experienced person who seeks to develop the character and competence of a younger person" (p. 31).

One mentor relationship that is commonly referenced is the relationship of Merlin to King Arthur. Whether real or fictional, the power of Merlin as a mentor is exemplified by his dedication to ensure that the young Arthur had all the experiences and wisdom to be great king. Merlin was a mentor not just for Arthur's sake, but for a better life for the people of Great Britain. He included lessons on the nature of life, understanding others, and responsibility of one for his fellow man. Many of these lessons were lost on the young Arthur. However, when he needs him, Merlin appears to counsel King Arthur and remind him of those early lessons.

Leonardo da Vinci had an unusual, yet very influential mentor in Fra Luca Pacioli. Pacioli was a Franciscan friar who also served as da Vinci's math teacher. Pacioli is credited with being the father of accounting. Da Vinci was so impressed with Pacioli's math theorems that he illustrated *De Divina Proportione*. It has been discussed that Pacioli encouraged da Vinci's connection between math and his art and engineering projects.

T. S. Eliot found a mentor who both stimulated his art of poetry, as well as provided psychological support. Ezra Pound was very outgoing and served as an agent to advance young Eliot's career. Gardner (1993) suggests that Pound could be responsible for Eliot's residence in England, the transition from philosopher to poet, introducing him to his first wife, meeting his prominent agent, and even his publications in America.

In his book *Iron John*, Robert Bly (1990) takes a story from the Brothers Grimm and illustrates the importance of mentors in the life of young men. In Bly's version, a wild man mentors a young man to recognize his own talent and strengths. In the process, the young man must leave his family, learn the importance of honesty, and learn to accept consequences. Even as the boy falls from being the son of a king to a lowly kitchen servant, the mentor supports him and encourages the boy that he can develop into the man he is intended to be. One of the lessons of *Iron John* is that the teachings of the mentor are always there for consideration and can guide young men throughout their lives.

Floyd (1993) suggests two types of mentors: the natural and the planned. The natural mentor develops a relationship with the boy through existing institutions such as schools, organized sports programs, neighborhoods, and churches. The natural mentor is in a place in the boy's environment to offer teaching, coaching, and counseling. Natural mentors are sought after as a guide to success in life. The planned mentor is becoming an alternative in a changing modern society. This type of mentorship is arranged for a specific audience of boys. Programs like Big Brothers Big Sisters and Boys to Men purposefully offer mentoring to boys who are looking for it or, in some cases, are recommended by social workers or the court system. Boys who feel excluded or unsuccessful in school may look elsewhere to find an older male for guidance. We'll discuss these two forms of mentorship in greater detail below.

NATURAL MENTORSHIPS

Natural mentorships can develop within the normal sequence of everyday life. Thomas was a former back-up musician for several up-and-coming rock bands that never quite made the big time. He kept current in the music scene, but made his living as a cabinetmaker. While installing a new kitchen in a client's house, he heard the distinct sounds of a garage band on the other side of the house. Thomas, being the consummate musician, of course had to check it out. Nick is a talented young man with interests in music, theater, and the martial arts. He recognized Thomas simply as the man who built kitchen cabinets. Thomas knew the ropes of the music scene, and with a few positive pieces of constructive feedback helped Nick's band improve the timing on the chorus of a song they had been working on for weeks. Thomas was now accepted as the band's new mentor.

During the course of the next 6 months, Nick's band began to play local adult nightspots (the early time period, of course) and cut their first CD. Although this began as a music- and business-related mentorship, the band now has discussed drug and alcohol issues very openly with Thomas. Thomas says he nearly cried with joy at having this opportunity. He now has a chance to share with a new generation of young men the lessons he learned from his mistakes.

Natural mentorships are like that. Sometimes they come out of nowhere and on occasion they come from a person who is part of the system. Mike was a borderline underachiever who found a mentor in his history teacher who influenced his life for many years. Mike enjoyed history and politics, but he had several teachers in his life that made the subject boring, so he sought his own education in these areas. In high school he had a track coach, Marty Strong, who was excited about politics and made history come alive with real and modern connections. Mike appreciated the lively debates in class with Coach Strong. He actually began to look forward to writing essays defending or attacking political stances in Coach Strong's class. Mike found academic success that year, but perhaps most importantly he made a connection to a teacher who influenced him like no others had.

Later that year, Mike was disappointed, but not shocked to learn that Coach Strong had taken a community college position over the summer. But, what really made the difference for Mike was that Coach Strong called him in August. Marty Strong was requesting Mike to work in his election campaign for local school board. True to form, Marty Strong was making American politics real for his student. His mentorship included Mike as an integral part of his successful school board campaign. Mike had found a natural mentor who made a transition from the classroom to his everyday life.

PLANNED MENTORSHIPS

There are occasions where a deliberate attempt to match a boy with a mentor is made. Planned mentorships can be provided by outside organizations or schools to connect boys with mentors for specific projects or for lifelong guidance. Planned mentorships do require the dedication of the mentor and the slow building of a meaningful relationship.

Big Brothers Big Sisters

Perhaps one of the most recognizable programs nationally is Big Brothers Big Sisters. This organization has served more than 200,000 children, ages 6–18, in 5,000 communities across all 50 states (Big Brother Big Sisters, 2005). This program is well developed and has deep understanding of the specifics needed for men to be good mentors. A comprehensive study by Teirney, Grossman, and Resch (1995) followed 487 students in a treatment group receiving support from Big Brothers for 18 months. Their findings indicate the following very impressive measurable influences of the Big Brothers Big Sisters programs. Participants were:

- 46% less likely to begin using illegal drugs,
- 27% less likely to begin using alcohol,
- 52% less likely to skip school,
- 37% less likely to skip class, and
- 35% less likely to involved in a physical confrontation at school.

> . . . participating minority students [in Big Brothers Big Sisters programs] . . . were more confident in their schoolwork performance, demonstrated modest gains in their grade point averages, and were able to get along better with their families (Teirney et al., 1995).

In addition, participating minority students were 70% less likely to initiate drug use when compared to their nonmentored peers, and overall, the participants were more confident in their schoolwork performance, demonstrated modest gains in their grade point averages, and were able to get along better with their families (Teirney et al., 1995).

Although these findings are impressive, there were some cautionary conclusions that should be seriously considered. Teirney et al. (1995) note that these results are due to a local, committed, and highly trained organization of mentors. In order for similar results to be produced, the standards and supports would have to be in place for successful mentorships to be developed. Secondly, the question arises if there are enough volunteers and funding to expand this type of program into more areas. The report suggests that the cost of support and supervision is running more than $1,000 per participant.

Unfortunately, the time and cost is a limiting factor for further implementation. However, local groups and some school districts are able to develop similar programs that are being recognized for their success.

Project HIGH HOPES

As part of a Jacob K. Javits federal grant funded from 1993–1996, Project HIGH HOPES sought to identify students with talent in science, engineering, and the visual and the performing arts (Baum et al., 1997). This study was specifically seeking to identify twice-exceptional students (students with special education needs who are also gifted and talented) in Connecticut and Rhode Island. After identification, students had the opportunity for talent development classes in which mentoring became a very valuable component. In Project HIGH HOPES, the students were identified for their special education need, as well as for their gifts (Baum et al.). These young men were hungry to be recognized for what they could do in science, engineering, and the arts, while in the regular school system they were known for what they could not do.

Marcus was an excellent athlete, tall, and well liked by his peers. He was very sensitive when it came to academic issues and carefully protected his dyslexia so that his peers would not associate him with other special education students. Marcus had been identified by the Project HIGH HOPES program for his engineering ability and looked forward to the talent development sessions each week. The unique situation for Marcus in this planned mentor arrangement was that his engineering mentor, Tim, was also dyslexic. This led to a very important mentorship that not only informed Marcus about academic options and career choices as he learned the skills of the practicing engineer, but perhaps most importantly, Marcus learned about how Tim survived school with dyslexia. This common bond actually was a well-anchored place in their relationship. Both Tom and Marcus could share their experiences with someone who shared the same type of learning disability and experienced its effect on their lives. Marcus is now pursuing a degree in engineering, thanks to the important support a planned mentor provided him at a crucial stage of his teenage years.

The Prism Metaphor

Mentoring has been demonstrated to have a positive influence on boys who are underachieving in school. The Prism Metaphor (Baum, Renzulli, & Hébert, 1995) draws on a metaphor of the light spectrum. The beam of light that an underachieving student projects can be separated out into the precursors of achievement by the elements of a prism shaped intervention that relies on the talents and skills of a mentor.

In this planned mentor model, a dedicated and trained teacher must sift through emotional difficulties, social issues, learning problems, and the possibilities of an inappropriate school curriculum to facilitate an individual student's attempt at the following (Baum et al., 1995):

- a positive relationships with adults,
- self-regulation of behavior,
- self-understanding,
- an interest-based curriculum, and
- a positive peer group.

Perhaps that special mentoring relationship that can guide our young men is best encapsulated in the following story. Esteban had benefited from a mentor in the construction industry when he was young. The contractor valued the work ethic and attention to detail that Esteban demonstrated on the work site. This contractor had even supported Esteban as he entered college and pursued an engineering degree. Esteban had developed a successful career as a civil engineer and his children were grown and now had their own careers. He wanted to give back to the community. Esteban saw an advertisement at work looking for mentors in an afterschool and Saturday engineering program for struggling second language learners.

Jose didn't get to see his dad often. He had a very good job that required him to be on the road managing the construction of a chain of new restaurants. Jose's mother valued education and urged Jose to check into the engineering program being offered at the community college.

From the first Saturday of the program, Esteban could see that Jose had the same characteristics he valued in his employees, the same characteristic that had caught the attention of his contractor many years ago. For the next year a half, Esteban and Jose worked on a variety of short- and long-term engineering projects, even entering some in statewide competitions. Both of these individuals invested intellectual and emotional resources and grew from their experience. Esteban was able to bridge the language gap for some of the more technical engineering vocabulary for Jose. The end result of this mentoring relationship was that Jose was able to gain acceptance into a school of engineering and is succeeding at the university level. By mentoring Jose, Esteban had completed a cycle of sorts, one that would hopefully continue to benefit other young men like he and Jose.

Conclusion

The successful ending to Jose and Esteban's story is just one of the many we've seen. Mentorships have played a powerful role in many boys' lives, helping them to realize their potential and ultimately change their attitudes about their futures. Mentors can also help boys realize and develop their areas of talent. More information about talent development in the home and in and outside of school is presented in Chapter 10.

CHAPTER 9 TOOLS

Finding a Mentor Worksheet

1. Who is the person who needs a mentor?

2. What are his passions or interests?

3. What is his learning style?

4. When is he available?

5. Where are the resources available?

6. What are some natural mentor possibilities in school? In the community?

7. What are some planned mentor possibilities in school? In the community?

Traits for a Successful Mentor Checklist

- ❏ Are you able to enjoy your work with students? Can you let them experience the joy of discovery?
- ❏ Can you recall the joys and frustrations you experienced when you were just learning and can you see and recognize that in your mentees?
- ❏ Can you demonstrate a process and share insights and mistakes made along the way?
- ❏ Can you withhold some of the answers and instead help mentees begin to pose their own questions?
- ❏ Are you prepared to provide guidance in areas of nonacademic interests and values?
- ❏ Will you allow boys to make their own decisions?
- ❏ Can you make suggestions without being too directive?
- ❏ Can you listen to boys' thoughts and suggest future plans of action?

Suggestions for Being
a Successful Mentor

- *Listening.* This is perhaps the most difficult skill of the mentor to master. This requires really being present and available and perhaps hearing words or dealing with emotions that are difficult.
- *Being there.* While most boys would never say that they appreciate your presence at an event, they actually crave the presence of a significant male who is watching them.
- *Don't fear confrontation.* No matter how simple it may be to avoid confrontation, let young men know what your values are. Let them know how you feel about certain topics
- *Practice what you preach.* You can say it many different ways, but if you are not "walking the walk" and modeling what you are saying you may in fact be doing even greater damage. You should be aware that you are being observed in each conversation for the way you express your anger and the way you handle relationships.
- *Be ready to teach and be honest.* The best example you can give your mentee is to be honest about your life and your experiences. Honesty leads to honest teaching and honest learning, what the mentee really needs from your relationship.

chapter 10

Developing Boys' Talent

arcus stares at a 2" x 8" slab of wood in the hands of today's instructor—a silver-haired engineer with an eye patch. With very few words, the visiting engineer shows a diagram drawn by Leonardo da Vinci of a spring-powered cart. Again, using few words, but demonstrating important techniques, the engineer assembles a simple model of the da Vinci cart that moves across the classroom floor under its own stored energy. The engineer now hands each student a pile of rubber bands, a flat block of wood, four eye screws, two thin wooden dowels for axles, two small wooden wheels, and two large wooden wheels. The challenge: to assemble a wooden car that can move across the floor under its own stored powered. Marcus is enthralled.

In 15 minutes, Marcus has assembled his vehicle and begins to wind its rubber bands. He proceeds to the school hallway, where every fifth floor tile is marked with an orange piece of tape to represent 5 feet of distance. Marcus places the vehicle on the starting line and lets it go. The model accelerates and slowly comes to a stop 20 feet from the starting line. Much to everyone's surprise, the vehicle now begins to roll backward, returning 10 feet under its own power. The engineer looks knowingly at the surprised student. Marcus returns to his worktable with a new understanding of the concept and begins a series of modifications that will enable his model to travel 53 feet down the school hallway under rubber band power. Marcus feels successful. He has been given the opportunity to explore his interest area of engineering and, at the same time, demonstrate that he has abilities that on some occasions are not elicited or nurtured in his regular classroom environment.

DEVELOPING BOYS' TALENTS

How do we discover and develop the talents of young men? Marcus was fortunate in that he was participating in Project HIGH HOPES, a 3-year program (1993–1996) funded by the Jacob K. Javits act (Baum et al., 1997). This program provided hundreds of students like Marcus an opportunity to explore and develop their talents during the school day. In this program, Marcus's talent in engineering was discovered, and then he had the opportunity to take special classes during the regular school day to help develop his interest and talent. Joseph Renzulli (1994), who researches and advocates for gifted and talented programs, has suggested that schools can be a place for talent development and a place where students can develop their innate abilities.

So, what does talent development mean? Perhaps it refers to facilitating the areas of interest of a student and going far beyond that. Once these interests are identified, we then can provide the specialized enrichment similar to the activities Marcus was participating in. Talent development then goes on to provide training in the skills of the practicing professional. For instance, after the rubber band powered car activity, Marcus went on to work with engineering mentors on a solar powered car experiment. In order to construct this vehicle, Marcus had to learn how to solder electrical wiring. This was a specific skill that he might not have picked up in the regular curriculum; however, it is a skill that he will be able to use throughout his life.

Why do we need talent development for our young male students? Talent development opportunities can be the crystallizing experiences that shape the path boys follow as they pursue their interests and produce products that benefit themselves and society. For Pulitzer Prize-winning scientist E. O. Wilson, his talent development came in the form of spending long hours in the backwoods of the Southern United States collecting and observing wildlife (Wilson, 1995); for former U.S. Secretary of State General Colin Powell, his talent was developed through opportunities that the military's Reserve Officers Training Corps program afforded him to understand leadership (Powell, 1996); and in the case of Eli and Peyton Manning, brothers who play quarterback for the New York Giants and Indianapolis Colts NFL teams, respectively, their talent was recognized and honed at an early age, which led to outstanding collegiate and professional football careers. Often, these crystallizing experiences do not occur in the regular school curriculum. So, we must also allow for enrichment activities that go beyond the regular curriculum to capture the interests of boys and help them develop their natural talents.

> Talent development opportunities can be the crystallizing experiences that shape the path boys follow as they pursue their interests and produce products that benefit themselves and society.

CREATING TALENT DEVELOPMENT OPPORTUNITIES

Before we can proceed to creating a plan to develop the talents of boys in schools, we must consider three factors: interest, motivation, and ability as expressed through multiple intelligences. Interest might be considered as the spark that gets things moving as a young man develops his talent. Motivation would be the force and determination that drives the boy to complete the assignment or project. Ability is that unique combination of intelligences that the student has developed or is developing to bring to bear on a school assignment or project.

Interest

Interest is a key factor in boys developing skills in a specific area of study. The school experience should present boys with a variety of topics from the core areas or disciplines (arithmetic, science, language arts, and social studies). However, it is the subtopics that allow boys to become experts. For example, it is interest that drives young boys to pursue every book, television show, and model created about dinosaurs. Teachers are always amazed when they find out the interest area of a boy who has otherwise been unresponsive in class. Some boys are fortunate to attend schools that offer special electives from the arts and even specialized discipline-specific courses (e.g., a course in oceanography). Many of the young men we have worked with over the years can tell you of the lesson, the teacher, or the experience that turned them on to the area that now has become their passion. It is this type of interest that drives a boy to a continuing search of the topic throughout his life and enables him to produce products about the topic (Albert & Runco, 1988).

Parents can recognize immediately when their boys have developed a profound interest in a topic. Suddenly everything has to revolve around the area of interest. These boys begin asking questions and doing investigations about their topic of interest at home when time limitations do not allow for such investigations in school (Neu, 1993). A boy's interest in a topic will fuel his investigation of the matter far more than any academic assigned task. It is often these childhood interests that propel boys into specific careers and the production of creative endeavors.

Motivation

Although every classroom teacher wishes that every lesson he or she teaches could capture the interest of each student and motivate him or her to excel, this is a highly unrealistic goal. Interest is just one component of motivation. Motivation itself is a complex topic and is the topic of hundreds of books and scholarly articles. For the purpose of discussing talent development, let's look at two categories of motivation that can be easily observable in boys. Motivation comes in two types: extrinsic (motivation that is attributed to outside factors, such as school demands, what peers are doing, or what parents require) and intrinsic (motivation that is driven by a personal desire to succeed, such as the completion of a project for personal use).

Extrinsic motivation is common in school systems and can be encouraged by parents. For instance, students who work toward a goal for the recognition of their teacher or peers show extrinsic motivation. Extrinsic motivation is very common and useful in many situations. The one drawback is that this form of motivation is situational. In other words, the reward must be meaningful to the individual boy or the boy may choose not to attempt the assignment. Boys with an overly developed need for extrinsic motivation begin to face real difficulty when no reward is apparent for completing a task.

Intrinsic motivation tends to be the drive that allows boys to complete tasks that they find personally meaningful. Find a young man who has learned the meaning of practice for the improvement of his music, art, or sport and you'll find someone who has an understanding of intrinsic motivation. Intrinsic motivation is doing the task because the process is important. In this situation, students are driven to succeed for personal fulfillment, without any concern for a tangible reward.

Ability as Demonstrated Through Multiple Intelligences

Howard Gardner (1999) has promoted the theory that traditional intelligence testing and standardized evaluations fall short of measuring the many intelligences that each student expresses in his or her possibilities of cognitive abilities. Simply put, Gardner believes that all people have nine different intelligences that they can draw from to produce products in a domain. Gardner (as cited in Checkley, 1997) defines intelligence as:

- the way we make sense of the world,
- the way we solve problems, and
- the way we produce culturally valued products.

These intelligences can be considered the tools that boys use to solve problems and produce projects (Baum, Viens, & Slatin, 2005). In our experience, by using a multiple intelligence approach, teachers will provide young male students with a substantial variety of outlets to display their ability. Too often, we believe, instruction is geared to only a few of the intelligences, and boys may be cheated out of opportunities to demonstrate what they actually understand and can produce.

We believe all people have some level of all nine of the intelligences, however, some of us are either born with more ability in an area or have developed some expertise in an area and have applied it to a domain. In other words, we are trying to develop our abilities from those of a novice to those of an expert in order to succeed in our careers and life. For example, the novice guitar player may use kinesthetic and rhythmic intelligences to learn to play guitar, while the individual with a few years of practice is using these same intelligences to perform a much more complex piece of music.

The idea that we bring our intelligences to bear on a domain springs from the variety of human endeavors and the appropriate skills needed. A domain can be defined as a discipline or a real-world activity that is valued by society. Many domains have unique requirements for combinations of intelligences. Later in this chapter you will be introduced to a group of students as they examine lizards, snakes, and frogs. The boys in this group are producing a representative product from the domain of the biological illustrator. This product required both the observation and pattern-seeking skills of the naturalist intelligence combined with the spatial intelligence and bodily-kinesthetic intelligence of the sketch artist. This combination of several intelligences to produce domain-specific, real-world projects is very common, to the point that we might not even be aware of the combination of skills and intelligences.

The following is a brief description of each of the multiple intelligences, as purported by Gardner (1999). The *linguistic* intelligence can be demonstrated by reading, writing, public speaking, storytelling, and a variety of day-to-day school tasks. Some of the skills include reading comprehension, poetic use of vocabulary, spelling, and creative writing. The domains or careers that require this intelligence would include the law, sports reporting, and the stand-up comedian or motivational speaker. Products that we can associate with this intelligence include the creation of a poem, a newspaper article, the execution of a debate, or even the performance of a story.

The *logical/mathematical* intelligence can be seen in boys with the ability to work with number and logic problems. Skills in this intelligence include problem solving, computation, and using abstract relations, such as calculating the number of points needed to achieve a new level on a video game. This intelligence far exceeds the rote memory work often required by ditto math sheets or textbook questions. Domains like accounting, engineering, computer programming, and investment trading use this intelligence on a regular basis. Products of the logical/mathematical intelligence may appear as charts, graphs, computer programs, and the use of mathematical proofs.

The *spatial* intelligence deals with the ability to manipulate objects in the mind's eye and includes directional abilities used by pilots and some athletes. This intelligence can be seen in various skills associated with the visual arts and can also be seen in chess players. For young engineers, like Marcus, this intelligence is their world. For instance, when Marcus was faced with a problem, he changed the problem into an image he could work with more easily. The photographer, sculptor, choreographer, cartographer, and even the surgeon depend on their abilities in the spatial intelligences for their domain. Products associated with this domain include elaborate constructions of buildings and models, creation of blueprints for the ultimate tree house, or the production of a video for a class assignment.

When we discuss the *kinesthetic* intelligence, we have to include everything from the fine motor skills used by the surgeon to the gross motor skills of the soccer player. This intelligence emphasizes moving the body to solve a problem or create a performance. Several domains that are highly valued by today's culture represent the use of kinesthetic intelligence including, but not limited to, athletes, dancers, artists, and actors. The products range from the wrestling match between two trained athletes, to the performance of a Tai Chi form, to acting in the school play, or even the painting of portrait. This is an area that boys develop early and cherish any opportunity to explore. However, we must carefully discriminate boys' need for movement from the purposeful movement developed in the kinesthetic intelligence. In other words, if a boy is fidgeting in his seat due to being uncomfortable with an academic topic or being overstimulated, this is not a demonstration of kinesthetic intelligence.

The *musical* intelligence can be seen in the professions of the conductor of the orchestra, the DJ, and the country/western singer. Gardner (as cited in Checkley, 1997) said "Musical intelligence is the capacity to think in music, to be able to hear patterns, recognize them, remember them, and perhaps manipulate them" (p. 12). So, what are skills of the musical intelligence? They include producing a specific type of music, the accurate critical analysis, and the composition of music. The domain also includes the products of performing the piece of music, writing it, and/or critiquing music. In boys, we can see this in the youngster who can always generate a rap, organizes a band to play at parties or school activities, or the boy who can compare the musical style and influence of The Doors to that of Nirvana.

The personal intelligences can be divided into two intelligences. The *intrapersonal* intelligence includes those attributes of knowing one's self. The *interpersonal* intelligence is concerned with relations with other individuals. For instance, the intrapersonal intelligence enables boys to develop a mental conception of who they are, and allows them to distinguish between feelings and make decisions that reflect their beliefs. The interpersonal intelligence is the understanding that other people have feelings and being able to recognize them in social situations. It also includes those skills needed to work with others. Examples of the domains that value the intrapersonal intelligence are the therapist, artist, activist, and motivational speaker. Products of this intelligence include the therapeutic intervention, the painting that expresses feeling, the drive to change a course of action of society because of a personal sense of justice, and a pep talk before the big game.

When we look at the interpersonal intelligence, people such as the educator, the coach, and the diplomat come to the forefront. These domains value the products of an excellent exploratory lab based on the student's interest and ability, the direction and feedback given to support a boy as he improves his goal blocking ability, and the instigation of peer mediation between two warring friends.

The *naturalist* intelligence can be seen most often when a boy is fascinated with the living world around him. This intelligence is highly misunderstood and misinterpreted. Some boys just can't keep their hands off any life form they come in contact with. The naturalist produces products like leaf collections, arrangements of rocks in symmetrical patterns in the woods to guide his path, or running records of the birds he sees. However, this intelligence is not limited to living things. Gardner (1999) pointed out that this intelligence is also demonstrated in the boy who groups his toys by size, shape, and color, or the young man who recognizes patterns in the dress or behaviors of his peers at school.

The remaining intelligence has less written about it, but we believe it is critical to the healthy development of all young men. Gardner (1999) has written sparingly about the *existential* intelligence, but he indicates that this intelligence contributes to the domain of the philosopher. The existential intelligence deals with those individuals who are constantly asking the "what if" questions. Thinkers and social activists such as Friedrich Nietzsche, Dr. Martin Luther King Jr., and Mahatma Gandhi are examples of men who demonstrate the characteristics of the existential intelligence.

TALENT DEVELOPMENT IN THE SCHOOL

A child's talent can be developed using several methods, both in the school and in the home. The following are just a few of the many methods that can be used to develop boys' talent in the school setting.

Using a Pathway Development Approach

Considering the importance of interest, motivation, and ability as demonstrated through the multiple intelligences, how can we provide talent development opportunities on a regular basis to our students? There are many ways we can provide educational modifications that give boys instruction that caters to their strengths and can help them circumvent their weaknesses, as well as give them opportunities to explore future careers and interests. One method to systematically interweave talent development with classroom instruction is the Pathways Model (Baum et al., 2005). We have seen boys across the nation flourish when educators integrate the pathways into the array of educational opportunities. The following is an introduction to the five basic pathways.

THE EXPLORATIONS PATHWAY

Bobby, Mark, and Lee were usually the last students to get excited about anything dealing with school, however, excitement lit up the faces of the three boys when they learned that a scientist would be visiting their sixth-grade classroom and bringing live animals along. Bobby was especially ecstatic that the guest speaker was going to be bringing in live snakes. The guest instructor could identify these budding naturalists immediately, as they volunteered to move the specimen boxes and to pass out the handouts for identifying poisonous and nonpoisonous snakes of Arkansas. However, the boys' teacher was having second thoughts about this enrichment activity and reported she was not feeling well to another sixth-grade teacher as soon as the live snake specimens began to appear. Unfortunately, she passed out when she saw the 6-foot rat snake, much to the amusement of our three young naturalists. The rat snake was then passed to some young ladies who stepped in to pass the snake to two reluctant young men. (It should be noted that not all boys are into snakes and other creatures and that these two young men who hesitated when handling the snake were observed to have excelled a few weeks later in an exploration activity that focused on rhythm and music.) Next in line were the boys who had been waiting for this moment. Bobby, Mark, and Lee could not wait to see each animal, and they had to touch each of the reptile and amphibian specimens.

Now, the students were put to work. Each student was given an observation worksheet and two specimens. Their task: to act like a herpetologist and determine the differences between reptiles and amphibians. They were instructed to observe five characteristics of the head of the specimen, then generate two descriptive qualities of those particular characteristics. Bobby chose the lizard's eyes for one of his five characteristics. He carefully described three qualities he observed about the lizard's eyes: The eyes were situated high on the head and were protected by eye sockets, and each eye also had eyelids for further protection. What Bobby really enjoyed about this task was the instructor's recommendations to draw as much of the observation as possible, and then support the sketch with words. Bobby was always sketching and doodling in class. This guest speaker even said that practicing herpetologists always draw specimens as a method of recording data.

This scenario provided an exploration into Bobby's strengths: a profound interest in the living things around him and his ability to draw. Bobby had been able to experience a practical science lesson that was challenging and he even learned the difference between reptiles and amphibians (outcomes required in his state's curricular frameworks). His teacher was able to observe Bobby's drawing talent in a new light; she saw that it was not just something this student did when he was bored in class. She also realized that Bobby actually had artistic talent and that Bobby could use drawings to represent his understandings and to communicate ideas.

Bobby's story illustrates the Explorations Pathway (Baum et al., 2005). This pathway has three goals for the education of boys:

- to promote a classroom learning environment that is stimulating with opportunities for experimentation of all types;
- to provide boys with learning experiences across a range of domains and intelligences; and
- to uncover cognitive strengths, interests, and learning style preferences of young men.

This pathway is actually what good education should be all about. When educational activities are stimulating and promote experimentation, we have seen boys become active learners who can't wait to go to school. Likewise, the chance to explore learning across domains and the use of a variety of intelligences give boys insight into fields of study that they might not be aware of.

> When educational activities are stimulating and promote experimentation, we have seen boys become active learners who can't wait to go to school.

Most importantly, this pathway is an opportunity to discover the strengths and interests of the boys in our classrooms. Reflect on your own education—how many times was a special topic or activity that a classroom teacher offered the one you remembered most? Chances are, you chose an area of study or a career path based on an area of strength or interest that was stimulated by a classroom lesson that offered opportunities beyond the regular curriculum.

THE BUILDING ON STRENGTHS (BRIDGING) PATHWAY

Abdul and Francis have just completed constructing an 11-inch paper tower made from 20 sheets of paper and a roll of tape. Abdul had suggested the design, based on the pillars that held up the highway overpass that he walked past daily on his way to school. Francis was good with his hands and meticulously rolled the papers so that each was level on the top and bottom. In the meantime, Abdul was drawing a blueprint to capture the details of their design.

The boys then stack encyclopedias one by one on their tower constructed of paper and tape. Each new placement of a book brings smiles and the anticipation of breaking the school record.

While this building activity fits into the math curriculum, these young men are actually preparing for the writing portion of their state's competency exam. These two future architects have kept a detailed blueprint of their structure. When the tower finally gives beneath the weight of 26 encyclopedias, the boys begin to take notes on the cause of the structural failure. Later, these two young men will begin to write a descriptive essay detailing the directions to build a similar tower, therefore bridging their strengths in building and design to literacy skills.

The Building on Strengths Pathway focuses on classroom methods and instructional techniques that attempt to support a strengths-based approach to academics and attempt to "bridge" student strengths specifically to literacy learning.

Another example can be seen in the use of storyboarding. This technique encourages students to use the same technique that film producers use to layout the details of their stories. Instead of writing an outline to begin the structure of a story, boys are encouraged to draw detailed pictures in frames that contain important elements of the story. They are encouraged to use their area of strength to produce a visual outline or representation of the details of their story before they start adding words. In other words, they are using their artistic strength to get the story in a medium that they favor, and then they will go back and use words to complete the written essay. For many boys who are struggling with the abstract nature of words, the creation of a visual representation allows them to use their strengths. They then feel much more positive about the writing experience and allow the internal procedures of the writing process to emerge with confidence.

The Understanding Pathway

Somewhere in upstate New York, very far from any ocean, and even further from a temperate climate that would be conducive to sea turtles laying eggs, there is a class struggling with the concept of population dynamics and survival rates among sea turtles. Thus the question arises: How do you teach an abstract concept in the classroom in order to enhance students' understanding? For years, educators attuned to the unique educational needs of boys have used videos to do this, but now they are turning to Web sites and other technological tools. Although these are great educational tools, there is still a low-tech option that is readily available to every teacher: simulations. In this particular simulation, the New York students line up holding cups filled with 100 red beans representing sea turtle eggs. Their task: to navigate beach hazards—dogs, egg hunters, sea gulls, and pollution—to reach the open sea. If they are "captured" by the beach hazards (played by other students), they must surrender 10 of their precious red beans, each of which represents the life of an individual baby turtle. Once they reach the open sea area (in this case, the playground), each participant must head to the roped off areas in the middle and sides of the activity area that represent the beds of sea grass to avoid the other predators in the sea—sharks and barracuda.

This simulation was developed by Project WILD (Council for Environmental Education, 2003), an international environmental educational program. Project WILD has developed a comprehensive collection of teacher-tested activities that, while not intentionally designed for boys, do provide the visual cues and high-interest topics with opportunities for movement that many boys prefer. For more information on Project WILD in your area, visit the organization's Web site at http://www.projectwild.org.

The above simulation is a great example of incorporating the Understanding Pathway in the classroom. The Understanding Pathway has two goals in the education of boys: to develop curricular options to enhance students' understanding and to create diverse assessment options for students to demonstrate their understanding. Developing curricular options that use simulations can assist boys in accessing a deeper understanding of an abstract concept. These boys were able to experience the learning through four areas:

- movement—for a boy pretending to be a turtle diving into the sea grass to avoid a shark and/or actually being pursued by a seagull or barracuda;

- low-level competition—the survival instinct of running from the predator and likewise the thrill of catching simulated prey;
- concrete to abstract—this simulation can make those unconnected vocabulary words on the board a living concept that boys can reference again and again; and
- visual representation of math—when the time comes to count the survivors, those numbers have a connection to what is going on daily in the oceans so far from the boys' classroom, and they can now visualize those abstract numbers as being physical numbers of baby turtles.

Not every boy who participated experienced the activity in the same way. In other words, their understanding of the important concepts may be coming from any of the four different areas or even perhaps from a combination of experiences.

After such a stimulating learning activity, how can we provide a variety of alternative assessments in order to allow boys to demonstrate their individual understanding? One way would be to take the assessment from products that would be valued by different domains and that require a variety of intelligences to produce. The following are some possible challenges for boys to produce domain-specific products:

- *Statistical Researcher Representing Data Through Graphs*: You are working for the Save the Turtles Foundation and you have just collected the data on the survival rates of young turtles during a 10-year period of time. Using this data, create line, bar, or scatter plot graphs to explain population dynamics, survival rates, and limiting factors, including features of the habitat during the past 10 years.
- *Environmental Activist*: You have heard that the town is planning to sell the beachfront property on the edge of town to developers who are planning to use the land to build a huge shopping mall. Please stage a protest using posters and speeches explaining that this proposed development will have a significant impact on the turtle population. Include informa-

tion about habitat needs for laying eggs, population dynamics, and limiting factors.

- *Nature Cinematographer:* You are working for Disney Films and have been asked to design a documentary film on animal life. You are to create a storyboard depicting the sea turtle population dynamics during the last 10 years using the data on the class chart. Please make sure your documentary includes information about population dynamics, carrying capacity, predator/prey relationship, and limiting factors, including features of the habitat.
- *Writer for a Popular Magazine: Outdoor Life* has hired you to write a story on the plight of the sea turtle. You should describe some of the natural history of sea turtles and should include information about population dynamics, carrying capacity, and limiting factors, including features of the habitat.

You may find as we have that the variety of student responses is endless. Each group of boys will bring its own unique understanding of the activity to the products for this activity. For instance, boys in New York developed elaborate, fact-filled protest speeches and chants to promote preservation of nesting habitats for turtles. They even wrote a rap song and encouraged audience participation as they performed it. In Texas, a group of boys meticulously assembled storyboards about developing safe turtle zones. One of the boys had seen a model used by the hotel industry in Mexico to promote turtle nesting. He eagerly shared this with his peers who drew complete pictures of the proposed safe turtle zone facility, as well as the camera angles and the location of the narrator in several scenes.

Perhaps most importantly, the understanding pathway allows boys to explore a topic deeper and spend more time on a topic of their choosing. In this way, we can find our future artists and scientists by examining their interests, understandings, and the depth of their products.

THE AUTHENTIC PROBLEMS PATHWAY

So, how do we facilitate young men to realize that learning has a connection to the real world? By using an Authentic Problems

Pathway approach, which uses real-world problems and expert roles to create authentic assessments of student learning.

Marcus, the young man who discovered his talent area through the engineering activity with the da Vinci vehicle, had a unique summer experience with Project HIGH HOPES. Students were presented with a real-world problem, a polluted pond on school property (Gentry and Neu, 1998). This pond had a spillway and bridge system. A small creek that flowed through an upper-middle-class neighborhood fed the pond. Although the pond supported many local flora and fauna, there were several problems apparent. There was an overgrowth of algae in one side of the pond, in some areas oil slicks coated the surface of the water, and the spillway and the far side of the pond were a collection point for a variety of solid refuse ranging from used automobile tires, to Styrofoam cups and cola cans.

The students were divided into groups based on their talent and interest area. They were then given the opportunity to form a corporation, an invitation to investigate the site, and the instructions to propose a solution to a panel of school officials. Marcus had been receiving specialized engineering training and joined an all-male corporation that was composed of an artist, a scientist, an actor, and two other engineers. Their intent: to use their various talents in a team effort.

These boys were also identified with a specific learning disability or ADHD. In addition, these boys were highly visual-spatial and preferred to express themselves this way rather than reading or writing. To investigate this real-world problem, Marcus' team armed themselves with disposable cameras and swarmed over the pond area. For these young men, the photograph was the best way to record the important information they needed to develop a solution. Within 2 hours, they had their pictures back and then began to assemble a huge storyboard to address the environmental and engineering problems.

The Authentic Problems Pathway is the ultimate answer to the question, "When are we ever going to use this stuff?" This is an opportunity for students to apply what they have learned in a real and meaningful way. Educators must present content knowledge in the context of a real-world problem in this pathway.

Renzulli and Reis (1997) developed a Triad Model for education that promoted the Type III investigation as a way that a student's passions are manifested in a product. They promote a student's ability to choose his or her own topic for investigation, as long as it addresses a real-world or authentic problem. The Type III investigation is just that—a problem chosen by the student that addresses an authentic problem, and is presented to an appropriate audience.

One of this book's authors (Terry) experienced the use of the Authentic Problems Pathway in his science classroom with one student, Karl. Karl was recognized as an outstanding linebacker. He was fearless and many of his opponents expressed that he lived to deal out pain to running backs and errant wide receivers that crossed into his territory. As his football coach and biology teacher, Terry knew that Karl was actually a very sensitive young man. He had an abusive father who no longer lived in his home, an emotionally unavailable mother, and an intense love of animals; a very interesting combination for a special education student who was struggling to maintain his academic eligibility with a 2.0 grade point average. Karl was identified with Oppositional Defiant Behavior and a mild form of dyslexia. He appeared in Terry's classroom after he had failed biology under another teacher. The school's assistant principal believed that Terry could apply leverage to a troublesome young man who had to repeat biology.

While taking Terry's class, Karl approached him with an idea for a science fair project. The school district required a Senior Project for graduation. Karl had seen "many bodies of the deceased," as he called them, on his drive to school each morning. Karl drove himself to school each day in an old Chevy truck with a gun rack and mud tires on the back. He lived in an area that was near a U.S. Government nuclear missile silo. The silo was fenced in for security reasons, but the fence, which was intended to keep intruders out, was in fact changing natural wildlife patterns along the highway, such as animal migration. In other words, Karl lived off a highway that was prone to road kill (animals hit and killed by vehicles). Karl, a demolisher on the football field, was concerned about those individual animals that were being struck down every evening on the roads near his home.

Karl asked Terry early in September if he could study the road kill on his drive to school for his required project. Yes, Terry responded, this would meet the requirement of the school district and the state. So, Karl began an 11-week odyssey of recording and documenting the animal bodies he had seen along the road. This investigation very quickly got out of hand, as Karl was gathering data on a very impressive level. Terry could not give him the skills he needed to complete his project, so he called on an old friend. Dale is a trained biologist for a southern state, who really enjoys going into schools to give enrichment lessons. Dale came into Terry's classroom and gave a great presentation that gave Karl the tools he needed to complete his study in the manner a practicing biologist would. Other students were present at this special lesson and each came away with a understanding of the experimentation of biology or method of record keeping that supported his or her own projects or interests.

In the end, Karl produced a study, a real-world application to a real-world problem, of road kill on rural roads that won him first place at the district science fair. In his project, Karl was able to show that some rural highways in the southern U.S. did disrupt certain wildlife patterns at different times of the year. His story is a great example of how the Authentic Problems Pathway approach can be used to identify and develop talent in boys.

THE TALENT DEVELOPMENT PATHWAY

For many years, the public school systems have provided a series of afterschool or special programs that meet the interests of students. Yet, many schools are falling short in the actual development of talent in today's young men. The Talent Development Pathway intends to purposefully provide a method to design structured talent development opportunities and to create opportunities to assess and nurture student talents.

When we discuss the talent development of boys, we must also consider the future of our society and the development of its most precious resources—the gifts, talents, and interests of its young people. Unfortunately, according to a report by the U.S. Department of Education (1993), the United States is failing to recognize and develop the potential of many students. When so many young men do not actualize their potential, we must consider finding fault with an educational system that fails to meet the diverse needs of today's boys. However, reports also state that vocational and technical schools are mounting a concentrated effort to identify the strengths and talents of students (Neu, Baum, & Cooper, 2005). Perhaps what is needed is an education that enables all people to discover their passions, gifts, and talents (Darling-Hammond, 1996).

A unique case in talent development can be seen in the story of Billy and John. Billy was dyslexic and found little use for school. He had attended special education pull-out programs for his reading disability, yet many of his teachers also felt he demonstrated gifted behaviors (Neu et al., 2005). He was large for his age and considered awkward at school. However, Billy had an out-of-school passion: He spent his weekends at Civil War reenactment camps dressing as a Union soldier. On one such occasion, he heard a story told by an older person that concerned an unusual phenomenon at the Battle of Shiloh in Tennessee. It seems that wounded soldiers had crawled through the mud to reach water. Among some of these soldiers, it was noticed that their wounds glowed in the dark, a strange event indeed. The story continues that those soldiers with glowing wounds tended to survive and recovered their health better.

At the same time, Billy began a friendship with John in his chemistry class. John is an excellent student and wanted more than anything to compete in the Intel Science Fair. After these two boys had completed several lab assignments together, John shared his dream of competing on the international level, but admitted that he had not developed a suitable research question. Billy suggested pursuing the question of the glowing wounds on the soldiers at the Battle of Shiloh.

So, let's look at this from a talent development lens. Billy and John had made several explorations into their different fields of study that they found interesting and motivating. Both young men had different sets of strengths to build on. Billy was creative, very visually aware, and more aware of the possibilities, while John was more analytic, precise, and procedure oriented. Billy and John had a deeper understanding of history and the science necessary to prove that this tale from the 1860s could actually be accurate. This was a real-world investigation that was worthwhile and captured their imagination. To top this off, a family friend had mentioned to Billy that a glowing bacteria had just recently been discovered that rode on planaria, a type of flatworm found in the Shiloh area. This was all they needed to begin their investigation.

Over the next year, Billy and John began their investigation into their project, entitled "Photorhabdus Luminescens Inhibition of Pathogens and its Possible Relationship to the Healing of Civil War Wounds That Glowed." They were able to get access to bacteria samples through the help of a family member who worked at a government research facility. Both young men found support and guidance from government research scientists. They were even able to take jobs at the facility performing basic cleaning duties.

Once they had learned the techniques for growing bacteria such as Staphylococcus sp., Bacillus thuringiensis, and Pseudomonas aeruginosa in a controlled and safe setting, they began a series of long and arduous testing that took up most of the summer. Billy and John simulated the wounds of the soldiers by using different growth media and varying temperatures. They devised a method of marking the plastic growth plates with a special grid of their own development so that they could measure the inhibition of bacteria growth by P. luminescens. In order to give themselves a break from this meticulous task, Billy and John would work until they felt their concentration slipping. Then they would play a video game for a 30-minute time period before returning to the task of measuring the thousands of dishes for bacterial growth.

In the end, Billy and John won the Siemens International Science Fair competition. Both of these young men are pursuing their areas of passion with the scholarship prize money. John is still working at the same government lab where they performed their summer experiments and hopes to become an organic chemist. Billy is using his scholarship to pursue a degree in American History, with a specialty in the American Civil War, of course.

Talent Development in the Home and Outside of School

Parents often are aware of the interests and talents that their sons display at home. One systematic approach to developing the talent of boys at home can be adapted from Renzulli's (1977) enrichment triad model. This model was originally developed for gifted and talented students, however, the model has proven to have educational benefits for all students. In essence, Renzulli discovered that creative producers, or individuals who produce products that benefit society, demonstrate a collection of behaviors that cluster into three areas. He describes the three areas as an interactive combination of above-average ability, task commitment, and creativity. The above-average ability would include interest in a topic and the demonstration of some success in that area. Task commitment can be best described as "sticking to it," or when a boy continues to work on a problem until he finally reaches a solution. The creativity aspect is that twist or unique solution that a boy brings to a problem.

Out-of-School Activities to Develop Boys' Talents

Keeping these three important characteristics in mind, there are three levels of activities that parents can provide or support in the talent development of their boys. The first would be general enrichment. In other words, parents can provide a variety of experiences for boys based on interests and even explore some new areas that might be unfamiliar to their son. For instance, if a boy is interested in LEGOS and spends hours building with them, perhaps a further enrichment would be to explore an activity in a similar 3-D art form, such as clay modeling.

Once an enrichment activity captures the interest of the young man, the next level would be to provide training in the advanced skills of the discipline. Often, these skills are beyond the parents' abilities or knowledge, so parents must find someone who practices the discipline regularly to help the boy acquire the necessary advanced skills. Staying with the clay sculpting example mentioned above, the practicing potter has techniques or "tricks of the trade" that enable him or her to produce products that have a unique look. There are specific skills to glazing clay products that boys can learn from professionals. These skills include the knowledge of how to use specialized equipment properly. Home improvement projects would be another example where advanced skills are needed. Although books and TV shows on home improvement can be helpful, a practicing carpenter knows and practices these skills on a daily basis and his or her understanding goes beyond the scope a remodeling book or television program can provide. These knowledgeable professionals can give boys the insight to develop the skills they need to take their talent to the next level. Skill education also may include training in thinking skills or creative problem solving.

The third level of talent development allows boys to choose a project to work on. Regular academic schooling has plenty of challenging activities, but few real opportunities to do an investigation based on one's own interests. These self-chosen projects have given boys more rewarding experiences outside of school, and in many cases, they have inspired the boys to pursue college educations (Neu, 1993).

Once an idea is developed, it may require more skill training. One young man who started off photographing animals at his local zoo soon realized he also needed to know how to use a video camera to record animal behavior. This led to the necessary acquisition of video editing, script writing, and storyboarding skills. The end result was an award-winning science fair project, done with the support of his parents, which took his classroom teachers by surprise.

NATIONAL ORGANIZATIONS

For years, parents have turned to organizations like the Boy Scouts of America, 4-H, and the YMCA to help boys develop their talent in specific areas. The Boy Scouts of America offer a wide range of activities for boys to explore. As boys progress through the program, they can choose topics and develop greater proficiency in various skills. 4-H was once thought of as an agricultural organization, however, it has kept pace with modern trends and now has significant opportunities for talent development in technology. 4-H has maintained its traditional role of fostering citizenship and leadership. The YMCA has been working with boys for years and has highly developed programs. All of these organizations welcome parent participation.

While these organizations are well-known, a search on the Web will yield a variety of lesser-known groups. A few examples include the Trailblazer program, developed by the U.S. Sportsman's Alliance, which introduces young people to outdoor activities; Trips for Kids, a biking adventure program with chapters around the country; or even the American Legion's various auxiliary programs that promote leadership and patriotism.

NATIONAL COMPETITIONS

Odyssey of the Mind (OM) is a national program that encourages creativity in the solving of unique problems. Parents can be trained to serve as coaches and can support their child's OM team in afterschool meetings or at local community centers. Destination ImagiNation also offers unique challenges in which boys can bring their talents to bear. Both of these programs post the problems to be solved early in the fall with competitions occurring in the early spring. The typical problem requires a solution to the problem that involves engineering ability, creative dramatics, and creative problem solving, as well as staying within a budget. Countless other competitions in a wide range of academic, artistic, and leadership domains can be found via a Web search, or by checking out the book *Competitions for Talented Kids* by Frances Karnes and Tracy Riley (2005).

SUMMER OPPORTUNITIES

Summer camps abound for boys to have opportunities to explore a multitude of areas. Many summer programs are now modeling their programs after talent development models. This includes in-depth learning into specific topics of interest, from dinosaur digs in Montana, to rainforest explorations in the Amazon, to video game programming camps in California.

Summer camps come in a variety of costs, types, and disciplines. Some camps are day camps for local students only, while others are residential "sleep-away" camps. Some camps offer tuition reimbursements and scholarships. Some are relatively inexpensive, while others are quite pricey. Across the nation, you'll find a wide variety of camps and programs, including those for academics, leadership, the arts, sports, specific talents such as writing or computer programming, and religious-based camps.

When looking for summer opportunities, it's best to start small, looking for programs at local universities, campsites, sports organizations, performing arts centers, museums, and churches. Once your child gets a taste of the summer camp fever and wants to pursue more opportunities, start looking at programs in nearby states or at national centers. One good resource for finding educational summer programs is Duke University's Educational Opportunity Guide. More information about this guide can be found at http://www.tipstore.tip.duke.edu/eog.asp. For older students, check out the various books published by Kaplan or The Princeton Review. And, don't discount the value of word-of-mouth. Talk to other parents whose children are involved in similar activities as yours. Contact local youth organizations such as the Boy and Girl Scouts of America to see if they keep listings, and get in touch with your child's counselor to see if he or she has any recommendations. If you want to get your child involved in summer programs, the opportunities are endless.

> Don't discount the value of word-of-mouth. Talk to other parents whose children are involved in similar activities as yours. . . . If you want to get your child involved in summer programs, the opportunities are endless.

MUSEUM AND ZOO PROGRAMS

There are a variety of museums that offer outreach programs. For example, the Eli Whitney Museum in New Haven, CT, regularly offers afterschool programs to develop the talents of budding engineers. In addition, the Audubon Society centers across the nation have regularly scheduled activities on weekends for the entire family. Most local zoos also have community education programs throughout the year that allow students to take part in the day-to-day activities of zookeepers and other staff. Contact your local museums or zoos to see if they offer any weekend, weekday, or summer programs.

COMMUNITY LEARNING

Several communities have highly developed community-wide learning centers that offer enrichment courses for adults and young people alike. Many community colleges also offer enrichment courses over the summer. Three boys mentioned in this book developed their interest in photography by attending workshops at their local community center. Typical offerings may vary from acting classes and foreign languages, to swimming and diving lessons. These classes are typically taught by an individual with a solid background in an area who is able to teach others the basic skills of the domain. Parents can encourage a young man to take a class based on his interests or one in an area that he has never investigated before.

COMMUNITY ARTS CENTERS

Investigate local community arts centers. Depending on the center, it may produce local theater groups, periodic musical performances, and art shows. Many offer individual or small-group instruction in the visual arts, or acting or musical performance. Many of these centers also offer both private lessons and summer or Saturday classes open to the public in a variety of artistic disciplines. Check your community or city's calendar also, as many art centers host citywide festivals and arts events each year, most of which are open to children. More importantly, these centers are the ideal grounds to find practicing artisans to mentor young budding artists and performers.

COMMUNITY SERVICE

A valuable lesson for parents to model is the importance of community service. Often, our roles as volunteers go unnoticed by our boys simply because we do not inform them of our own community involvement. Parents should allow their children the opportunity to participate in community service activities.

There are many organizations that welcome family participation in community service projects. Some do have age requirements. For instance, Habitat for Humanity only takes volunteers over the age of 16 for construction sites due to federal child labor laws. However, Habitat for Humanity does have a Campus Chapters and Youth Program (CCYP), which provides for younger boys to participate in a variety of community projects (Habitat for Humanity, 2006).

The United Way and the American Red Cross are other organizations that are open to accepting volunteers. Both of these organizations have extensive local chapters that have specific projects in neighborhoods across the U.S.

Parents and teachers can also watch their local newspapers to find community service projects or campaigns in their areas. Often, local organizations inform the newspapers when they need help with a specific project or are requesting donations of some sort. Articles about various activities in the community can also be helpful. Pay attention to the news; for instance, an article about a local wetlands project would garner the necessary contact information to help a boy interested in aquatic science find the perfect out-of-school talent development opportunity.

The number of school-based relief projects has been very impressive across the nation. Recently, we've seen relief projects such as a young man in New York who collected T-shirts to send to Hurricane Katrina victims and a boy in Arkansas who was collecting books for schools destroyed by the hurricane. Classroom teachers have been known to sponsor food drives for needy families in the area or school supply collections for students in third-world countries. Boys need to know that they can contribute to all types of relief efforts both on their own and with a school's support.

The Most Important Opportunity for Talent Development

Most importantly, parents should be vital support systems in the talent development of their son by providing opportunities, making time to pursue interests, discussing and exploring interests with their boy, and following their child's lead. Although programs, summer camps, and community courses are great support systems, they are not a substitute for the vigilant parent who is constantly aware and willing to provide an opportunity for a boy to explore his area of interest. Likewise, in the hectic lifestyle so many of us have adopted, sometimes just making the time to take a boy to a lake to fish or to drive him to the skateboard park sends the message that we support his pursuit of interests.

Most of all, sometimes letting the boy determine the next experiment and following his lead lets him know that you value his interests and support him as a developing individual. This can be frustrating to an adult, especially if we may see some inherent problems with the idea. As adults we sometimes forget that our learning has occurred over several years and that our sons have to learn for themselves. It is OK for an experiment or project to fail. Parents, remember that a failed project just gives you the opportunity to continue to support and encourage your son.

> As adults we sometimes forget that our learning has occurred over several years and that our sons have to learn for themselves. Parents, remember that a failed project just gives you the opportunity to continue to support and encourage your son.

What would a talent development opportunity look like at home? Let's look at a possible project for a young man with abilities in math. If we know that the boy in question is interested in planning and budgeting, then we could supply a real-world problem. For instance, planning the family vacation can become an excellent opportunity to use math skills in an everyday context. In this case, lets look at two possible avenues in which math talent can be developed. The first is having your son plan the financial budget for the vacation. The other is to have him plan the navigation routes and itinerary for the trip. To produce a viable solution for the budget problem, the boy would need to master the following skills:

- using Excel or another spreadsheet program to plan a budget,
- comparing and contrasting rates by investigating a variety of hotels in the area and examining the price versus any special benefits (pool or near a site of interest), and

- understanding a cost analysis of varying modes of transportation (i.e., driving versus flying to the destination).

To plot the navigation of the trip and plan the itinerary, the boy would need to practice the following skills:
- reading a standard highway map or atlas,
- using the scale located on the map to plot the distance between each point,
- using mileage per hour to figure the time between each destination, and
- using basic math skills to determine the amount of time to allocate to each destination.

By allowing a young man to learn actual skills and then apply them to a meaningful situation, he will not only have an opportunity to develop a talent, but he will also have a chance to contribute to solving a real-world problem that will benefit the family. Providing for talent development activities at home has unlimited possibilities. Below are a few suggestions for additional activities boys can do at home to help develop their talents. Some of these activities will be great for you to work on and share with your son. Others may be better suited for your son to work on alone. Be sure to give him any support he may need as he completes talent development activities.

If your child has math talent, he may enjoy:
- developing a scale blueprint of your house or apartment,
- producing a topographic (3-D) representation of his room,
- creating his own Sudoku puzzles, and
- investigating Web sites with math word problems, like http://www.stfx.ca/special/mathproblems or http://www.mathstories.com.

If your child shows talent in history, he may enjoy:
- investigating the family history using tape recordings or video cameras,
- creating grave rubbings to record the local history in the graveyard,
- checking out local historical societies,

- joining a reenactment society, and
- volunteering at a local historical site or history museum.

If your son has language arts talent, he may enjoy:
- writing Haiku poems, complete with watercolor background illustrations;
- writing letters to the editor of the local newspaper;
- composing a play for family members, friends, or neighbors to participate in;
- maintaining a journal; and
- creating and telling tall tale short stories.

If your child displays talent in science, he may enjoy:
- keeping a Christmas bird count record for the Audubon Society,
- investigating kitchen chemistry,
- starting a rock collection,
- maintaining a record of the family aquarium with observational commentary, and
- taking up model rocketry and measuring the distance traveled by different rockets.

If your child's talent is in learning foreign languages, he may enjoy:
- taking a foreign language or culture course with a parent at a community center,
- watching a children's show on a Spanish-language television channel,
- developing friendships or pen pal relationships with students from other countries, and
- reading magazines, newspapers, or Web sites in other languages.

If your son displays creative modes of self-expression, he may enjoy:
- experimenting with a magic kit or magic tricks,
- learning to make quilts or other sewing projects,

- building and painting miniature models, and
- starting a collection of any sort.

If your child shows talent in the performing arts, he may enjoy:
- trying out for roles in community plays or children's theatre groups,
- joining a chorus or other singing group,
- learning to play a musical instrument, and
- playing improvisation games.

If your son has visual arts talent, he may enjoy:
- painting with watercolors or making chalk art,
- sculpting clay to make pottery,
- arranging flowers,
- remodeling or redesigning his room, and
- learning to use a digital camera and digital photo editing programs.

If your child shows talent in using and manipulating technology, he may enjoy:
- learning a new computer program or operating system,
- exploring video editing techniques and programs,
- building a family Web site,
- starting an online blog,
- creating slide shows or presentations for important events, and
- learning how to set up computer servers and other basic programming skills.

Chapter 10 Tools

Da Vinci's Car: A Talent Development Activity

Introduction:

Engineering has been considered a strength area of the child with spatial skills. Students with strong spatial skills seldom have instruction modified to elicit this strength area. This activity has been designed to capitalize on spatial strengths by presenting a problem faced by Leonardo da Vinci. As da Vinci approached this problem through the use of testing models, students will follow his example as they explore basic concepts in engineering and design. Little or no verbal directions are needed, as students use visual cues to actually construct the original model, then test and modify the model to increase the distance achieved by their car. There are many possible solutions that can be generated by students to this problem.

Behaviors to Be Observed:
- Actively manipulates materials
- Tries to predict outcomes
- Understands the main concepts of today's topic
- Shows clarity of thought and focused plan of action in product
- Puts materials together in a unique way
- Explains the logic of alternative solutions
- Shows problem solving by pursuing an unprompted investigation

Organization for Learning:

Set up materials table. Arrange worktables in a manner that allows the students to move to different locations with ease. Make sure there is easy access to a hallway or other area in which the completed vehicles have plenty of room to run.

Materials:
- 2 wooden dowel axles
- 2 small front wheels (available at most hobby centers, just make sure the dowel axle fits the hole snugly)
- 2 large rear wheels (can be purchased or cut from Masonite)

- 4 eye screws
- Small nails
- Hammer
- Several larger rubber bands per student
- 1 ½" x 3" soft wood board per student

Procedures:

Boys will be introduced to the work of Leonardo da Vinci, who had conceived of a spring-powered vehicle using the mechanisms commonly found in wind-up clocks. Show students the diagram of the car on p. 202 and ask students, "What do you think this is? How might it work?" Demonstrate the spring power used to run a clock and ask for student feedback. Show students a mock up of da Vinci's cart that has been altered to run on rubber bands. Wind up the cart and let it travel across a table or floor. Ask students for the differences they notice between the design of the cart and automobiles they are familiar with. Take out enough parts to assemble a demo four-wheeled car. Model the construction technique with a limited amount of teacher talk.

Key points for students to observe that will enhance the performance of the model include:

- using a nail to start the eye screw hole;
- placement of the wheels on the axles;
- anchoring a nail on the front to attach the rubber bands (This should be done before the wheels are assembled to prevent the breaking of an axle.);
- attaching a rubber band to the back axle; and
- winding up the back wheel.

Allow time for students to complete their models. Emphasize that they will need to make adjustments to increase their car's distance after they test their model each time. While students are constructing their model, mark off a testing track at 5-foot intervals. A floor with 12-inch tile is common in most public schools and is ideal for the test track, but you can always use masking tape to mark off appropriate intervals. Typically, students finish their prototypes at different times. As students finish, have them test their vehicles on the track. Make sure to keep accurate records for each test they conduct. Also, be sure to debrief each student after each test and elicit students' alterations for extended runs.

Assessment:

1. Record the distance traveled by each car.
2. Check students' understanding of the engineering principles involved.
3. Does the student make multiple modifications to the car to increase the distance it travels?
4. Keep a running record of the following behaviors. Does the student:
   a. actively manipulate materials?
   b. try to predict outcomes?
   c. understand the main concepts of today's topic?
   d. show clarity of thought and a focused plan of action?
   e. put materials together in a unique way?
   f. explain the logic of alternative solutions?
   g. show problem-solving skills by pursuing an unprompted investigation?

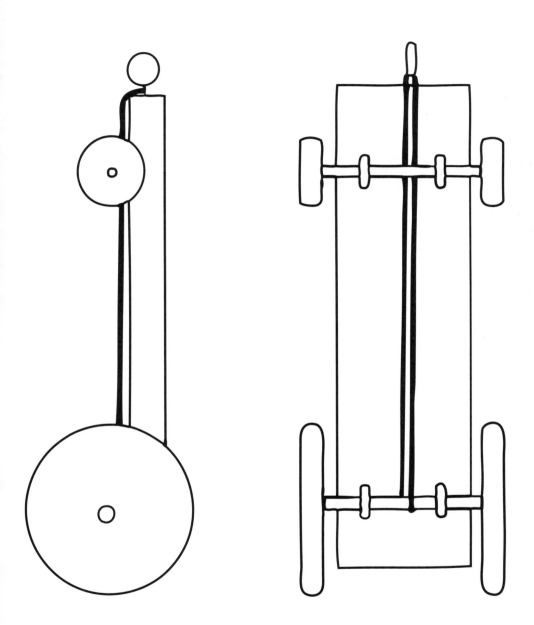

What's the Difference?
An Experiment in Herpetology

Introduction:

It is safe to say that most boys have a fascination with dinosaurs at some point in time. So, when we bring in the last, miniature remnants of the dinosaurs (modern-day reptiles and amphibians), educators are sure to get the full and undivided attention of the majority of the male students in the room. This lesson will be using living specimens, so certain precautions should be taken to ensure the well-being of all live animals. Specific directions for the care and feeding of various reptiles and amphibians can be found via a Web search, by asking a local pet store, or in a field guide. Students will be conducting observations that will lead to the comparing and contrasting of specimens in an attempt to produce a product that demonstrates their skills as a naturalist, an artist, or even a logical thinker.

Behaviors to Be Observed:
- Displays curiosity by asking relevant questions
- Shows previous knowledge related to the topic
- Actively manipulates materials
- Clearly communicates the results of the project
- Systematically tests hypothesis
- Tries to predict outcomes
- Represents ideas in the form of a model
- Finds means of overcoming obstacles in problem solving

Organization for Learning:

The room should have long tables for specimen display and for student work areas. Be sensitive to some students' fear of reptiles and amphibians. Caution: Some animals are very sensitive to human touch—for instance, amphibians have very sensitive skin that can absorb any chemicals or common oils on human hands, and some are very susceptible to overheating if they are held close to the midbody region for a long period of time.

Materials:

- Several terrariums or other suitable containers
- A species of salamander or newt (red spotted newts are easily available)
- Any one of a number of available lizard species
- A turtle (check with your state for any restrictions)
- A local species of frog
- Your favorite snake or whichever species is less expensive at the local pet store
- Observation paper (included at the end of this lesson)
- Pencils with erasers
- Access to Web sites such as http://enature.com for pictures of local specimens

Procedures:

Determine which boys have pets at home and if they have ever spent time just sitting and watching reptiles and amphibians. How many of them watch TV shows on reptiles and amphibians? Ask the students if they are interested in herpetology. Did they know that the word *herpetology* literally means the study of creeping things?

Place a container with one of the specimens on each table of students. Give them the observation worksheet. The observation worksheet has eight squares with different titles. Give the students an overview of how to conduct an observation for this activity. They need to choose four characteristics of the animal (a characteristic would be the head or tail) and then list two attributes (specific descriptions) for each characteristic. Stress that field biologists get to draw their observations when working in remote areas. As a herpetologist, students will get to draw their observations. They will not be graded on the quality of their drawing. They can use words to further describe their observations.

After students have completed making observations on the four characteristics of one specimen, change the containers so that they can make a new set of observations based on the new specimen in front of them. Ideally, they will make two observations, one of a reptile and one of an amphibian. With this set of data, students can now compare and contrast the differences and similarities of the five characteristics of their reptiles and amphibians.

Typically, a specialist in science will conduct the classroom lesson, while two classroom observers take note of specific students' behaviors during the activity using the Talent Discovery Checklist on page 210.

Assessment:
1. Which students are constantly asking questions?
2. Which students want to know more about their species? Are they searching for additional Web sites related to their animal?
3. Keep a running record of the following behaviors. Does the student:
   a. actively manipulate materials?
   b. try to predict outcomes?
   c. understand the main concepts of today's topic?
   d. show clarity of thought and a focused plan of action?
   e. put materials together in a unique way?
   f. explain the logic of alternative solutions?
   g. show problem-solving skills by pursuing an unprompted investigation?

AMPHIBIANS

<table>
<tr><td>

Head

</td></tr>
<tr><td>

Legs

</td></tr>
<tr><td>

Tail

</td></tr>
<tr><td>

Skin

</td></tr>
</table>

REPTILES

<table>
<tr><td>

Head

</td></tr>
<tr><td>

Legs

</td></tr>
<tr><td>

Tail

</td></tr>
<tr><td>

Skin

</td></tr>
</table>

Talent Discovery Checklist

Rater: _____ Date: _____ Science Area: _____

Directions: For each student listed, mark a " + " in the appropriate space when you first observe the student exhibiting any of the behaviors listed in the first column.

STUDENT BEHAVIORS	STUDENT								
Displays curiosity by asking relevant questions.									
Shows a lot of knowledge related to today's topics.									
Actively manipulates materials.									
Communicates clearly the results of the project.									
Systematically tests hypothesis.									
Tries to predict outcomes.									
Represents ideas in the form of a model.									
Finds means of overcoming obstacles in problem solving.									

Following the team's discussion concerning student behaviors observed, each rater should assign a holistic score for each student based upon the following key:
3 = Place student in talent development class
2 = Defer judgment
1 = Placement in talent development class not appropriate at this time

STUDENT NAME									
HOLISTIC SCORE									

When Boys Struggle

oys can find themselves needing professional counseling support as they deal with emotional issues that are specific to their gender, as well as those that face all youth. This chapter focuses on some of the more difficult cases we have worked with. These case studies of four individual boys who have taken the path back to successful lives are included to demonstrate that the healing process for some boys takes time. This chapter will tell the stories of these young men and give general recommendations that are common to many young men who are struggling. Specific counseling suggestions will be associated with each individual case, but these can be applicable to a wide range of young men. Again, these are themes gleaned from the multitude of young men we have worked with over the years. We also want parents and teachers to understand that there is hope for our troubled boys in the long run.

Dean: A Case Study of a Highly Creative and Social Boy With School Problems

A very athletic boy, Dean held his school's pull-up record on the Presidential Fitness test. He was a leader and a valued choice on any afterschool athletic team. It was not unusual for students to ask Dean for help with their math assignments. Although Dean had an IQ score of 138, his school placed its focus on his social/emotional issues, not on his gifted behaviors. He was very frustrated in school and had even thrown a chair at his teacher. Dean's parents had tried to work with the school district; however, their own problems at home seemingly contributed to some of Dean's social and emotional issues.

Years ago, after days of observation in Dean's classroom, a very interesting incident occurred that allowed for further insight to Dean's abilities. The teacher handed out a math worksheet. Every student sat down and began to do his or her work. The teacher returned to her desk and began her daily paperwork routine. Dean sat back in a corner desk all by himself well away from the teacher. He finished his math worksheet in 10 minutes. The walk to his teacher's desk to turn in his paper was quite diagnostic. Geometrically, we know that the shortest distance between two points is a straight line. Dean went to the opposite corner of the room and he picked up some extra pencils. He angled toward the math center and picked up seven wooden sticks; he then stopped two desks over and had a conversation with another student, taking something from her desk. Smiling very sarcastically at the teacher, he put his math paper down on the corner of her desk. She didn't notice, but he stole two paper clips, a pen, and some rubber bands off her desk. Dean went back in the other direction picking up materials as he went. When Dean returned to his desk, he began to work feverishly below his desk. Dean finished his math paper 10 minutes faster than anyone else in his class. His teacher took his paper to use as the answer key without even looking at it, because she knew he never missed a problem.

So, what was Dean doing under the cover of his desk? The students had been studying medieval history in social studies class, and Dean was constructing a catapult. He completed the catapult while his peers were finishing up their math problems. Dean then began to launch spit wads at his unsuspecting peers as they finished the math worksheet. This catapult was a wonderful piece of engineering; it was handheld, concealable, accurate, and it had great range, hurling spit wads from the back of the room as far as the door in front of the classroom.

Later, when we questioned the classroom teacher about Dean's math ability, she revealed that he was above grade level in math and always turned in his math assignments; however, he did act bored with some of the math lessons and tended to be disruptive. Dean's previous chair throwing incident occurred after an argument in math. The classroom teacher had done a math problem incorrectly on the board and Dean had tried to correct her. The teacher admitted that she didn't listen to Dean's explanation and correction, and his frustration grew until he finally lost control and threw a chair.

Dean is currently pursuing an engineering degree at a major university in New England, demonstrating much success in that effort. The opportunity to trace the path he took from his public education experience, as exemplified with the situation in the math class, to his current academic success, is crucial to understanding other students who are struggling to make it in the educational system. Students like Dean can be found daily in schools across the U.S. Further examination of Dean's case will shed light on specific strengths and interventions that later facilitated his success in school.

Dean's story provides us with a look at the needs of a gifted boy struggling in school and what actually worked for him.

Recommendation: Recognize Strengths

It is imperative when working with gifted boys who are struggling academically that we focus on their abilities and strengths. These are the attributes that will carry them through life and provide avenues for careers. Dean had six strength areas that were extremely apparent: aptitudes in math and art, and skills in leadership, creativity,

> It is imperative when working with gifted boys who are struggling academically that we focus on their abilities and strengths. These are the attributes that will carry them through life and provide avenues for careers.

and athletics. In addition, he had the support of both of his parents, even though they were going through a divorce.

Dean faced the challenge of completing uninteresting tasks and the harsh criticism of educators on a daily basis. Dean desperately wanted recognition for his strengths and talents rather than his challenges, yet he continued to lack opportunities to demonstrate these in an academic setting. His biggest academic turnaround occurred after entering high school, where his math educators began to recognize and acknowledge his talent. His sixth-grade teacher (the one whose classroom was described earlier) was not a math expert and had failed to recognize his high ability in this area. With this newfound recognition and support, Dean soon excelled in his honors and Advanced Placement math classes at the high school. The high school teachers were able to identify and nurture his math ability. Dean finally felt some success and began to look forward to new challenges.

Recommendation: Find Male Role Models

Another significant issue evident in Dean's case is the need for positive male role models for bright, struggling boys. Only 9% of all elementary teachers are men, down from 18% in 1981 (National Education Association, 2006). Dean had a tough family situation and although his father did attempt to spend as much time with him as possible, he was not always available for Dean on a consistent basis. It was clear that Dean needed a male role model to guide and support him. Dean's female sixth-grade teacher realized this need and began to coordinate with the baseball coach, a male Dean felt he could trust and look up to. Today, Dean is quick to point out that the male role models he had in middle school and high school provided the guidance and support that facilitated his successful completion of high school and entry into college.

Recommendation: Give Boys an Outlet for Their Emotions

Starting as early as the age of 2, we treat boys and girls differently. Pollack and Cushman (2001) describe this difference as the "boy code" and details its effect in his book, *Real Boys Workbook* (for more about the boy code, see Chapter 12). The boy code consists of expectations placed by society on boys from an early age. Part of this unwritten code is that boys are not encouraged to, and may even be denied opportunities to, express their emotions. Often, boys are taught that an open expression of emotion is unmasculine. The boy code had done a number on Dean. While his emotions raged over his family's divorce, he had no real outlet to express these feelings. He could be exuberant on the soccer field or angry at the umpire's call in baseball, but Dean was expected to hold his emotions in when he was in other situations. His art became a healthy outlet to express those emotions that the boy code had prevented him from revealing. Dean's current reflections indicate that no matter how he was feeling at the time, his artwork provided a safe place to "unload" his fears and anger about his home situation.

Recommendation: Recognize That Boys Know What They Don't Want to Be Like

Another interesting theme that emerged when dealing with struggling boys is that they know what they *don't* want to be like. The disturbing point is that when boys are asked what they want to be like when they grow up or what teacher they like, boys invariably respond with a negative example to demonstrate behaviors they intend not to copy. When boys can describe what they don't want, rather than a positive example of what they do want, we have a real problem with directionality. Dean would clearly state that he did not want to be like his father. No wonder these young men flounder, as they have no example to follow. Boys must be introduced to positive examples for them to emulate, while at the same time we must recognize that they build a sense of what they don't want by describing negative examples.

Recommendation: Introduce Multiple Ways for Students to Demonstrate Understanding

Many common educational practices are not receptive to a boy's need for movement and hands-on and experiential activities. Dean was definitely an active learner who demonstrated his knowledge in a variety of ways. Dean commonly turned in illustrations to accompany homework assignments. It was not unusual for teachers to believe Dean was not paying attention in class because he was constantly drawing. On closer examination, his notebook recorded all the main ideas and many times the illustrations on the side of his paper were visual representations of the topic of the lesson. In high school, Dean was able to combine his abilities in art and math for the first time. This led to Dean's pursuit of a degree in engineering, a field that values multiple representations of a product.

Dean is just one of many young men that we have worked with. His story is a great case study, because we can see what the effects of positive interventions lead to over time. Dean is currently nearing the completion of a college degree. Like so many boys, all he needed was the opportunity to develop socially and emotionally by having a positive outlet for his abilities and being able to use them to express his depth of knowledge.

Recommendation: Be Aware That Boys Need Self-Actualization

In the boys we have worked with that are successful, we have found that they found a niche or interest area early on that helped them develop a positive self-image and gave them goals and direction. Those boys who were struggling typically gave up a passion area and were without a niche during the time period their school problems occurred. When our troubled boys demonstrate a commitment to a purpose or positive activity, working through school problems is soon to follow. A similar indicator of success is increased independence. When young men are willing to take responsibility for their behavior, they are truly growing into successful men.

Matt: A Case Study of a Boy Who Found a Way to Communicate

Matt came to our attention as a failure in the school system who needed immediate intervention. Matt started his school career as a shy, reserved young boy who earned good grades and never got into trouble. In his middle school years, things became more intense in Matt's life due to normal developmental processes, cognitive frustration in school, and some emotional frustration at home. He still maintained a normal perspective: playing sports and interacting with his peers. Matt was ahead of the curve cognitively, but he began to trust his teachers less and less and began to slip academically. Discord within the family played a factor, but it was clearly coupled with the increasing demands of school. Matt's repression of anger over his home situation and his frustration at school began to take its toll and manifest as destructive behaviors. In addition, he lost interest in sports, as they were no longer able to relieve his aggression.

In his room, Matt began to write ominous messages on his walls. Then, he began to include destructive illustrations and specific written threats targeting his family and school. His parents were concerned, but thought it was just a phase. Matt changed the way he dressed and the music that he listened to. He soon would not appear in public in anything other than black clothes, and even began to highlight his face with black eyeliner. Matt's gothic appearance began to intimidate some of his teachers and became a major concern for his parents.

In art class, Matt really allowed his destructiveness to come out. His complex tapestries and paintings began to encode veiled threats in symbolism. Matt's overall emotional health was suddenly in question. Some of his art was so graphic that the art teacher notified a social worker. After further investigation, Matt was questioned about the details in his artwork. Matt offered to translate and verbally stated the encrypted messages in the presence of school authorities. This act of being honest and complying with the principal resulted in Matt's arrest, as some of the messages encoded in his art were specific threats to teachers.

Matt took a hard route. He did attend an alternative school for boys with emotional or behavior problems and received extensive counseling. Eventually, Matt worked his way back into the public school system and earned his diploma. Currently, Matt is attending a junior college and is now looking for entrance into a university. Many of those teachers from his "gothic days" would not recognize him today. Matt has stopped using the black eyeliner and no longer wears primarily black clothes and leather accessories. He has held the same job for more than 2 years and for the first time in years, Matt seems content and happy with his life.

Recommendation: Educating Teachers to See Beyond the Presentation

Matt gave the public appearance of being untouchable. In fact, many of his teachers were worried about having him in their classrooms. In nature, we would call Matt's appearance *warning coloration*, or a type of camouflage that warns others to stay away. As Matt became increasingly frustrated, he projected more of this standoffish behavior. He chose to wear the black clothes and leather accessories to display the message that he was tough and independent. In reality, Matt was crying for help. This is a great challenge to classroom teachers. In today's classrooms with large numbers of students, teachers tend to focus on higher yield students. Matt was so discouraging of positive interactions that his teachers then reciprocated his feelings by staying as far away from him as possible. His destruction of property and threats (particularly against teachers he perceived to be unwilling to go beyond the norm to try reach students) became what everyone focused on, rather than a constructive intervention.

Matt later found teachers who were able to see through the warning camouflage to address a sensitive young man who needed an outlet for expression. Some of the teachers who were able to see through Matt's disguise were accustomed to working with "hard case" boys or boys who were on a track for incarceration. These teachers realized that Matt was not yet a lost cause. Matt later was very appreciative of those teachers who could look beyond his antisocial projections and who would not give up on him.

Recommendation: Avoiding the Self-Fulfilling Prophecy

Perhaps even more confounding was that the camouflage of the tough gothic rocker began to reinforce a negative self-image for Matt. His teachers' avoidance of him, an unwilling student, forged his belief that he was in fact incapable, weird, and unable to fit in, and that his teachers had no interest in helping him figure out his current situation. Matt's feigned disinterest is a common theme in many boys with school problems. With repeated practice, he began to actually buy his own act.

Matt knew he didn't fit in the regular education system. We knew that his perception of a special education classification would further remove him from the educational system. For Matt, the key was to set up opportunities in which he saw a different side of himself and felt comfortable letting others see a different aspect of himself. To break the self-fulfilling prophecy, we had to catch Matt in an accomplishment or positive action and ask him how this felt. Matt was so conditioned for failure that he predicted he would always fail. He could not recognize his own success. Through time, reinforcement for positive accomplishments, and the gradual realization that he was worthwhile, Matt internalized that he could do much more than he once believed.

Recommendation: Overcoming Limitations Inherent to the School System

One limiting factor in Matt's case was his slow spiral downward without obvious reasons. The school social worker did recognize that Matt was heading for trouble, however, she was constrained by procedure and had to work within the system. Without a diagnosis of a specific disability, Matt was in limbo in the school system. While his behavior was self-contained, he had no ability to grapple with change and was slowly withdrawing further and further away from his parents and teachers. His destructive outlet was his only outlet. Although Matt was never self-destructive or physically aggressive to others, he did destruct school property and creatively remodeled his room in what he considered to be art. When a boy like Matt is promoting his anger through art and writing for the public, he is sending a clear message: "I am not able to express my frustration through conventional channels."

Boys often draw violent scenes. Matt was a talented artist and used his skill to develop complex murals and graffiti to express his anger. He often drew graphic depictions of violence to a teacher or a peer that he shared with others to get a reaction. In truth, this expression may have kept him from doing physical damage to self and others. We believe that it was his way of drawing attention to the fact that he wanted help but did not know how to ask for it.

Unfortunately, it wasn't until Matt discussed the meaning of the symbolism of his art that the school district had the required data to make an intervention. Matt was a unique individual and required some creative measures, but the social worker was limited by protocol. The psychotherapist consulting on his case developed a specialized program for Matt, but because it was outside the regular school system's capabilities, it had to be implemented in an alternative school setting.

Recommendation: Building Trust With an Adult

"Are you one of them?" This was the question on Matt's mind whenever he had an interaction with an adult. Matt was searching for an adult who operated out of the system and was willing to get involved in hearing about the concerns of a very unusual boy. For some adults, it was difficult to differentiate between Matt's call for help and the adults' fear of his potentially destructive and harmful behaviors. In addition, some of the adults just didn't have the time for his case.

According to Matt, one of the first adults who was able to cut through the threats approached trust through the use of communication with an edge. The teacher addressed the fears other adults had, and talked to Matt directly, instead of avoiding him.

He soon realized that this adult was here to stay and could serve as a translator at the critical junction of the unacceptable behavior. This professional realized that Matt did not necessarily need a diagnostic label other than to receive services from the school system. Unfortunately, to receive services Matt would have to be classified with social and emotional difficulties.

To Matt, many of the adults he came in contact with were hypercritical. He didn't like what he saw and he could see what the world was really like. His perceptions of the incongruence and the frustration led him to decide that he didn't want to play the game that the educational system required of him any more. Even as Matt visibly improved socially and emotionally, he still questioned the sincerity of adult teachers. After completing a history project successfully, Matt was complimented by his history teacher during a Planning and Placement Team (PPT) meeting. When asked, "Why didn't you acknowledge the compliment Mr. P gave you?" Matt was quick to respond with "Why should I? I don't like him."

Matt did develop an understanding with his father. Through the support of counseling, they worked together and built open lines of communication. Matt's father was still not impressed with Matt's taste in modern music, but was willing to acknowledge that it held meaning for Matt. The counseling professional was instrumental in developing the trust relationship that helped Matt to communicate effectively, instead of retreating into his antisocial, untrusting world.

Recommendation: Finding Other Boys Like Themselves

Boys who are struggling have a knack for finding other young men like themselves. Whether it is through clubs in the middle school or perhaps passing another student in the hall with Pokémon cards, these boys are looking for others who share their interests. Again, all four case studies in this chapter created friendships with young men with similar outlooks and interests. Although some of these were not positive influences, they were a venue to seek support and build relationships with others.

One fear expressed by parents is the socialization of boys who don't fit in with their local high school community's peer groups.

Matt was an outsider, however, when he began to associate with the student-artists who were a positive influence on him, he developed a new circle of friends. Many boys who appear as social outcasts find circles of friends at the university level. University life proves that there are many other individuals with similar interests and quirky behavior. In many cases, some behaviors and interests may even lose their novelty, as in Matt's case, when he realized he didn't have to look different to be an artist.

Recommendation: Being Aware of Perceived Classifications That Are Inaccurate

We have seen a variety of misidentifications of boys in the last few years, primarily highly creative boys who may have been misdiagnosed as having ADHD (Cramond, 1994). Unfortunately, these boys are boxed in for behaviors that could be valued in the world of work. The remedy is simple: Look beyond the obvious.

Professionals must push through the presentation of behaviors and the popular classification, whether it is accurate or not, and see other possible explanations. One key to recognizing boys who appear to be demonstrating ADHD behaviors is to explore their products. If the boy is creating art or building objects, you have to look to see if there is a discrepancy between the quality of his product and his test scores and schoolwork. A boy who is producing creative and outstanding products outside of the school environment may not need a special education classification as much as he needs a different educational environment. Another common indicator is the inconsistency of one's behaviors, depending on the environment and the task. Too many of our boys are categorized and labeled for isolated behaviors in certain environments, while they demonstrate quite different behaviors in a different environment.

> **A boy who is producing creative and outstanding products outside of the school environment may not need a special education classification as much as he needs a different educational environment.**

Greg: A Case Study of a Boy Who Began to Disappear

Greg was very popular with his peers, earned good grades, and enjoyed a variety of activities, including sports. Greg was basically your average American boy.

Things began to change for Greg in eighth grade. After his parents' bitter divorce, Greg was notably distraught. He began to slowly withdraw from school. His grades went down quickly. Greg dropped out of athletics and soon began to drop out of classes. His mother called him in sick on a regular basis. Greg was considered an above-average student and his school failure was a mystery to teachers and administrators.

His mother constantly challenged the school to test Greg for special education services. She sought desperately for the school to classify him as having a nonverbal learning disability. She also had Greg tested by outside evaluators to determine if he was possibly gifted and to see if he had ADHD. The school did classify Greg as socially emotionally maladjusted (SEM).

What followed was a long siege between a parent and the school system. Greg's mother was constantly attacking the school. The school was providing services for her son, but they were not appropriate to Greg's mother. Greg's school performance began to deteriorate further. He began to skip his special education class. After a couple of years, Greg had accumulated a number of incompletes in his classes due to excessive absences or a lack of work being turned in.

Greg was definitely spiraling out of control. He began to party heavily and his entire group of friends changed. Greg had an older girlfriend who introduced him to heroin. After a bitter argument and a break up with his girlfriend at a party, Greg drank an excessive amount of alcohol and got behind the wheel of his car. Traveling at a high rate of speed, he missed a turn and hit a telephone pole. After he was almost killed in this wreck, Greg needed an immediate intervention.

Recommendation: Planning Substance Abuse Interventions

Greg had withdrawn from the few outlets for emotional and physical exertion and expression he had, such as soccer and hockey, so he turned to drugs and alcohol. His way of coping with his problems became self-medication. Greg, it seems, had a history of earlier experimentation with drugs and alcohol, and there was pattern of alcohol use in his family. The more overwhelmed Greg became with school or family issues, the more apt he became to continue using drugs and alcohol, for lack of other coping skills.

Greg saw adults model the use of drugs and alcohol, so it became a natural avenue for him to follow. With no other outlets for his expression, he internalized much of his frustration and began to manifest oppositional behaviors. The court order that forced Greg to attend substance abuse counseling was a step he took with resistance. Greg's only motivation at first was knowing that the only way he would get his driver's license back was to attend all of the mandatory meetings. The skilled counselor was able to reach Greg, and by the end of the mandatory sessions, Greg was sharing and learning from others in the group.

Recommendation: Supporting Students in Breaking the Double Bind

Greg is an unfortunate example of a young man caught in a double bind with his mother (Miller, 1979). After the divorce and Greg's slow disappearance from school, his mother began to blame the school for Greg's behaviors. She vented regularly on anyone who would listen. She was certain that Greg's problems were based in the school's lack of adequate educational services. In essence, Greg's mother was attempting to manipulate the world around Greg so that his issues would not be his fault. When Greg was successful in an academic task, then it was obviously attributed to an outside support service the mother had arranged. Greg was so enmeshed in this that he refused to contradict his mother in public. He would not attend PPT meetings and abdicated his voice to his mother. All the while, he longed to move out of her house and away from her influence, yet she was providing for him, protecting him, and allowing him to evade his school responsibilities. Hence, the double bind: If Greg did what he felt he needed to do, he would anger his mother, yet he could not stand to be under her supervision and longed for an independent life.

Recommendation: Overcoming Atrophy of Academic Skills

While Greg floundered, it became apparent that he was in fact lagging behind his peers academically from a lack of use of his academic skills. Greg's former strengths, such as writing and an interest in scientific experimentation, disappeared from his school performance. Even in a hands-on science lab, which sparked Greg's interest for 20 minutes, Greg balked at writing about his discoveries, for what he would later describe as a fear that his peers would laugh at his spelling. Greg had an extensive vocabulary when he decided to use it, however, he was out of academic shape. His years of school avoidance had manifested into an academic regression. Greg, who had once been an A and B student, could no longer accomplish the same academic tasks as his peers.

In Chapters 4 and 5, we discussed development of academic skills for boys. In the cases of Greg, Matt, and Jonathan (who we will discuss later in this chapter), as with many other boys that have difficult periods in their education, these academic skills must be relearned and applied in a meaningful manner. Greg unfortunately, did not value study skills until he was faced with the shame of not graduating from high school. He did receive his diploma a year later than his peers, but he is currently diligent in his studies and is taking advantage of any tutoring possibilities and study skill courses on the junior college level.

Recommendation: Participating in an Alternative School Setting

The public school setting decided that Greg did indeed require alternative placement. As mentioned in Chapter 6, there are times when this is a very important avenue to pursue. Greg was demonstrating school avoidance. He was now several years behind his peers and would have to take make-up classes with underclassmen. Greg openly said he would not attend classes with younger students, as this would embarrass him. He also would not attend a study skills course, because of its association with special education. It was still easy for Greg to convince his mother to call him in sick, rather than attend these classes.

The alternative school setting provided Greg with an environment away from his peers, in which he could not simply disappear, and in which drugs were not available. Greg did want to graduate, and the alternative school's emphasis on learning strategies allowed Greg to redevelop his academic skills.

Recommendation: Making Connections to Successful Adults

Greg will tell you that it was the influence of successful adult men outside of school that made the difference and helped him turn around his life. In essence, we noticed that Greg did work well with male tutors who would not fall for subterfuge. Several of his tutors challenged Greg and held him accountable in a way that he was compelled to respond to. These male tutors and mentors did not let him disappear behind the manipulative screen of his mother. Instead, they held him accountable and expected results. Many boys need to see positive, successful adult role models to help them find success in their own lives.

Recommendation: Removing Sex, Alcohol, and Drugs as Outlets

Particularly in the case of Greg, but all too common in boys we have worked with, sex, alcohol, and drugs are outlets when boys see no other possibilities. Boys with no outlets for emotions turn to drugs and alcohol as a form of self-medication to dull the pain. On occasion, Greg would sneak into his mother's liquor closet and drink to excess just so he "wouldn't have to think." Although drug use is down on the national average, adolescents report that is more accessible in schools (National Center on Addiction and Substance Abuse, 2006). This includes an increase in the abuse of prescription drugs.

Counseling and rehabilitation programs, particularly those that show boys positive male role models who have overcome their own addictions to find successful, happy lives, should be sought out to help boys overcome their substance abuse problems. Encouraging boys to find other outlets for their emotions, such as sports, the arts, writing, or peer counseling programs, can also be helpful.

Recommendation: Developing Tools to Overcome Shame

Time after time we have realized that many of the troubled boys we have worked with were sensitive guys who had no support for their emotions. As Pollack and Cushman (2001) and Thompson and Kindlon (2000) have said, expectations on boys and stereotypical pressures create an environment of shame. When boys are conflicted by what society tells them they should be doing, yet are unable to fulfill this expectation or perhaps disagree with it, the reaction of society and their peers is to put them down. In addition, boys who learn differently or have learning difficulties usually are sensitive to their inability to succeed academically and seek to hide their disability to avoid feeling ashamed of it.

Boys who are sensitive and would like to share their tenderness or express their feelings are quickly taught that this is not expected of boys and that they should be ashamed of these feelings. Crying is the age-old example of a behavior that boys are taught to be ashamed of. When they see that girls have this freedom to question their feelings and share them and are encouraged to do this, and then boys get rebuked and teased for the same behaviors, a definite barrier is built to avoid that shame from reappearing.

Greg was very sensitive and had intense emotions to share, but was ashamed of crossing the

> **Boys who are sensitive and would like to share their tenderness or express their feelings are quickly taught that this is not expected of boys and that they should be ashamed of these feelings.**

line drawn at school and at home and becoming too emotional. While he wanted to grieve the loss of his family due to his parent's divorce, his friends on his soccer team who had gone through a similar experience put him down for his emotional state. Greg later realized that they had the same feelings he did, but they just submerged them. They were also shamed by others and only knew how to handle their grief in one way.

At this writing, Greg has been clean and sober for some time now. He is successfully holding down a job and saving money. Greg has been able to separate from his mother's influence, but still lives in her house. He is performing well at a local college and looks forward to earning a degree in business.

JONATHAN: CASE STUDY
OF A HIGH-ABILITY UNDERACHIEVER

Jonathan maintained a C or D average, but he "aced" almost every test he took, regardless of its subject matter. Jonathan was a self-proclaimed geek and had a select group of friends who were geeks and typically high achievers. His closest friends shared a passion in Dungeons and Dragons and Mech Warrior, a science fiction strategy game where the players control futuristic fighting robots. Jonathan would design elaborate game scenarios, writing up pages of dungeon descriptions. Although Jonathan was an exceptional Dungeon Master known for his meticulous detail, his teachers had quite a different picture of his work ethic. Jonathan did maintain passing grades because of his high test scores, but he never did his homework. On the occasion that a teacher put more emphasis on a specific project, Jonathan would always do just enough to pass the class. Jonathan loved to debate issues with his teachers in class. There were more than a few teachers in Jonathan's school who dreaded his presence in their class and moved aggressively to keep a lid on Jonathan's questioning ways.

Jonathan was a classic example of a highly able underachiever. Jonathan was self-nominated for the gifted and talented program, but several teachers rejected him because of his habitual lack of doing homework. He was self-nominated again the next year and was tested. Of course, his scores were well within the district's gifted range, so he was allowed to enter the gifted program on a probationary basis.

Jonathan's story is used in this chapter for a couple of reasons. One, unfortunately, is that despite interventions of educators, social workers, and counselors, sometimes the best teacher is life itself. Jonathan was very good at taking tests. When he decided to join the military, Jonathan scored one of the highest scores on the ASVAB exam ever recorded in his southern state. This earned him a choice of military positions. Jonathan, of course, selected military intelligence. After surviving a grueling boot camp experience, he was assigned to a foreign language school to begin his military intelligence training. Unfortunately, Jonathan again resorted to old habits. He did not keep up with his training and lost his opportunity to continue in his chosen area of military service. The military has a unique way of assigning individuals to undesirable duties for the rest of their contracted time.

Jonathan's story is important. We must all learn as educators and parents that we cannot win every fight. Jonathan is brilliant and had opportunities to succeed, but made personal choices that sidetracked an otherwise promising career. While he did produce certain academic products to the level in which he graduated from high school, he is just recently finding an avenue for personal success.

Recommendation: Availability of a Teacher

Each of the boys described in this chapter sought a teacher who they could relate to. Whether it was in their strength area or a teacher who just had the time to listen, finding a teacher the boy could relate to was challenging. These are not just ordinary educators and do not always connect with every student. The teachers these boys sought and found tended to be creative and nonconforming. These teachers also cultivated respect by challenging their students and demanding results of them.

Jonathan sought out teachers who would relate to his science-fiction-oriented world. After he tested them to his satisfaction, he would respond and actually turn in homework in their classes. What Jonathan was really looking for was a teacher who was available to teach outside the box. Jonathan could handle the text material, but what he sought was the connections and the sharing of challenging ideas.

Recommendation: Allowing the Boy to Fail

Sometimes the best and most difficult lessons in life are learned by failure. Most parents avoid letting their sons fail at all costs. School systems also find ways to ensure success. Jonathan was a highly capable young man who had always been able to squeeze by in school. It wasn't until his failure at his dream military job and the ensuing humbling postings that Jonathan appreciated the value of studying. After leaving the military he did pursue a college education with renewed vigor.

Jonathan did not understand that his choices were responsible for his success or failure. In other words, when he chose to play Dungeons and Dragons all weekend and not do his homework, he received a failing grade. However, he knew he could always ace the test and make up the percentage points he lost by not turning in homework.

Recommendation: Developing Skills to Educate the Underachiever

There is a good possibility that everyone has a family member or perhaps a friend who they consider to be an underachiever. In fact, underachievement is a complex combination of factors that are difficult to unravel. With Jonathan, the lack of connection to the school curriculum was a real problem. Because he felt what was being taught was not relevant to the real world, Jonathan chose not to cooperate.

In the four cases studies mentioned in this chapter, each boy expressed the need to keep it together, no matter what emotional turmoil he was suffering internally. This need to control emotions, yet secretly expressing vulnerability and sensitivity was a constant pressure that many times fueled their downward spiral.

After reading these four case studies, it is important to remember that these boys are all doing well and have achieved a level of success in their lives. Their stories are here to remind us that boys sometimes have difficulty along the way. Although we have to work through the challenges, it is sometimes helpful to hear about those young men who have overcome their problems.

CHAPTER 11 TOOLS

Listening to Boys

Dr. William Pollack (2000) offers these tips for listening to boys:

- Honor a boy's need for timed silence, to choose when to talk.
- Find a safe place, a shame-free zone. Connect through activity or play. Many boys express their deepest experience through action talk.
- Avoid teasing and shaming.
- Make brief statements and wait; do not lecture.
- Share your own experiences (if relevant). It lets your boy know he is not alone with issues.
- Be quiet and really listen with complete attention.
- Convey how much you admire and care about and love the boy.
- Give boys regular, undivided attention and listening space.
- Don't prematurely push him to be independent.
- Encourage the expression of a full and wide range of emotions.
- Let him know that real men do cry and speak.
- Express your love as openly as you might with a girl.
- When you see aggressive or angry behavior, look for the pain behind it. (p. xxxiv)

Is My Child in Trouble? Checklist

Typical observable warning signs of a boy in trouble include:

- ❏ Lack of cooperation with authorities
- ❏ Does not follow up on school assignments and with homework
- ❏ Oppositional behavior
- ❏ Not fitting in with school or community groups
- ❏ Begins hanging with incongruent group (or pack) of peers
- ❏ An amalgam of sorts, displays different behaviors and attitudes in different settings
- ❏ Withdrawal from family member and friends
- ❏ Refuses to communicate with teachers
- ❏ Lethargic behavior

Note. Warning signs information from Mays, 2005.

Does My Child Have a Substance Abuse Problem?

Symptoms of substance abuse to watch for in boys include:

- ❏ Sudden personality changes that include abrupt changes in work or school attendance, quality of work, work output, grades, discipline
- ❏ Unusual flare-ups or outbreaks of temper
- ❏ Withdrawal from responsibility
- ❏ General changes in overall attitude
- ❏ Loss of interest in what were once favorite hobbies and pursuits
- ❏ Changes in friends and reluctance to have friends visit or talk about them
- ❏ Difficulty in concentration, paying attention
- ❏ Sudden jitteriness, nervousness, or aggression
- ❏ Increased secretiveness
- ❏ Deterioration of physical appearance and grooming
- ❏ Wearing of sunglasses at inappropriate times
- ❏ Continual wearing of long-sleeved garments particularly in hot weather or reluctance to wear short-sleeved attire when appropriate
- ❏ Association with known substance abusers
- ❏ Unusual borrowing of money from friends, coworkers, or parents
- ❏ Stealing small items from employer, home, or school
- ❏ Secretive behavior regarding actions and possessions, including poorly concealed attempts to avoid attention and suspicion such as frequent trips to storage rooms, restroom, basement, etc.

Note. Substance abuse information from Teens With Problems, 2005.

chapter 12

Cracking the "Boy Code"

Guiding Boys Beyond Stereotypical Expectations

ust the mention of the word *boys* brings to mind a host of stereotypes. Stereotypically, boys are well-known for eating anything, running around and constantly moving, and wanting to blow up things or take things apart. The old adage, "boys will be boys" is partially true. We have discussed that, in fact, boys do have different needs, they do learn differently, and they can benefit from different instructional strategies. However, the "boys will be boys" attitude can lead to stereotypical expectations that are embraced by our culture. Building on these cultural expectations, William Pollack (Pollack & Cushman, 2001) has deftly identified key components of a boy code that influences our expectations of young men.

1. Do not cry (no sissy stuff).
2. Do not cower, tremble or shrink from danger.
3. Do not ask for help when you are unsure of yourself (observe the code of silence).

4. Do not reach for comfort or reassurance.
5. Do not sing or cry for joy.
6. Do not hug your dearest friends.
7. Do not use words to show tenderness and love. (p. 77)

The following chapter is a discussion of some of the more prevalent stereotypes boys face, including Pollack's (1998) boy code, with additional twists or concerns shared by boys and young men who we have worked with. It is important to recognize the expected behaviors the boy code stereotype dictates. Boys are aware of these unwritten expectations in their daily lives and must deal with the negative ramifications from peers if they break expected behaviors. However, with proper support systems in place, these stereotypical expectations can be overcome.

Stereotypical Message to Boys: Be Independent and Take Care of it Yourself

Many boys strive to be independent and are reluctant to admit when they are confused or stuck and need help. Jack was very insistent on remitting his point, "I don't need any help from you." Jack had been known to give a whole new meaning to the cliché, "doesn't play well with others." He refused to work in cooperative groups in class. He was a perfectionist and believed that only he could get it right.

Jack was also creative and enjoyed solving problems. When his school formed an Odyssey of the Mind (OM) team, he wanted to be a part of the solution. The issue for Jack was that OM is an international creativity competition that requires teams to work to together to find solutions to problems. This teamwork aspect is so important to OM that the organization evaluates just how well the team works together in the spontaneous part of the competition, where teams are asked to solve a previously unknown problem in a short amount of time.

Fellow team members were reluctant to allow Jack on their team, but he did bring some skills the team needed. The team chose a long-term problem involving the construction of a tower with balsa wood sticks that weighed 9 grams each. This structure would be required to support as much weight as possible. Past winners had held more than 150 pounds of weight before shattering.

Jack had two things going for him: supportive team members who tolerated him and a coach who understood how Jack thought. Ron, his coach, was a practicing engineer who had been volunteering to help coach OM teams for years. Ron was much like Jack when he was in school and knew how to guide Jack in the ways of working with a team. His team members and his classroom teachers noticed the changes that occurred in Jack over the next few months. He became much more available in conversations and was noticed to actually be concerned about the feelings of others. Jack had slowly realized that there were issues beyond his own. These changes came about as Jack realized that working with and trusting others had a benefit.

Breaking the Stereotype: Developing Relationships
That Encourage Cooperation Between Boys

The independent spirit is valuable and has a place as boys develop into men. At the same time, boys must learn that it is OK to ask for help and to work with others. Team sports are one avenue for boys to learn the value of working together. Boys in athletics learn quickly that each player has a role and everyone must work together to succeed. Programs and competitions such as OM and National History Day also give boys a chance to work with others in a cooperative effort in which they can feel successful.

A big part of Jack's perception of himself was his inability to accept help and his insistence on completing tasks alone, based on trust issues.

> **The independent spirit is valuable and has a place as boys develop into men. At the same time, boys must learn that it is OK to ask for help and to work with others.**

While working with Ron, Jack learned that he was trustworthy and learned to trust his teammates. Jack also saw Ron model an appreciation of other people's ideas. Ron played a major role in helping Jack overcome some of his perfectionist tendencies by exhibiting the trial and error aspects of problem solving over and over again.

Boys in a supportive environment can and will ask each other for assistance (Neu, 1993; Sax, 2005). These supportive environments require an informed coach or teacher to set the stage and maintain a nonshaming environment for boys (Pollack, 1998). This type of environment accepts the boy for who he is, supports him when he struggles, and lets him know that is OK to fail, but also challenges boys to succeed.

STEREOTYPICAL MESSAGE TO BOYS: AVOID FEMININE THINGS

Brendan lived with his mom and two sisters. A feminine influence was very real for him. He was constantly concerned about what his mother would think. Brendan and his mother had a wonderful relationship, and he was very open with her in a variety of discussions. A good student, Brendan usually made the honor roll. When he was given the chance to produce a product that really represented who he was, Brendan frequently chose to make videos.

However, in seventh grade, things began to change. Brendan admits he was able to see the difference a dad made in the life of his friends. He also relates the pressure from peers to avoid those "girl things" that he had grown up with and always accepted. He began to explore "guy things" with his friends. At first, his mother supported his explorations and encouraged Brendan to join the Boy Scouts of America. But, by his ninth-grade year, she saw such a change in her son that she thought he needed counseling. Her otherwise sensitive boy was now embracing violent video games and skateboarding, and in her opinion, acting rather barbaric.

Breaking the Stereotype: Confronting and Exploring
What Is Perceived as Masculine and Feminine

Bly (1990) is very clear that young men must separate from their mothers and older men should be there to assist them. Gilligan (2006) has suggested that some boys are pushed out from the protection of their mothers too early. Unfortunately, in our modern culture, the father sometimes is not ready in the wings to support the boy toward further growth and development. As boys explore the different perceived masculine and feminine qualities within themselves, they need an older male to guide them.

Brendan is a very fortunate young man with an intelligent mother who did her homework. As Brendan explored these male behaviors, she realized that he didn't need psychotherapy, but rather the influence of a good male mentor. Although she was not used to these behaviors, she learned to tolerate them. Brendan, in turn, had a remarkable experience in high school. He was able to integrate his feminine, sensitive side as he explored the art of film. As a junior in high school, his video skills blossomed. Brendan had a highly creative male visual arts teacher who guided him in the development of his art. This teacher was able to guide Brendan into the sensitive side of his characters and was still able to develop and value traditional male traits.

Perhaps most interesting was that Brendan helped make the theatre arts department, another area of his passion, a "cool" activity for guys to do at his school. After he participated in several performances, other young men decided that theatre wasn't necessarily a "sissy" thing to do. Brendan is unusual in his development of an integration of perceptions of male and female expectations. He navigated the perils in his local high school successfully and helped other boys overcome stereotypical classifications of behaviors.

The guidance of a male role model can help boys bridge the perceived differences between male and female characteristics. This guidance should include an understanding that a mixture of traits should be valued, appreciated, and accepted. Today's schools are more tolerant of stereotypical feminine behaviors, but as mentioned in Chapter 2, there is still room for improvement.

STEREOTYPICAL MESSAGE TO BOYS: DON'T EXPRESS FEELINGS UNLESS IT IS ANGER AND KEEP YOUR FEELINGS TO YOURSELF

Josh was 6-feet tall and weighed 230 pounds. He was rough-looking, very masculine, and could intimidate anyone with a quick glance. He loved football for the contact aspect of the sport. Josh once said he was addicted to hitting people. However, Josh had a different side that many people found very unusual: His parents were very affectionate in public with each other and their kids. So, if Josh wanted to show you he cared about you, he gave you a hug. Here was an All-State defensive tackle who was not afraid to show his emotions. Josh would cry openly at the end of a game if he felt his performance was sub par and like he let his teammates down. No one questioned Josh's public display of emotions. In fact, Josh was a positive influence on his teammates and by his junior and senior year, "Josh Hugs" had become an acceptable form of contact among boys on the football team.

Breaking the Stereotype: Helping Boys Express Emotions

In the case of Josh, he had a home environment that nurtured the expression of emotions. As with many other interventions to the boy code, boys need a model that they can see and emulate. This real example will give them a visual image that will support them in their efforts to express emotion. When an athlete shows joy or even cries on national television, it has a huge impact. Several boys have expressed the impact of watching an awards ceremony like the induction service into the Football Hall of Fame and seeing a sports hero openly cry for joy.

The best way to help boys express their emotions is to model that same behavior in the home and at school, however, the media is now becoming a major positive influence in this area. Several of the young men we talked to stated that character portrayals in the movies and TV have actually encouraged them to be more open with their feelings. It is interesting that these young men name stereotypical unemotional males as "cool," but also discuss sensitive men as being persons they would like to have as friends.

STEREOTYPICAL MESSAGE TO BOYS: THERE IS NO PLACE FOR EMPATHY

Robert had worked hard in his 3 years of high school football. He had sweated and bled, he had endured hours in the weight room, and now in the final minutes of the district championship game—he was empathizing with the opposing team. The opponent was not accustomed to losing; in fact, they had won the district championship three times previously, and the weight of the sadness from their loss could be seen in each player even as they gallantly struggled to keep the game respectable. Robert was able to say after the game that he was proud of his opponents and he could feel their grief. His opponents had also experienced the same grueling workouts, the hours of practice, and the joy of winning that his team had, but now they were losing to Robert's team in an all-out rout. "Don't get me wrong," Robert was quick to point out.

> We have won this game and the Bears have earned this win, but even while we were beating them I was proud of them. They gave their best and we defeated them. I realized they had worked just as hard as we had to get to this game. Now we go home champions, but they go home defeated. I have been defeated before (by them) so I know how it feels. I am glad we won, but at the same time I respect their sacrifice and hard work during the season.

In expressing these thoughts, Robert was showing empathy, an emotion many boys are taught to hide.

Breaking the Stereotype: Encouraging Empathy
as a Natural Trait for Boys

In reality, close investigation will reveal that many boys are sensitive and empathic. Too often, this sensitivity has to dive deep to remain hidden and undiscovered by peers who see this as a sign of weakness. This masking of sensitivity starts very early. Several of our young men report being in classroom situations in which another boy was punished publicly or teased by others and admitted they could feel the pain of the other boy, but could not bring themselves to express their empathy to others.

Robert says he was always empathic to some degree but was given permission to express it after a series of lessons in his global studies class. This class had a unique curriculum of sociology, anthropology, geography, and economics. The teacher had run a simulation in which volunteer students fasted for 48 hours for a fundraiser for a children's fund in a Central American country. For Robert, 48 hours without food drove home the point of world hunger in a manner different from any other lesson. Robert refers to this as an opening of the floodgates. With the discovery that empathy was acceptable in some venues, Robert began to volunteer for other civic activities. He later volunteered for a church mission to Guatemala and saw firsthand the conditions that he had heard of in his class. These experiences gave Robert the go-ahead that empathy is important and OK to express.

While Robert's example is not easy to replicate, the key element is for boys to make a connection and identify with others. Empathy can only be developed through opportunities to walk in another's shoes or to actually engage in a form of service to others. There are a variety of service agencies that welcome volunteer support, such as the American Red Cross, Habitat for Humanity, Special Olympics, and the United Way. The tragedy of recent disasters by Hurricanes Katrina and Rita in the Gulf Coast, the tsunami in Indonesia and Thailand, and Hurricane Stan in Central America has provided an avenue for boys to participate in fund-raising for people they have never met. It has been very encouraging to see young men in schools around the country contributing to fund raising and developing empathy for others in an accepting environment.

STEREOTYPICAL MESSAGE TO BOYS: ACT TOUGH

Karl, Robert's teammate, displayed no sympathy for the fallen football rivals. Karl was a middle linebacker and relished the macho antics of wrestling heroes. He taunted the other team's offensive players quite carefully, lest he draw the attention of his coach or be caught by a referee for unsportsmanlike conduct. If his coach caught him belittling the defeated opponents, his punishment would stretch out for many weeks after the football season ended. Karl was playing the macho role. On the other hand, his teammates did not know that Karl often showed empathy toward nature, especially the animals that lived in his region. Karl wrote poetry, but was so terrified that his friends would call him "gay" that he never shared his work. He did find that he could put together poetic rhymes to taunt an opposing team or to tease another team and that this form of poetry was OK and acceptable with his teammates.

Breaking the Stereotype: Men and Boys
Don't Always Have to Be Tough

Karl also did not want his teammates to know about his soft spot for animals. He did not hunt and was deeply affected by the loss of pets or the sight of animals dead along the side of the road. If his rough and tumble peers had seen him cry over the death of an animal, his tough image would have suffered. Karl was very protective of his tough-guy image. He said it was a way of protecting himself from emotions. As long as he could pronounce himself better than someone else, Karl did not have to deal with his own emotions.

Educators, coaches, and parents alike can encourage boys that they always don't have to be the tough guy. Through his school's job-shadowing program, Karl was given the opportunity to work with a local veterinarian. To Karl, this was still a masculine job, because this veterinarian specialized in large animals, including the state's police drug enforcement dogs. Although Karl was responsible for some of the mundane jobs, such as cleaning the kennels and walking the animals, it quickly became apparent that there was more to Karl when he interacted with these animals. Here, he could be soft and caring with the animals he worked with. Years later, Karl's wife thanked the teacher who arranged the internship. She attributes Karl's slow release of his tough-guy image to a teacher who allowed him to show his compassion toward hurt animals.

Once again, it's important for adults to model that young men don't always have tough in every occasion.

STEREOTYPICAL MESSAGE TO BOYS: ALL BOYS TEASE AND BULLY OTHERS AT SOME TIME

Taylor was short and stocky and wore glasses. He had only met his father once and his mother was struggling to make ends meet by working as a cook in a truck stop and collecting food stamps. Taylor's clothes were not always clean, and he tended to wear the same shirt for several days. However, this aspect alone did not set Taylor apart from his peers in this rural farming community; in fact, he had peers who were in worse financial shape than he. Taylor was a constant target of bullying. He was diagnosed with ADHD and tended to miss parts of conversations or discussions. Taylor also tended to ask "dumb" questions in class. This constantly drew the negative attention of several boys in his class. One classmate, Devin, in particular found many ways to torture Taylor in the classroom, gym, or hallway, or even on the bus. On one rainy day, Devin was waiting around a school corner with a handful of mud. As Taylor turned the corner, Devin pushed Taylor up against the wall and smeared the mud in Taylor's face. Devin then wiped the excess off on Taylor's shirt.

Taylor did have supportive teachers and administrators. He just had difficulty breaking the bully to victim cycle. However, after his incident with Devin, Taylor's mother remarried and moved to a town with a larger school district. Taylor's life subsequently changed. He was cautious. He carefully chose friends. Taylor became active in church activities and went out for sports. Taylor broke out of the cycle of being a victim. With a newfound confidence, he actually volunteered for a peer antibullying program at his high school. Taylor found that his new life as an athlete and church leader gave him influence over other boys. Taylor made certain that bullying was not to be tolerated.

Fifteen years later, Taylor confronted Devin. Devin had been in a terrible auto accident a few years earlier than the confrontation. Taylor held angry feelings for Devin for years, and at the time of Devin's wreck, Taylor wished out loud and even prayed that Devin would die. Now, a few years after Devin's accident, a much more mature Taylor was able to tell Devin how devastating the bullying had been. He laid out specifically how it had made him feel and the anxiety it caused. Taylor was also able to express how he had come to terms with the constant torment that Devin had dished out. Taylor then said, quite simply, "I forgive you." Devin was quite humbled by the experience and apologized to Taylor with tears in his eyes.

Breaking the Stereotype: Moving Away From Hurtful Behaviors

Bullying and teasing are not normal behaviors, but they do occur. As discussed in Chapter 7, there are definite patterns for both the bully and the victim. The lesson from the story of Taylor is that these patterns can be overcome. Perhaps it will be through the actions and influence of young men like Taylor that more boys will have examples to refrain from bullying. By understanding the role of the bully and the victim, boys can overcome these destructive behaviors.

Schools and parents need to form partnerships that support both the victim and the bully. Schools that have enacted antibullying programs have been successful in creating safe school environments in which all boys can learn without fear of bullying.

STEREOTYPICAL MESSAGE TO BOYS: LISTENING TO AN OPPOSING VIEW OR GIVING IN DURING AN ARGUMENT MEANS YOU ARE WEAK

Nine boys are sitting in a circle with four adult men. The topic is controversial: The adults are trying to teach the boys how to actually listen to another person's opinion. Juan is trying to express to Larry why he is mad at him. This is very difficult for Juan, as he tries to identify his feelings and then put them into words. Larry is having a problem just sitting still and following the discussion. The adult men in the group are encouraging Juan and demonstrating ways in which he can express his ideas.

Meanwhile, other adults are stressing to the rest of the boys that this is not a competition to be won or lost, but the process is what is important. Their message is clear: You don't have to win every argument. Larry feels like he is losing the argument and just wants to leave the group. With some skill, an adult recommends a compromise that both boys are quick to realize works for them. Juan and Larry agree to shake hands and accept the compromise position. They feel like they have both won and the other boys in the room have just seen a mature way of handling a tough situation.

Breaking the Stereotype: Teaching Listening and Mediation Skills

This scenario demonstrates that boys need direct instruction on listening skills and have to see these skills modeled. Larry's argument was, "I spend most of my day listening in school, why do I have to listen to you?" This is true; most boys spend a large amount of cognitive energy trying to listen in school. However, Larry also admitted that he didn't want to lose the argument, because the next day at school he might be considered weak for giving in. With continued guidance and instruction, boys and young men can successfully listen and mediate life situations. To break the stereotype, boys must see males modeling listening and mediating skills.

Often, men and boys want to solve a problem and not listen to the feelings expressed by others.

STEREOTYPICAL MESSAGE TO BOYS: VIOLENCE IS COOL AND A WAY TO GET WHAT YOU WANT

Adam was quick to react to anything that he thought was an insult or a challenge. Adam was tall, good-looking, athletic, and could be very persuasive when he talked. His father was physically violent at home. In fact, a common family leisure activity was watching the former WWF wrestling program on TV. Adam talked about violence and threatened to be violent frequently. He was well known for not backing down. Unfortunately for Adam, violence struck home when his brother was killed in a drug deal and he felt the effect of very real violence from the other side. The loss of his brother had a very sobering effect on Adam. He went from rage, to paranoia, to vengeance, and through the guidance of a friend, he finally found solace in religion.

Carlos, on the other hand, had been in three separate situations where violence had landed him in police custody. He was very quick to respond with the solution of " . . . pop the sucker up the side of the head," as a remedy for most of his school or social problems. Carlos had little tolerance for those who did not fight over any minute argument. After 3 years of therapy and social work interventions, Carlos now is beginning to see that there are other ways to solve problems.

Breaking the Stereotype: Recognizing Violence for What It Really Is

Boys have and will always be fascinated by power, whether it is the power of a machine or the power over others that violence implies. In an earlier chapter, we noted that incorporating themes of action, machines, sports, or even violence could be motivating factors for boys to improve their reading skills. So, if this fascination with power is such a dominating force, how can we deal with it?

After the school shooting tragedy occurred at Columbine High School in Littleton, CO, many schools have adopted a "no tolerance" policy that is very restrictive to any mention of violence, much less actual physical blows. Boys have discovered the hard way that the imposed limits of the "no tolerance" policies have long-ranging effects. Several young men we have worked with have discovered legal difficulties when they crossed the line. Such policies are having an effect on the number of disciplinary infractions and are resulting in a reduction of incidents, yet they are not teaching boys the lesson of not resorting to violence.

> **Boys who emerge from environments that demonstrate violence as a manner for settling disputes require guidance and dedication from a mentor or therapists for long periods of time to learn alternative methods of solving their problems.**

What is needed is a conscious effort to bring boys together with concerned parents and trained professionals. A forum, perhaps outside of school, in which role models can speak openly to boys about the dangers of violence, could be successful. Programs like Boys to Men (see Chapter 9) that bring boys who demonstrate at-risk behaviors into a therapeutic safe environment have been successful in getting across a message about the potential for solutions other than violence; however, internalizing the lessons takes time and dedication. Boys who emerge from environments that demonstrate violence as a manner for settling disputes require guidance and dedication from a mentor or therapists for long periods of time to learn alternative methods of solving their problems.

STEREOTYPICAL MESSAGE TO BOYS: DON'T RAT (TATTLE) OR TURN IN ANOTHER BOY

Terrance had just had an altercation with another high school boy. Adrian was interested in the young lady that Terrance was in a rocky relationship with. Terrance was defending his territory, and

Adrian was trying to expand his. Both had competed over different young women before, so this was not unusual. When words could no longer convey the conflict, it became physical. Adrian raised his head to make a verbal comment, which gave Terrance an advantage, and by redirecting Adrian's force, Terrance shoved him into the wall of the English classroom with enough force that Adrian left a distinct body print on the sheetrock. Terrance backed off to laugh at his opponent, while Adrian repositioned himself and checked the room. No teacher was around and only a few classmates were in the room, and they didn't notice the action until they heard the loud thud of Adrian's body impacting on the sheetrock.

Well, Mr. Brian, the English teacher, was never known for being punctual or for being very observant, yet on this day he entered his classroom and knew there was a problem. When he saw the body print on the sheetrock, he asked who had caused the imprint to occur. Immediately, the boys' code of silence came into play. After interrogating all of the boys in the room, the teacher and the assistant principal got no answers. Even the two boys who had the disagreement were not about to say anything. They were under heavy scrutiny by every boy in the room. Would one of them break?

Breaking the Stereotype: Allowing Boys to Speak the Truth

A deep message that appears is that this stereotype teaches that truth has little meaning depending on the situation. Boys have been trained for years to not "tattle" on their peers. Boys know that when the truth is told someone is going to be punished. A double message often occurs: Sometimes teachers and parents want the truth, but at other times, parents and teachers don't want other boys to turn in their peers for every minor infraction. This groundwork, combined with the boy stereotype of sticking together, makes the boy who is willing to express the truth a target for ridicule.

When boys are allowed to speak the truth in an accepting environment without repercussions, what boys are willing to say becomes very different. Most of the boys we have talked with want justice, but openly state that they feel that parents and educators manipulate truth in order to impose rules that the boys may not necessarily agree with. This is one very complicated stereotype that takes special effort and support for young men to overcome. Adult men and women, parents, and teachers who are not afraid to speak the truth regardless of the situation are the best model for showing boys it is OK (acceptable) to speak the truth. Seeing the good examples encourages them to speak the truth without fear of consequence.

STEREOTYPICAL MESSAGE TO BOYS: EDUCATION IS NOT IMPORTANT, AS LONG AS YOU CAN GET BY

In his interview with us, James noted, "It is not cool to be smart, but it is not cool to be a loser like Mike [a special education student] either. You got to do enough to slide by." This comment was a major concern to us. James was not the only boy we'd talked with to make a similar comment. Boys are being told by their peers that success in school puts them at risk of being labeled a "nerd" and therefore, being different. On the flip side, if you are a slow learner or have learning difficulties and let others know it, you are still considered different, and in James' words, a "loser."

Equally disturbing is the tendency of young men to do only what is necessary to complete school. Too often these young men do not see the connection between hard work in high school and success in future careers. Unfortunately, the consequence for many of these students is the failure to complete graduation requirements. This is resulting in only 65% of young men graduating from high school in recent years (Green &Winters, 2006).

Breaking the Stereotype: Education Leads to the Fulfillment of Dreams

Many of the young men we interviewed about their recollections of school showed another disturbing trend. They realized a few years after they left high school that they were not on the track to get higher paying jobs. They simply did not have the training and felt they did not have the academic skills to try to enter into a college. These same young men also point out they never saw a connection to school and later career success.

As many a parent, coach, or teacher will tell you, there are times that boys will not hear a message from a person they are familiar with. Enter the professional athlete or motivational speaker. Well-known sport heroes or other famous people can be a powerful influence on young boys to help them realize that education is important.

Another effective means is introducing the boy to the biography of an individual he admires or respects. Bibliotherapy can be a pathway for some boys to benefit from the wisdom of others. Reading books about boys who have succeeded gives boys a pathway to follow and suggests role models for boys to emulate.

From an education standpoint, teachers must make a concentrated effort to connect curricular content with real-world applications. Again, many of the struggling young men we talked to report that classroom instruction is presented in isolation with no meaning. The result is that students ask the question "When are we ever going to use this?" Educators must make instruction more engaging and connected to real-world problems and skills to provide our boys some understanding of when they will actually use what they are learning.

STEREOTYPICAL MESSAGE TO BOYS: YOU DON'T HAVE TO WORK TO GET ANYWHERE

"No pain, no gain."
"We fall so we can learn how to get up."
These are not just clichés, and they are not coming from just the overly macho side of male development. Although boys admire these sayings, they rarely understand the ramifications. Consider the time an athlete dedicates to practicing his skills and the hours of repetitive practice that the musician reserves for the mastery

of his art. So many of our boys are clueless to the time it takes to master one's body and mind.

Sometimes we hear a similar argument being made for academic skills, such as writing and spelling. What is the difference here? Athletes, artists, and musicians will tell you that poor practice only reinforces poor habits. Boys need to be taught to practice smarter, not harder. Practicing smarter improves the skill and reinforces a skill that will be used successfully. The same is true for the practicing of academic skills, only without the glamour associated with sports or music.

As educators, we must be aware that meaningless practice has contributed to this problem. Many individuals cannot get past the ideas of "Well, if it was good enough for me, it is good enough for them," and "It worked in the past." Perhaps if they realized that the young men they are teaching and working with have no connection to this ethic they might change their approach. Time and time again, the boys we have worked with related stories of teachers who could not make that connection and did not teach boys to practice smarter, not harder.

Breaking the Stereotype: Demonstrating the Importance of Hard Work and Challenge

Educators and parents need to guide boys into understanding that using their talents in challenging situations and taking on hard tasks leads them to improve themselves and achieve rewarding goals in life.

Challenge is a very positive form of adversity that has confronted many a young boy and man. Our culture applauds those who overcome physical challenges. Of the boys and young men we have talked to, a specific moment of pride was gleaned from overcoming difficult tasks, especially if that challenge was personal, rather than one issued by a school setting that might not have a real-world application. Educators and parents need to guide boys into understanding that using their talents in challenging situations and taking on hard tasks leads them to improve themselves and achieve rewarding goals in life.

Boys today are facing a variety of stereotypes that confront them with different interpretations of what it is like to be a man. These stereotypes are being thrust at them by culture, peers, and their own beliefs. We have presented methods for boys to break these stereotypes. To do this will require adult guidance and ultimately acceptance by the boys themselves.

CHAPTER 12 TOOLS

Parent Recommendations

- *Explore strengths and interests.* Be aware of your boy's interests and strengths. Look for opportunities to explore activities. For instance, if your son is interested in dinosaurs, subscribe to a museum newsletter and take advantage of any upcoming dinosaur-related activities. In the same way, present your son with several new and different activities so he can explore new areas.

- *Opportunities to meet and work with other boys.* Search for opportunities in which groups of boys work together. The chance to work with other boys is not limited to sports or national organizations such as the Boy Scouts of America. Try to find local art groups or even neighborhood clean-up and environmental activities.

- *Locate specialized programs.* There are many specialized programs available to boys today. These include everything from highly competitive robotics competitions, to video production training with the local cable company. These specialized programs provide advanced training in skills not normally part of the regular school curriculum.

- *Encourage mentorships and relationships with older male family members.* Ask yourself who in your family has a worthwhile hobby, interest, or skill that may interest or benefit your son. These types of mentorships can blossom into a wide variety of opportunities for boys, from gourmet cooking or specific sporting skills, to auto mechanics and chess mastery.

- *Develop "Gentlemen's Night."* There are times that males should and need to be together. In modern society, men gather to play poker, go bowling, or admire and converse over a new vehicle. Make a point of picking a night on a regular basis to play a game, read a book, or do an activity that is just for the gentlemen of your household or neighborhood.

- *Don't rescue; support boys in the face of adversity.* Perhaps one of the most difficult scenarios each of us face as parents, teachers, or someone who cares about a specific young man is defining the difference between rescuing a developing boy from adversity and supporting him in a time of need. We have all fallen and struggled in life. Sometimes we just have to listen and support our boys as they work their way out of a troublesome situation.

- *Young men are resilient and can survive.* As parents and teachers, we sometimes worry about the trials faced by boys or even perhaps mistakes we feel we have made in their guidance. The incredible thing about boys is that they can face adversity and survive. Talk to a young man who has come from less than favorable circumstances and he will tell you that resiliency is a characteristic that has helped him to overcome a variety of trials.

Recommendations for Breaking the Boy Code

- Provide a place and time to give your son undivided attention.
- Tell him that what he has to say does matter to you.
- Fathers, express your feelings to your son and model that it is OK to share feelings.
- Examine what you believe a boy should be like. Should you revise these beliefs to fit today's generation of boys?
- Encourage independence in decision making, but take into consideration the individual boy and allow it to happen at his pace.
- Tell your son that it is OK to cry.
- Respect your son for who he is.
- Use stories to teach morals or life lessons.
- Use short sentences to get his attention and give him direction.
- Provide a connection with nature. The outdoors has accepted, healed, and invigorated many a boy.

chapter 13

The Future

A visit to Wakefield High School in Arlington, VA, provides dramatic evidence of the power of boy-friendly strategies and supports. Wakefield High School consists of 84% minority students. Half of Wakefield's students are receiving free and reduced meals, an indication of the high degree of poverty present in the student population (Beitler, Bushong, & Reid, 2004). In 1997, the faculty of Wakefield High committed itself to a self-study of the achievement gap of Wakefield's minority population. One of the findings was the particularly low enrollment of Black and Latino males in Advanced Placement (AP) courses. The staff's research and experience with high school boys confirmed that boys generally have less motivation than girls of the same age, particularly for challenging academics. There was a prevailing attitude among the boys at this school that it wasn't cool to look too smart. The staff at Wakefield set out to put specific structures in place that would increase the number of Latino and Black male students in AP-level courses in preparation for college and graduate school (Beitler et al.).

One of the main strategies employed has been the establishment of the cohort program. Under the direction of counselors Alan Beitler and Al Reid, as well as gifted resource teacher, Delores Bushong, 76 boys in grades 9–12 attend weekly lunchtime counseling groups, attend other cohort sponsored activities such as a yearly college trip, and provide ongoing support to one another. Students need to have earned all A's and B's during one quarter in ninth grade to be selected for the cohort. Once in the cohort group, these boys become a team, under the direction of Coaches Beitler, Reid, and Bushong. One out of every six Latino or Black males at Wakefield are now in a cohort group and the results have been dramatic. In the year 2000, when the cohort groups began, there were 7 Black and Latino males taking 14 AP classes. In 2004, when the first group of cohorts was finishing their fourth year in the program, there were 28 Black and Latino males participating in 43 AP classes, and all 20 seniors who had completed the first 4-year cohort group were enrolled in college for the fall of 2004, with 18 of them enrolled in 4-year schools (Beitler et al., 2004).

Other than the cohort groups, the students at Wakefield participate in a totally mixed-gender program. They are clearly benefiting from some of the counseling interventions that were conclusions of the Cambridge study (Younger & Warrington, 2005), particularly that of using mentors to mediate and negotiate for their students, while at the same time challenging their students to do more and better work. As we talked to the senior cohort group, they were able to identify the differences in their lives, not only those their coaches had made, but the difference it has made to have teammates or peers who were facing the same challenge that they were facing. One boy said, "I can't talk to the guys I grew up with about Shakespeare, but with these guys, I can." Talking to the students, it's clear that it has not only been the mentor and peer support, but also the different strategies that their teachers have employed in the classroom, that have made all the difference for them.

The senior boys talked about how so many of the teachers have taught in different ways than just reading and writing. The boys talked about how they have responded to learning through class seminar discussions and have benefited from being able to demonstrate their understanding in alternative ways such as projects, rather than just in writing. Finally, the boys were able to describe the qualities of the teachers who made the difference for them. What came through over and over again was the power of connection. As one boy described it, "You can tell if they are a real person and they are interested in you as a person."

How are we going to rescue boys from the downward spiral in which they are now involved? The answer is complex. It involves both academics and social/emotional interventions. It involves making an effort in the school, home, and community. We must find ways to focus on what boys do well and provide them with opportunities to develop these natural tendencies and strengths. We must reverse the current trend to provide a one-size-fits-all school system that focuses on remediation of certain weaknesses while ignoring other strengths. We must find ways to increase the connection that boys feel when they are at school. We must find ways for boys to feel safe from bullying, feel they have the opportunity and encouragement to discuss their feelings, and feel that there are adults in their lives who will provide caring and leadership. We must also make it clear that there are many ways to be a successful male that go beyond the traditional concept of what is acceptable male behavior.

Wakefield High, Twin Ridges, Thurgood Marshall, the Montgomery County GT/LD program, Project HIGH HOPES, the Raising Boys Achievement study at Cambridge University, and many other programs and studies are showing that it is possible to change the current downward trend and help boys succeed in school. It is up to all of us, as concerned educators and parents, to learn from these examples and

> **We must find ways to focus on what boys do well and provide them with opportunities to develop these natural tendencies and strengths. We must reverse the current trend to provide a one-size-fits-all school system that focuses on remediation of certain weaknesses while ignoring other strengths. We must find ways to increase the connection that boys feel when they are at school.**

make a difference in our boys' lives. We hope we have provided you with the knowledge and guidance you need to help your boys succeed in school and life.

References

Albert, R. S., & Runco, M. A. (1988). Independence and the creative potential of gifted and exceptionally gifted boys. *Journal of Youth and Adolescence, 18*, 221–230.

Armstrong, T. (2000). *Multiple intelligences in the classroom* (2nd ed.). Alexandria, VA: Association for Supervision and Curriculum Development.

Bailey, K., Moulton, P., & Moulton, M. (1999). Athletics as a predictor of self-esteem and approval motivation. *The Sport Journal, 2*(2), 1–5.

Bandura, A. (1994). Self-efficacy. In V. S. Ramachaudran (Ed.), *Encyclopedia of human behavior* (Vol. 4, pp. 71–81). New York: Academic Press.

Baron-Cohen, S. (2003). *The essential difference: The truth about the male and female brain.* New York: Perseus.

Barry, D. (1995). *Dave Barry's complete guide to guys.* New York: Random House.

Baum, S. (2005, April 15). *The alphabet children.* Keynote session presented at annual meeting of The Association for the Education of Gifted Underachieving Students, Denver, CO.

Baum, S. M., Neu, T. W., Cooper, C. R., & Owen, S. V. (1997). *Evaluation of Project HIGH HOPES* (Project R206A30159-95). Washington, DC: U.S. Department of Education.

Baum, S. M., Renzulli, J. S., & Hébert, T. (1995). *The prism metaphor: A new paradigm for reversing achievement* (Collaborative Research Study No. 95310). Storrs: The National Research Center on the Gifted and Talented, University of Connecticut.

Baum, S. M., Viens, J., & Slatin, B. (2005). *Multiple intelligences in the classroom: A teacher's toolkit.* New York: Teachers College Press.

Behncke, L. (2002). *Self-regulation: A brief review.* Retrieved June 1, 2006, from http://www.athleticinsight.com/Vol4Iss1/SelfRegulation.htm

Beitler, A., Bushong, D., & Reid, A. (2004). Making this team. *Principal Leadership, 6*(10) 16–21.

Big Brothers Big Sisters. (2005). *Our impact.* Retrieved June 10, 2006, from http://www.bbbs.org/site/c.diJKKYPLJvH/b.1632631/k.3195/Our_Impact.htm

Bishop K. M., & Wahlsten, D. (1997). Sex differences in the human corpus callosum: Myth or reality? *Neuroscience and Biobehavioural Reviews, 21*, 581–601.

Bly, J. (1990). *Iron John: A book about men.* Reading, MA: Addison-Wesley.

Caputo, K., & Neu, T. W. (2006). *Breaking the cycle: A qualitative study of bullies and victims.* Unpublished manuscript.

Center for Disease Control. (n.d.). *ADHD: A public health perspective conference.* Retrieved March 30, 2006, from http://www.cdc.gov/ncbddd/adhd/dadabepi.htm

Checkley, K. (1997). The first seven and the eighth: A conversation with Howard Gardner. *Educational Leadership, 55,* 8–13.

Cloud, J. (2003, Oct. 27). Inside the New SAT. *TIME, 162*(17), 48–56.

Colangelo, N., Assouline, S. G., & Gross, M. U. M. (2004). *A nation deceived: How schools hold back America's brightest students* (Vol. 1). Iowa City, IA: The Connie Belin and Jacqueline N. Blank International Center for Gifted Education and Talent Development.

Cooper, C. R., Baum, S. M., & Neu, T. W. (2004). Developing scientific talent in students with special needs: An alternative model for identification, curriculum, and assessment. *Journal of Secondary Gifted Education, 15,* 162–169.

Council for Environmental Education. (2003). *Project WILD Aquatic: K–12 curriculum and activity guide.* Houston, TX: Project WILD.

Coy, D. R. (2001). *Bullying.* (ERIC Document Reproduction Service No. ED459405)

Cramond B. (1994). Attention Deficit Hyperactivity Disorder and creativity: What is the connection? *The Journal of Creative Behavior, 28,* 193–210.

Dake, J. A., Price, J. H., & Telljohann, S. K. (2003). The nature and extent of bullying at school. *Journal of School Health, 73,* 173–180.

Darling-Hammond, L. (1996). The right to learn and the advancement of teaching: Research policy and practice for democratic education. *Educational Researcher, 25,* 2–12.

Dedman, B. (2000, Oct. 15). *Examining the psyche of an adolescent killer.* Retrieved May 17, 2006, from http://www.treasury.gov/usss/ntac/chicago_sun/shoot15.htm

DeVoe, J. F., & Kaffenberger, S. (2005). *Student reports of bullying: Results from the 2001 School Crime Supplement to the National Crime Victimization Survey* (NCES 2005–310). Washington, DC: U.S. Government Printing Office.

Dixon, J. P. (1983). *The spatial child.* Springfield, IL: Charles C. Thomas.

Floyd, N. (1993, Oct.). Mentoring. *Education Research Consumer Guide,* 1–4.

Freedman, M. (1993). *The kindness of strangers: Adult mentors, urban youth, and the new voluntarism.* San Francisco: Jossey-Bass.

Gardner, H. (1983). *Frames of mind.* New York: Basic Books.

Gardner, H. (1993). *Creating minds.* New York: Basic Books.

Gardner, H. (1999). *Intelligences reframed: Multiple intelligences for the 21st century.* New York: Basic Books.

Gay, Lesbian, Straight Education Network. (2000). *The GLSEN lunchbox: A comprehensive training program for ending anti-gay bias in schools.* Washington, DC: Author.

Gentry, M., & Neu, T. W. (1998) Project High Hopes summer institute: Curriculum for developing talent in students with special needs. *Roeper Review, 20,* 291–295.

Gilligan, C. (2006, Jan. 30). Mommy, I know you: A feminist scholar explains how the study of girls can teach us about boys. *Newsweek, 147*(5), 53.

Goldberg, G. L., & Roswell, B. S. (2002). *Reading, writing and gender.* New York: Eye on Education.

Golden, R. (Producer). (2001). What the silenced say [Motion picture]. (Available from PEAK Parent Center, 611 North Weber, Ste. 200, Colorado Springs, CO 80903)

Gray, C. (2000). Gray's guide to bullying: Part I. The basics. *The Morning News, 12*(4), 1–24.

Green, J. P., & Winters, M. A. (2006). *The boys left behind.* Retrieved June 1, 2006, from http://www.nationalreview.com/comment/greene_winters 200604190558.asp

Gross, M. U. M. (1994). Radical acceleration: Responding to the academic and social needs of extremely gifted adolescents. *Journal of Secondary Gifted Education, 5*(4), 27–34.

Gurian, M. (2005). *The minds of boys: Saving our sons from falling behind in school and life.* San Francisco: Jossey-Bass.

Habitat for Humanity. (2006). *Involving children and youth in Habitat's work.* Retrieved May 26, 2006, from http://www.habitat.org/ccyp/youth_programs/default. aspx

Hallowell, E. (1999). *Connect.* New York: Pocket Books

Hanlon, H., Thatcher, R. & Cline, M. (1999). Gender difference in the development of EEG coherence in normal children. *Developmental Neuropsychology, 16,* 479–506.

Hazler, R. J., Carney, J. V., Green, S., Powell, R., & Jolly, L. S. (1997). Areas of expert agreement on identification of school bullies and victims. *School Psychology International, 18,* 3–12.

Jenkins, S. (2005, Jan. 29). He saw, she saw. *Washington Post,* D-1.

Karnes, F., & Riley, T. (2005). *Competitions for talented kids.* Waco, TX: Prufrock Press.

Kelly, D. M. (1993). *Last chance high: How girls and boys drop in and out of alternative schools.* New Haven, CT: Yale University Press.

Kerr, B. A., & Cohn, S. J. (2001). *Smart boys: Talent, manhood, and the search for meaning.* Scottsdale, AZ: Great Potential Press.

Kimura, D. (2002, April 1). Sex differences in the brain. *Scientific American, 1992*(267), 119–125.

Levine, M. (2003). *The myth of laziness.* New York: Simon and Schuster.

Li, Q. (2005). *Cyberbullying in schools: Nature and extent of Canadian adolescents' experience.* Paper presented at the annual meeting of the American Education Research Association, Montreal, QC, Canada.

Martin, S. B., Jackson, A. W., Richardson, P. A., & Weiller, K. H. (1999). Coaching preferences of adolescent youths and their parents. *Journal of Applied Sport Psychology, 11,* 278–293.

Massachusetts Association of Vocational Administrators. (2003). *Brief of amicus curiae.* Boston: Author.

Mays, P. J. (2005). *Precursor behaviors that indicate potential problems for boys in school.* Unpublished manuscript.

Metz, M. H. (2003). *Different by design: The context and character of three magnet schools.* New York: Teachers College Press.

Miller, A. (1979). *Drama of the gifted child.* New York: Basic Books.

Mooney, J., & Cole, D. (2000). *Learning outside the lines.* New York: Fireside.

Mortenson, T. (2005, February). *What's still wrong with the guys?* Retrieved June 2, 2006, from http://www.postsecondary.org/last12/152guys.pdf

National Association for Single Sex Public Education. (n.d.a). *Single sex education.* Retrieved November 30, 2005, from http://www.singlesexschools.org

National Association for Single Sex Public Education. (n.d.b). *Advantages for boys.* Retrieved November 30, 2005, from http://www.singlesexschools.org/adboys.html

National Center for Health Statistics. (n.d.). *Suicide.* Retrieved May 17, 2006, from http://www.cdc.gov/ncipc/fact_book/26_suicide.htm

National Center on Addiction and Substance Abuse. (2006). *More than a quarter of underage drinkers meet clinical criteria for alcohol abuse or dependence.* Retrieved May 30, 2006, from http://66.135.34.236/absolutenm/anmviewer.asp?a=437

National Education Association. (2006). *Wanted: More male teachers.* Retrieved June 1, 2006, from http://www.nea.org/teachershortage/03malefactsheet.html

National PTA. (2006, March 13). *Recess is at risk, new campaign comes to the rescue.* Retrieved June 2, 2006, from http://www.pta.org/ne_press_release_detail_1142028998890.html

National Research and Development Center on School Choice. (2006). *Frequently asked questions about school choice in the United States.* Retrieved June 3, 2006, from http://www.vanderbilt.edu/schoolchoice/faq.html

National School Safety Center. (2006, January). Retrieved January 25, 2006, from http://www.schoolsafety.us/?School-Crime-and-Violence-Statistics-p-9.html

Neu, T. W. (1993). *Case studies of identified gifted students with emotional or behavioral disorders.* Unpublished doctoral dissertation, The University of Connecticut, Storrs, CT.

Neu, T. W., Baum, S. M., & Cooper, C. R. (2005). Talent development in science: A unique tale of one student's journey. *Journal of Secondary Gifted Education, 16,* 30–36.

Neu, T. W., & Caputo, K. (2005). *A proposed anti-bullying program for Eastern Connecticut school systems.* Unpublished manuscript.

Newkirk, T. (2002). *Misreading masculinity: Boys, literacy, and popular culture.* Portsmouth, NH: Heinemann.

Newman, T. (2005). Coaches' roles in the academic success of male student athletes. *The Sport Journal, 8*(2), 13–18.

No Child Left Behind Act, 20 U.S.C. §6301 (2001).

Odean, K. (1998). *Great books for boys.* New York: Random House.

Olweus Bullying Prevention Program. (2003). *Evidence of effectiveness*. Retrieved February 3, 2006, from http://www.clemson.edu/olweus/evidence.html

Organisation of Economic Co-operation and Development. (n.d.). *Education at a glance: OECD indicators*. Paris: Author.

Paluska, S. A., & Schwenk, T. L. (2000). Physical activity and mental health: Current concepts. *Sports Medicine, 29*, 167–180.

Perlstein, L. (2004, May 31). School pushes reading, writing, reform. *Washington Post*, A-1.

Peterson, J. S., & Ray, K. E. (2006). Bullying and the gifted: Victims, perpetrators, prevalence, and effects. *Gifted Child Quarterly, 50*, 148–168.

Pollack, W. (1998). *Real boys: Rescuing our sons from the myth of boyhood*. New York: Random House.

Pollack, W. (with Shuster, T.). (2000). *Real boys' voices*. New York: Random House.

Pollack, W., & Cushman, K. (2001). *Real boys workbook*. New York: Villard Books.

Powell, C. (with Persico, J.). (1996). *My American journey*. New York: Ballantine.

Randall, P. (1996). *A community approach to bullying*. London: Trentham Books

Renzulli, J. S. (1977). *The enrichment triad model: A guide for developing defensible programs for the gifted and talented*. Mansfield Center, CT: Creative Learning Press.

Renzulli, J. S. (1994). *Schools for talent development: A practical plan for total school improvement*. Mansfield Center, CT: Creative Learning Press.

Renzulli, J. S., & Reis, S. M. (1997). *The schoolwide enrichment model: A how-to-guide for educational excellence* (2nd ed.). Mansfield Center, CT: Creative Learning Press.

Resnick M. D., Bearman, P. S., Blum, R. W., Bauman, K. E., Harris, K. M., Jones, J., et al. (1997). Protecting adolescents from harm. Findings from the National Longitudinal Study on Adolescent Health. *Journal of the American Medical Association, 278*, 823–832.

Rigby, K. (2002). *New perspectives on bullying*. Philadelphia: Jessica Kingsley.

Sax, L. (2005). *Why gender matters: What parents and teachers need to know about the emerging science of sex differences*. New York: Doubleday.

Scarpaci, R. T. (2006). Bullying: Effective strategies for its prevention. *Kappa Delta Pi Record, 42*, 170–174.

Shaywitz, B. A., Shaywitz, S. E., Pugh, K. R., Constable, R. T., Skudlawski, P., Fulbright, R. K., et al. (1995). Sex differences in the functional organization of the brain for language. *Nature, 373*, 607–609.

Sheras, P. L., & Tippin, S. (2002). *Your child: Bully or victim? Understanding and ending schoolyard tyranny*. New York: Fireside.

Sjostrom, L., & Stein, N. (1996). *Bullyproof: A teacher's guide on teasing and bullying for use with fourth and fifth grade students*. Wellesley, MA: Wellesley College Center for Research on Women.

Stahl, L. (2003, May 25). *The gender gap: Boys lagging*. Retrieved November 20, 2005, from http://www.cbsnews.com/stories/2002/10/31/60minutes/main527678.shtml

Suckling, A., & Temple, C. (2001). *Bullying: A whole-school approach.* Philadelphia: Jessica Kingsley.

Taylor, S. E., Klein, L. C., Lewis, B. P., Gruenewald, T. L., Gurung, R. A. R., & Updegraff, J. A. (2000). Biobehavioral responses to stress in females: Tend-and-befriend, not fight-or-flight. *Psychological Review, 107,* 411–429.

Teens With Problems. (2005). *Is my child a substance abuser?* Retrieved June 3, 2006, from http://www.teenswithproblems.com/drugabuse.html

Teirney, J. P., Grossman, J. B., & Resch, N. L. (1995). *Making a difference: An impact study of Big Brothers Big Sisters.* Philadelphia: Public/Private Ventures.

Thompson, M., & Kindlon, D. (2000). *Raising Cain: Saving the emotional life of boys.* New York: Ballantine.

Thoneman, A. (1998, November). *Teaching against homophobia.* Paper presented at the annual meeting of the Australian Association for Research in Education, Adelaide, Australia.

Torrance, E. P. (1984). *Mentor relationships: How they aid creative achievement, endure, change, and die.* Buffalo, NY: Bearly Limited.

Trautman, M. L. (2003). 20 ways to identify and reduce bullying in your classroom. *Intervention in School and Clinic, 38,* 243–246.

Trulson, M. E. (1986). Martial arts training: A novel "cure" for juvenile delinquency. *Human Relations, 39,* 1131–1140.

Tyre, P. (2006, Jan. 30). The trouble with boys. *Newsweek, 147*(5), 44–52.

USA Today staff. (2003, December 22). Boys academic slide call for accelerated attention. *USA Today,* A17.

U.S. Department of Education, National Center for Education Statistics. (2003). *The nation's report card: Reading highlights, 2002* (NCES Report 2003-524). Washington, DC: Author.

U.S. Department of Education, Office of Educational Research and Improvement. (1993). *National excellence: A case for developing America's talent.* Washington, DC: U.S. Government Printing Office.

Wallis, C. (2006, March 27). The multi-tasking generation. *TIME, 167*(13), 48–56.

Weinfeld, R., Barnes-Robinson, L., Jeweler, S., & Shevitz, B. R. (2006). *Smart kids with learning difficulties: Overcoming obstacles and realizing potential.* Waco, TX: Prufrock Press.

West, T. G. (1997). *In the mind's eye.* Amherst, NY: Prometheus Books.

Wilson, E. O. (1995). *Naturalist.* New York: Warner Books.

Younger, M., & Warrington, M. (2005). Raising boys' achievement (Research Report No. 636). London: Department of Education and Skills.

About the Authors

Terry W. Neu received his Ph.D. from the Talent Development Program at the University of Connecticut and currently serves on the faculty of Sacred Heart University in Fairfield, CT. Terry also currently serves as Vice President of the Association for the Education of Gifted Underachieving Students (AEGUS). He has done extensive work with gifted students with disabilities, modifying the classroom environment for these students, as well as developing a challenging dually differentiated curriculum to meet their unique needs.

Terry also has consulted nationally and internationally on teaching strategies for gifted students with disabilities and emotional or behavioral disorders, and how to differentiate instruction. He has also written several articles and chapters on these topics. Terry has also worked with several of the Jacob K. Javits educational research grants, including Project HIGH HOPES.

Before entering the field of gifted education, Terry taught in the Arkansas public school system at White County Central in Judsonia. He was a secondary science and history teacher for seven years, four of which were spent working with secondary gifted and talented students. He earned his master's degree from the University of Central Arkansas.

Terry also is very involved in service learning and leads a delegation of undergraduate students to Tierra Blanca, El Salvador, each spring. Each year the delegation has a different project to construct, from elementary schools, to community centers. Terry has two children, Rachel and Jacob, and resides in Storrs, Connecticut.

Rich Weinfeld has long been an advocate for appropriate educational programming for all students. He currently provides advocacy to parents of students with a wide range of learning challenges, training to parents and staff on various educational topics, and consultation to schools and school systems regarding appropriate programming for all students. Rich serves on the national board of directors of the Association for Educators of Gifted Underachieving Students (AEGUS).

He previously served as Montgomery County (Maryland) Public School's first full-time Instructional Specialist for Gifted and Talented/Learning Disabled Programs. Rich has presented many workshops regarding best educational practices that help all students to succeed. He has also coauthored several articles regarding programming for smart kids with learning challenges. He is also coauthor of the best-selling book *Smart Kids With Learning Difficulties: Overcoming Obstacles and Realizing Potential,* and the upcoming book *School Success for Kids With Asperger's Syndrome.*

Rich received his bachelor's degree from American University and his master's degree from Trinity College. He is certified in administration and supervision. For more information about his current endeavors, visit his Web site at http://www.richweinfeld. com

About
the Contributor

Ken Caputo first began teaching and working with children as a swim and water safety instructor at the age of 16. Through high school and into college he expanded his teaching to include work with adults, individuals with handicaps, and the Special Olympics. In 1989, he was introduced to the martial arts, and soon chose to pursue a career as a professional martial arts instructor. Ken is an owner/operator of a martial arts school in North Windham, CT. He is now a fifth degree master in the art of shaolin kempo karate, and has helped more than 200 students ranging in age from 9–62 to receive their black belts.

He has worked extensively in the local schools, teaching character development and confidence building through the martial arts. He has spent more than 20 years in the field, helping children deal with the difficulties of bullying, peer pressure, low self-esteem, and physical and metal disabilities, as well as the day-to-day stresses faced by today's children. Ken continues to live and work in the Windham community, operating his martial arts school of 300 students with the help of his wife, Lisa.